Bartender's Bible

1001 Mixed Drinks and Everything You Need to Know to Set Up Your Bar

Gary Regan

A JOHN BOSWELL ASSOCIATES/KING HILL

PRODUCTIONS BOOK

HarperCollins*Publishers*

The Bartender's Bible

Design by Barbara Cohen Aronica

LIBRARY OF CONGRESS CATALOG CARD NUMBER 91-55104
ISBN 0-06-016722-X

91   92   93   94   95   HC   10   9   8   7   6   5   4   3   2

ACKNOWLEDGMENTS

This book is dedicated to my mother, who tolerates me living so far away from her, and to my wife, who tolerates me living so near.

I would like to thank all of the people who shared their recipes with me, including Marvin Paige and Mary Conelly of Claire Restaurant, New York City; Bob Jackson, Deven Black, Rod McLucas, Robert Smyth, John Pierse, and Stuffy Shmitt of the North Star Pub in New York City; Vic Alasio, Luke Farrelly, David Ridings, probably some friends whose names I did not jot down when they gave me recipes, and more than a few strangers who have given me recipes in various bars over the years.

Thanks is also due to my wife, Mardee, for all of her support and her help in testing the recipes, to Stuffy for being a friend, and to the entire staff at the North Star Pub, who have put up with my taking time off work and boring them with trivia I've gleaned while writing this book.

CONTENTS

Everything you need to know about setting up your bar, including what gadgets to use, what bar equipment to buy, types of glasses, and how to prepare the perfect garnishes.

A connoisseur's guide, from Kentucky corn whiskey to sour mash. Drink recipes range from the classics to such contemporary concoctions as J. R.'s Revenge, Pendennis, and Sazerac.

What makes a great brandy, and why the right snifter makes it even greater. Cognac, Armagnac, and all the other premier brandies of the world are analyzed.

4 · GIN 48

The sophisticated spirit with more than a hint of juniper and a lot of fascinating lore. From the Gin and Tonic to the Ramos Fizz, Widow with a Secret, Delmonico Cocktail, and Blue Cowboy.

5 · RUM 83

Rum is the essence of the Caribbean, the official drink of the British Navy, and the distilled product of simple sugar cane. This chapter covers all rums—light, amber, golden, dark, and aged, or añejo. Drinks range from the famous Planter's Punch and Bacardi Cocktail to the more contemporary Hat Trick and Sly Goes to Havana.

6 · SCOTCH 122

From the Highlands, Lowlands, and islands of Scotland comes the liquor with the taste (literally) of Mother Earth. Here's a clear explanation of the real differences between blended and single malt Scotches and a simple tasting chart that details some of the highlights of the best, most available single malts. Mixed drinks have the classic ring, including the Rusty Nail, Balmoral, and Highland Sling.

7 · TEQUILA 139

This unique South of the Border liquor is truly a drink of ritual. Drink it straight up with (properly applied) salt and lime, or in mixed drinks like the famous Tequila Sunrise and the less widely known Compadre and Tequila Mockingbird.

8 · VODKA 157

Literally "little water," this neutral spirit is the most chameleonlike of liquors. The chapter covers the vodka landscape from the Cape Codder to the Gorky Park.

The Bartender's Bible

INTRODUCTION

A bartender, as a rule, is a person who enjoys the company of others, endeavors to solve problems, listens to the woes of the world, sympathizes with the mistreated, laughs with the comedians, cheers up the down at heart, and generally controls the atmosphere at his or her bar. A bartender is the manager of moods, the master of mixology.

Certain scenarios are played out over and over again in bars everywhere. The questions are basically the same; only the details vary: What's in a true Singapore Sling? How long has the Martini been around? What's the difference between a Fix and a Fizz? A reference book is as necessary to a bartender as alcohol and ice.

This book is an up-to-date, comprehensive guide that tells you how to set up a bar and what liquors, mixers, condiments, garnishes, and equipment you will need. In addition, you'll find anecdotes and histories of your favorite potables, along with the recipes for over 1,000 cocktails and mixed drinks. All of the old standards are here, and so too are the newest drinks to gain popularity in bars from coast to coast.

DRINKING

In moderation, at the right time, with the right people, drinking is one of life's greatest pleasures. Beyond its ability to help us relax, what is it about drinking that makes it so appealing? Here is my answer: Drinking is ritual.

Drinking brings with it the clinking of glasses, the special words of friendship in different languages all over the world: cheers, *salud, sköl, kampai.* Raise your glass and propose a toast. Drinking has to do with friendship, good times, warm and tender moments, camaraderie, celebration, commiseration, birth and death, sealing a deal, remembering a friend—the very things that life itself is about. Even abstainers need not miss out on the ritual of drinking. When proposing a toast, raising a glass of ginger ale has no less meaning than raising a glass of fine Champagne. Life *requires* ritual, and sharing a drink along with a common cause or admiration for a friend, or even just the touching of glasses to say "Hail fellow well met" provides that ritual.

NOT DRINKING

In the carefree sixties, a popular bar in my hometown in Lancashire, England, was Yates' Wine Lodge. Everyone from the mayor to the mortician drank at Yates', where Australian white wine was served in three-ounce glasses and roast beef was carved before your eyes and piled onto crusty bread slathered with mustard. The atmosphere was dense, smoky, and downright earthy, with everyone laughing, talking, and sorting out the ills of the world. From time to time during any evening at Yates', your eyes were bound to wander upward to the glass-partitioned manager's office, which seemed to be jammed in between the ceiling and the wall, and where bespectacled eyes were ever watchful of your behavior. And as your eyes began their descent back to your Australian white, they would always lock onto the sign posted directly below the office:

"WINE IS A GOOD SERVANT
BUT A TERRIBLE MASTER"

Now we are almost into the next century, and alcohol awareness is acute in our society. We all know that overindulging can cost us and others dearly, and most people are treating drinking with the care and respect that it deserves. However, that doesn't mean total abstinence for most of us, and since we are drinking less, we should be having more fun with the drinks that we do have. If you are going to have something to sip on, why not have a special drink and make it with special ingredients that deserve savoring.

This book brings over 1,000 drink recipes to you. Some are old friends, though you may never have learned the correct proportions to make them; others will sound vaguely familiar, but you probably never knew quite what went into them. All of these recipes are designed to be easy to make and serve in the proper glasses, at the correct temperature, and with the classic garnish.

Cheers,

Gary Reg

HOW TO FIND A DRINK IN THIS BOOK

To absolutely guarantee that you could flip without thought to any given drink recipe in this book, it would have to be printed at least four times under different headings. A Harvey Wallbanger, for example, would have to be listed under Vodka, Galliano, Fruit Juices, and finally under *H* for Harvey. Since this is not practicable, every writer of a recipe book must select which way it is to be categorized. Here is all the information you need to find any drink in this book easily. The index in the back of the book lists:

1. All drinks alphabetically.
2. All drinks under a heading of every major liquor in each drink; e.g., Harvey Wallbanger is listed under Vodka and under Galliano. If the liquor is a secondary ingredient, the word *in* will appear before the title of the drink.
3. All drinks in distinct categories, such as Sours, Collins, and Daisies.

Within the book, the drinks are listed alphabetically under the predominant liquor in that drink. A Harvey Wallbanger is listed under Vodka. All drinks that contain larger amounts of a cordial than a liquor are grouped together in the Cordials chapter, listed alphabetically according to the predominant cordial.

Simply listing all drinks alphabetically, without separating them into liquor categories, doesn't help when you are experimenting with the contents of your liquor cabinet or trying to remember what went into that drink you had at your hotel in Jamaica. If you know that it was mainly rum, turn to the Rum chapter. Acapulco . . . that was it, and there it is.

If you want to make a specific drink, say, a Rusty Nail, you more than likely know that Scotch is the main ingredient. You will find this drink in the Scotch chapter. If you don't know the main ingredient, simply turn to the alphabetical index and look under *R*.

When you want to make something special for Uncle

Harry, who drinks bourbon, go straight to the Bourbon chapter and select a recipe. A Ragged Company is an interesting choice.

There are also some extra chapters that group drink recipes under some specific categories:

Tropical Drinks contains many exotic potions, such as the Mai Tai and the Scorpion.

Wine Drinks encompasses beverages containing still and sparkling wines as well as fortified wines, such as sherry and port.

Beer and Beer Concoctions covers just about everything you can do with ales, lagers, ports, and stouts.

Hot Drinks lists such favorites as Irish Coffee and Hot Buttered Rum.

Party Punches is a chapter of recipes for drinks made for large parties of people.

Nonalcoholic Drinks contains recipes for drinks with no alcohol in them.

Versatile Cocktails includes blueprints for recipes that can be made with a variety of liquors.

1 · THE WELL-STOCKED BAR

The job of making drinks is infinitely easier when all of the things you need are close at hand. When setting up the bar for a small cocktail party, read the recipes for the drinks you'll be serving and make sure that you have all the ingredients, including the correct glasses, garnishes, and equipment. To set up a small bar for everyday use or to furnish a well-rounded basement bar, check the appropriate lists below. Be forewarned, however; there will always be someone who wants a liqueur that you don't have. You know, the one he drank on a riverboat on the Ganges back in 1927; it tasted a little like kirsch, except that it reminded him of cornflakes with sliced bananas at the time.

Any extra time that you take to squeeze fresh fruit juices for use in your cocktails or mixed drinks will be time well spent. I can guarantee that, long after your party is over, your guests will talk about the difference between fresh and store-bought juices. So few people bother with fresh juices that it becomes a point well worthy of some praise.

Similarly, if a drink calls for crushed ice, don't use ice cubes unless you absolutely must. Manual ice crushers are relatively inexpensive, and if you don't possess one you can simply wrap some ice cubes in a lint-free tea towel and bash it with a rolling pin. Have some fun; imagine it's the boss!

Some recipes in this book call for raw eggs, a standard ingredient in many classic recipes. While all of the incidents of salmonella poisoning in the United States have occurred in food service establishments, *not* in home settings, the possibility of salmonella development in eggs is a real one. Investigation shows that the incidents that have occurred were caused by improper storage conditions; that is, the eggs were not kept under refrigeration at all times. Salmonella is killed by heating; since the eggs used in recipes in this book are used raw, you will need to decide for yourself. If you are not comfortable with eating raw eggs, you should simply avoid these recipes.

LIQUID ASSETS

LIQUORS

SMALL BAR

Bourbon
Brandy—Cognac and brandy
Gin
Rum—light and dark
Scotch, blended
Tequila, white
Vodka
Whiskey—blended and Irish

BASEMENT BAR

Add:

Añejo Rum
Armagnac
Canadian Whiskey
Citrus-flavored Vodka
Gold Tequila
Russian Vodka
Single Malt Scotches—one Highland, one Lowland, and one Islay
Spanish Brandy

LIQUEURS, CORDIALS, AND MORE EXOTIC LIQUORS

SMALL BAR

Amaretto
Anisette
Cointreau or Triple Sec
Crème de Cacao—white and dark
Crème de Cassis
Crème de Menthe—white and green
Grand Marnier
Kahlúa
Pernod or Ricard
Sambuca, white

BASEMENT BAR

Add:

Applejack or Calvados
Bailey's Irish Cream
B & B
Bénédictine
Chambord
Chartreuse—green and yellow
Crème de Bananes
Crème de Noyaux
Curaçao—white and blue
Drambuie
Frangelico
Fruit-flavored brandies—apricot, blackberry, cherry
Galliano
Irish Mist
Kirsch
Kümmel
Maraschino liqueur
Melon liqueur
Pimm's Cup
Rock and Rye
Saké
Sambuca, black (Opal Nera)

Schnapps, flavored peach and peppermint
Sloe Gin
Southern Comfort
Strega
Tia Maria
Tuaca
Vandermint

BEER

SMALL BAR

Lager

BASEMENT BAR

Add:

Ale
Porter
Stout

WINES AND FORTIFIED WINES

SMALL BAR

Red Wine, dry
Sherry—cream and dry
Vermouth—sweet and dry
White Wine, dry

BASEMENT BAR

Add:

Blush Wine
Port—tawny and ruby
Rosé Wine

MIXERS

SMALL BAR

Club Soda
Cola
Diet Soda
Fresh Lemon Juice
Fresh Lime Juice
Lemon-Lime Soda (such as 7-Up)
Orange Juice
Tomato Juice
Tonic Water

BASEMENT BAR

Add:

Beef Bouillon
Coconut Cream
Cranberry Juice
Fresh Orange Juice
Ginger Beer
Grapefruit Juice
Pineapple Juice

CONDIMENTS

SMALL BAR

Angostura Bitters*
Grenadine
Ground Black Pepper
Horseradish
Rose's Lime Juice (sweetened concentrated lime juice)
Salt—regular and coarse
Superfine Sugar

*Whenever just "bitters" is called for in a drink, this is the one
to use.

Tabasco Sauce
Worcestershire Sauce

BASEMENT BAR

Add:

Cinnamon Sticks
Eggs
Grated Nutmeg
Ground Cinnamon
Heavy Cream
Light Cream
Orange Bitters
Orgeat Syrup (an almond flavoring)
Peychaud Bitters
Whole Cloves

GARNISHES

SMALL BAR

Cocktail Olives
Cocktail Onions
Oranges
Lemons
Limes
Maraschino Cherries, preferably with stems

BASEMENT BAR

Add:

Bananas
Celery
Cucumber
Fresh Mint
Pineapple
Strawberries

To Prepare Garnishes: Although it is preferable to have garnishes prepared before guests arrive, it is also important to make sure that they are as fresh as possible. Cut a small amount just before opening the bar and replenish when necessary.

LIME AND LEMON WEDGES
1. Cut the "knobs" from the top and tail of the fruit.
2. Slice the fruit in half around the center, or from top to bottom.
3. Cut each half into 4 equal wedges.

To use, squeeze the juice from the fruit wedge into the drink just before serving. Shield the glass with your other hand to make sure that the juice doesn't squirt into anyone's face.

TWISTS
These are usually made from lemons, although lime and orange twists are sometimes called for.

1. Cut a slice from both the top and the tail of the fruit thick enough to expose the inside pulp.
2. Using a paring knife, cut through the peel into the fruit from top to tail.
3. Insert the bowl of a bar spoon into the cut and work it up and down between the peel and the fruit to separate the peel from the pulp.
4. Remove the whole peel from the fruit (it will come off easily). Reserve the pulp for juice.
5. Cut the peel into 1/4-inch strips, cutting lengthwise from the top to the bottom of the fruit.
6. When serving, twist the peel, colored side down, over the drink. This releases volatile oils into the drink. Now rub the colored side of the peel along the rim of the glass and drop the twist into the drink.

ORANGE SLICES
1. Cut the top and tail from the fruit, slicing deep enough to expose the pulp.
2. Cut the orange lengthwise in half, slicing from top to tail.
3. Set each orange half cut side down and cut each half crosswise into 1/4-inch-thick slices.

4. Cut into the center of each slice, starting on the flat pulp edge and reaching just up to—but not into—the peel.
5. Slip the cut onto the lip of the glass so that the orange hangs half in and half out of the glass.

Muddling: If you are muddling large quantities of ingredients for a batch of drinks, then you should use a good-quality ceramic mortar and pestle. Place the ingredients in the mortar and crush the ingredients together with the pestle so that the dry ingredient (usually sugar) dissolves in the liquid ingredient (such as bitters) or in the moisture produced by crushing fruit segments or fresh herbs (such as mint sprigs). When muddling ingredients for a single cocktail, you may want to skip the mortar and pestle and muddle in the glass that will hold the drink. Make sure that the glass is sturdy; you may want to hold it in a tea towel while you are muddling in case it breaks. Using the bottom of the glass as a mortar and the back of a barspoon or teaspoon as a pestle, muddle the ingredients together carefully against the glass.

EQUIPMENT

BARSPOON: A long, flat-headed spoon with a twisted shaft, the barspoon is used for stirring drinks in a mixing glass and for muddling.

BLENDER: A heavy-duty electric blender is used for mixing "frozen" drinks. I highly recommend buying a professional model, as grinding ice requires a strong motor.

BOSTON SHAKER: The Boston shaker consists of two flat-bottomed cones, one of which is glass and fits inside the other, which is usually stainless steel. When shaking, make sure that the metal half is on the bottom. This gives you better control and ensures that when you break the shaker apart, the bottom half won't slip and drop to the floor.

BOTTLE OPENER: A crown cork bottle opener is essential.

CHAMPAGNE STOPPER: A spring-loaded stopper for Champagne bottles will help to keep the carbonation in the wine.

CHURCHKEY OR CAN OPENER: Used for opening cans of fruit juices or bouillon, a churchkey makes for easier pouring.

CITRUS REAMER: Used for extracting juice from an orange, lemon, or lime. I prefer the old-fashioned glass variety with the bowl to catch the juice. Make sure that no seeds make their way into the drinks. Rolling and pressing the fruit on the work surface or warming it under hot water will increase the juice yield.

CORKSCREW: Although a waiter's corkscrew is more professional, use a wing-type corkscrew if it will make life a little easier.

GLASS PITCHER: This is an attractive way to keep fruit juices or preseasoned tomato juice for Bloody Marys close at hand.

ICE BUCKET AND TONGS: A decorative, well-insulated ice bucket will be attractive on the bar and keep your ice frozen longer.

ICE CRUSHER: A manual ice crusher can prove to be very useful. If you don't have one, place ice cubes in a lint-free tea towel and crush them with a rolling pin.

JIGGER: A good, double-headed jigger will provide 1½- and ¾-ounce, or 1- and 1½-ounce measurements. Since there is no ½-ounce measure, keep in mind that ½ ounce equals 1 tablespoon.

MEASURING CUP: Use a transparent, 1-cup measure with easy-to-read delineations for quantities larger than 1½ ounces.

MEASURING SPOONS: I recommend having two sets available, one for wet and one for dry ingredients.

MIXING GLASS: This glass is used to mix most cocktails that don't call for fruit juices. It is preferable to use a glass with a pouring spout that will prevent ice from falling into the glass when pouring. The mixing glass should hold at least 16 ounces (2 cups) of liquid. Many professional bartenders prefer to use the glass half of a Boston shaker along with a Hawthorn strainer.

MUDDLER: A ceramic mortar and pestle is ideal for muddling sugar with mint or fruit.

PARING KNIFE: Used for cutting fruit for garnishes. Make sure that it is sharp and well cared for.

STANDARD SHAKER: This usually consists of three

JIGGER STANDARD MEASURING BOTTLE
SHAKER SPOONS OPENER

MEASURING STRAINER CHAMPAGNE
CUP CORKSCREW STOPPER

MIXING GLASS CITRUS REAMER

ICE BUCKET
AND TONGS

BARSPOON CHURCHKEY OR PARING KNIFE
CAN OPENER

BLENDER   MUDDLER   BOSTON   GLASS
                        SHAKER   PITCHER

pieces: the lid, the strainer, and the receptacle. Before shaking drinks, make sure that the shaker is assembled properly. Hold the shaker with your forefinger over the top, the thumb of your other hand on the bottom, and your pinkies crossed around each other to prevent the shaker from coming apart. Never put carbonated beverages into a shaker.

STRAINER: The Hawthorn strainer has a spring coiled around its head. The spring fits neatly inside the Boston shaker's glass to hold it in place.

Your bar should also have a good supply of straws, swizzle sticks, cocktail sticks or toothpicks, and coasters or cocktail napkins for service.

GLASSWARE

It is essential to have the right glassware at your disposal in order to serve drinks properly. Good-quality, sparkling clean glasses make a huge difference to the drinker. Remember, drinking is, in part, ritual, and all aspects of any ritual should be perfect. Here, then, is a comprehensive list of the glasses you should have at your disposal in a well-stocked bar:

Balloon Wine Glass, 8–14 ounces
Beer Mug, 10–12 ounces
Brandy Snifter, 6 ounces and up (some run to 24 ounces)

Champagne Flute, 6–8 ounces
Cocktail, 4 ounces
Collins, 10–14 ounces
Highball, 8–10 ounces
Irish Coffee, 8–10 ounces
Old-Fashioned, 6–10 ounces
Pilsner, 12–14 ounces
Pousse Café, 3–4 ounces
Punch Cup, 6–8 ounces
Sherry, 2–3 ounces
Shot Glass, 1½–2 ounces
Sour, 4–6 ounces

BALLOON WINE

CHAMPAGNE
FLUTE

BRANDY
SNIFTER

SHERRY

COCKTAIL

SOUR

IRISH COFFEE   PUNCH CUP   BEER MUG

PILSNER   POUSSE CAFÉ

COLLINS   HIGHBALL   OLD-FASHIONED   SHOT

2 · BOURBON

Generally known as the king of American whiskies, bourbon is a robust spirit that gets much of its distinctive flavor from corn, its main ingredient, and from the charred oak casks that are used to age it.

The staple of such cocktails as the Mint Julep and the Sazerac, was first made by distillers who were intent on beating the tax man. Somehow, this liquor, which some call the finest of American whiskies, is enhanced by the romantic picture of moonshiners in the Appalachian Mountains actually "perfecting" bourbon. However, it should be noted that the Reverend Elijah Craig of Georgetown, Kentucky, is generally recognized as the first to distill Bourbon County Whiskey in 1789.

In 1791, the government introduced excise taxes on whiskey, and the distillers of Pennsylvania revolted. Tax collectors were tarred and feathered, and riots ensued in what came to be known as the Whiskey Rebellion. It was the first time that federal forces were used to uphold the law. Of course the tax man will always win, as will the grim reaper, but the distillers temporarily escaped his reach. They fled to the mountains of Kentucky, where corn was plentiful and the water, flowing from layers of limestone, was pristine. The quality of any whiskey is directly proportional to the quality of the water used in making it.

PRODUCTION

Two types of stills are used in most liquor production: the pot still and the continuous still, sometimes called the Coffey, or patent still. The pot still resembles an upturned funnel; it has a large, bowllike base and a tall, tapering tower. Vapors from the liquid being distilled travel up the tower and through a spiral tube surrounded by cold water; the cool temperature of the water condenses the vapors into the liquor being sought. This type of still is not as efficient as the continuous still, but it renders a more flavorful product.

The continuous still has two main parts, a rectifier and an analyzer, which both resemble tall, wide tubes. They are both filled with steam, and the liquid being distilled enters a pipe that travels down the rectifier. The liquid being distilled is heated by the steam almost to the boiling point when it reaches the analyzer, which is, in simple terms, just a tank full of steam. The alcohol from the primary liquid immediately vaporizes and is channeled, along with the steam, back into the base of the rectifier, where it mixes with the steam surrounding the pipes, bringing in more liquid to be distilled; thus the process is continuous. At a point about two-thirds up the rectifier, the vapors hit a cold plate that condenses them into liquor, which is then channeled out of the rectifier and diluted with water.

Bourbon must be distilled from a mash of at least 51 percent corn. It is distilled in a continuous still and then aged in charred virgin oak casks. These casks must never again be used for the maturation of bourbon, and the vast majority of them are sold to Scotch distillers for the aging of single malt Scotch. A more detailed explanation of the general process used to make all American whiskies appears in the chapter Whiskey (page 180).

SOUR MASH

There is always time at any bar for a good argument about sour mash. This is what it is:

1. Mash is a term given to the cooked milled cereal (grist) and water used in the distillation process.
2. When the grist is strained from the mash, what remains is a liquid known as "wort." Yeast is added to the wort to cause fermentation, which produces an alcoholic mixture known as "beer." This beer is then distilled into whiskey.
3. Sour mash whiskey, which is usually a style of bourbon, differs from any other whiskey because a proportion of mash already used in a previous distillation, hence "sour," is added to the fresh mash about to be used, and the resulting wort is allowed to ferment for three to four days before being distilled.

SOUTHERN COMFORT

This product is actually more like a prepared cocktail than either a bourbon or a liqueur, but since most people know that Southern Comfort has something to do with bourbon, I have decided to describe it in this chapter.

In the late nineteenth century there was a cocktail known as Cuffs and Buttons, a marriage of bourbon and peach liqueur in which fresh peaches were marinated. The fruity taste of the peaches made the bourbon much more acceptable to people not enamored with the taste of straight whiskey. A bartender in Missouri changed the name of this drink to Southern Comfort, and it was so popular that a distiller has marketed the blend of bourbon and peach liqueur as Southern Comfort ever since.

▌ BOURBLE

2 ounces bourbon   ½ ounce lemon juice
½ ounce Cointreau or
    triple sec

In a shaker half-filled with ice cubes, combine all of the ingredients. Shake well. Strain into a cocktail glass.

2 BOURBON AND BRANCH

2 ounces bourbon   4 ounces bottled water

Pour the bourbon and water into a highball glass almost filled with ice cubes.

3 BOURBON BLACK HAWK

2 ounces bourbon   1 maraschino cherry
1 ounce sloe gin

In a mixing glass half-filled with ice cubes, combine the bourbon and sloe gin. Stir and strain into a cocktail glass. Garnish with the cherry.

4 BOURBON BLACK HAWK #2

2 ounces bourbon   1 teaspoon superfine
½ ounce sloe gin   sugar
1 ounce lemon juice   1 maraschino cherry

In a shaker half-filled with ice cubes, combine the bourbon, sloe gin, lemon juice, and sugar. Shake well. Strain into a cocktail glass. Garnish with the cherry.

5 BOURBON COBBLER I

1½ teaspoons superfine   1 maraschino cherry
   sugar   1 orange slice
3 ounces club soda   1 lemon slice
Crushed ice
2½ ounces blended
   bourbon

In an old-fashioned glass, dissolve the sugar in the club soda. Add crushed ice until the glass is almost full. Add the bourbon and stir well. Garnish with the cherry and orange and lemon slices.

6 BOURBON COBBLER II

1 teaspoon superfine   2 ounces bourbon
   sugar   1 strawberry
3 ounces club soda   1 lime wedge
Crushed ice   1 pineapple wedge

In a large wine glass, dissolve the sugar in the club soda. Almost fill the glass with crushed ice. Add the bourbon. Garnish with the strawberry and the lime and pineapple wedges.

7 BOURBON COOLER

2 ounces bourbon
4 ounces lemon-lime soda
1 lemon wedge

Pour the bourbon and the soda into a highball glass almost filled with ice cubes. Stir well. Garnish with the lemon wedge.

8 BOURBON COUNTY COWBOY

2 ounces bourbon
1/2 ounce light cream

In a shaker half-filled with ice cubes, combine the bourbon and cream. Shake well. Strain into a cocktail glass.

9 BOURBON CRUSTA

1 tablespoon superfine
  sugar
1 lemon wedge
Peel of 1 orange, cut into
  a spiral
Crushed ice
1 1/2 ounces bourbon
1/2 ounce Cointreau or
  triple sec
2 teaspoons maraschino
  liqueur
1/2 ounce lemon juice

Place the sugar in a saucer. Rub the rim of a wine goblet with the lemon wedge and dip the glass into the sugar to coat the rim thoroughly; discard the lemon wedge. Place the orange peel spiral into the goblet and drape one end over the rim of the glass. Fill the glass with crushed ice. In a shaker half-filled with ice cubes, combine the bourbon, Cointreau, maraschino liqueur, and lemon juice. Shake well. Strain into the goblet.

10 BOURBON DAISY

2 ounces bourbon
1 ounce lemon juice
1/2 teaspoon grenadine
1/2 teaspoon superfine
  sugar
1 orange slice
1 maraschino cherry

In a shaker half-filled with ice cubes, combine the bourbon, lemon juice, grenadine, and sugar. Shake well. Pour into an old-fashioned glass. Garnish with the orange slice and the cherry.

11 BOURBON FIX

1 teaspoon superfine sugar	Crushed ice
1 ounce lemon juice	2 ounces bourbon
2 teaspoons water	1 maraschino cherry
	1 lemon slice

In a shaker half-filled with ice cubes, combine the sugar, lemon juice, and water. Shake well. Strain into a highball glass almost filled with crushed ice. Add the bourbon. Stir well and garnish with the cherry and the lemon slice.

12 BOURBON FLIP

2 ounces bourbon	¹/₂ ounce light cream
1 egg	¹/₈ teaspoon grated nutmeg
1 teaspoon superfine sugar	

In a shaker half-filled with ice cubes, combine the bourbon, egg, sugar, and cream. Shake well. Strain into a sour glass and garnish with the nutmeg.

13 BOURBON MILK PUNCH

2 ounces bourbon	¹/₄ teaspoon vanilla extract
3 ounces half-and-half	¹/₄ teaspoon grated nutmeg
1 teaspoon superfine sugar	

In a shaker half-filled with ice cubes, combine the bourbon, half-and-half, sugar, and vanilla extract. Shake well. Strain into an old-fashioned glass and garnish with the nutmeg.

14 BOURBON MILK PUNCH #2

1 teaspoon superfine sugar	5 ounces milk
2 ounces bourbon	¹/₄ teaspoon ground cinnamon

In a highball glass, dissolve the sugar in the bourbon by stirring with a teaspoon. Add 6 ice cubes and the milk. Stir well. Garnish with the cinnamon.

15 BOURBON MILK PUNCH #3

2 ounces bourbon
½ ounce dark crème de
  cacao

5 ounces milk
¼ teaspoon grated
  nutmeg

In a shaker half-filled with ice cubes, combine the bourbon, crème de cacao, and milk. Shake well. Pour into a highball glass and garnish with the nutmeg.

16 BOURBON OLD-FASHIONED

3 dashes bitters
1 teaspoon water
1 sugar cube

3 ounces bourbon
1 orange slice
1 maraschino cherry

In an old-fashioned glass, muddle the bitters and water into the sugar cube, using the back of a teaspoon. Almost fill the glass with ice cubes and add the bourbon. Garnish with the orange slice and the cherry. Serve with a swizzle stick.

17 BOURBON SANGAREE

1 teaspoon superfine
  sugar
2 teaspoons water
1½ ounces bourbon
Crushed ice
2½ ounces club soda

½ ounce tawny port
1 lemon twist
⅛ teaspoon grated
  nutmeg
⅛ teaspoon ground
  cinnamon

In a highball glass, dissolve the sugar in the water and bourbon. Almost fill the glass with crushed ice and add the club soda. Float the port on top. Garnish with the lemon twist and dust with the nutmeg and cinnamon.

18 BOURBON SLING

1 teaspoon superfine
  sugar
2 teaspoons water

1 ounce lemon juice
2 ounces bourbon
1 lemon twist

In a shaker half-filled with ice cubes, combine the sugar, water, lemon juice, and bourbon. Shake well. Strain into a highball glass. Garnish with the lemon twist.

19 BOURBON SOUR

2 ounces bourbon
1 ounce lemon juice
½ teaspoon superfine
   sugar

1 orange slice
1 maraschino cherry

In a shaker half-filled with ice cubes, combine the bourbon, lemon juice, and sugar. Shake well. Strain into a whiskey sour glass; garnish with the orange slice and cherry.

20 BOURBON SWIZZLE

1½ ounces lime juice
1 teaspoon superfine
   sugar
2 ounces bourbon

1 dash bitters
Crushed ice
3 ounces club soda

In a shaker half-filled with ice cubes, combine the lime juice, sugar, bourbon, and bitters. Shake well. Almost fill a collins glass with crushed ice. Stir until the glass is frosted. Strain the mixture in the shaker into the glass and add the club soda. Serve with a swizzle stick.

21 DIXIE DEW

1½ ounces bourbon
½ teaspoon white crème
   de menthe

½ teaspoon Cointreau or
   triple sec

In a mixing glass half-filled with ice cubes, combine all of the ingredients. Stir well. Strain into a cocktail glass.

22 DIXIE STINGER

3 ounces bourbon
½ ounce white crème de
   menthe

½ teaspoon Southern
   Comfort

In a shaker half-filled with ice cubes, combine all of the ingredients. Shake well. Strain into a cocktail glass.

23 FANCY BOURBON

2 ounces bourbon
½ teaspoon Cointreau or
triple sec
¼ teaspoon superfine
sugar

2 dashes bitters
1 lemon twist

In a shaker half-filled with ice cubes, combine the bourbon, Cointreau, sugar, and bitters. Shake well. Strain into a cocktail glass and garnish with the lemon twist.

24 FOX AND HOUNDS

1½ ounces bourbon
½ ounce Pernod
½ ounce lemon juice

½ teaspoon superfine
sugar
1 egg white

In a shaker half-filled with ice cubes, combine all of the ingredients. Shake well. Strain into a cocktail glass.

25 JILLIONAIRE

2 ounces bourbon
½ ounce Cointreau or
triple sec

½ teaspoon grenadine
1 egg white

In a shaker half-filled with ice cubes, combine all of the ingredients. Shake well and strain into a cocktail glass.

26 JOHN COLLINS

2 ounces bourbon
1 ounce lemon juice
1 teaspoon superfine
sugar

3 ounces club soda
1 maraschino cherry
1 orange slice

In a shaker half-filled with ice cubes, combine the bourbon, lemon juice, and sugar. Shake well. Strain into a collins glass almost filled with ice cubes. Add the club soda. Stir and garnish with the cherry and the orange slice.

27 J. R.'S GODCHILD

2 ounces bourbon   1 ounce milk
½ ounce amaretto

In a shaker half-filled with ice cubes, combine the bourbon, amaretto, and milk. Shake well. Pour into an old-fashioned glass.

28 J. R.'S GODFATHER

2 ounces bourbon   ½ ounce amaretto

In an old-fashioned glass almost filled with ice cubes, combine both of the ingredients. Stir to mix the flavors.

29 J. R.'S REVENGE

3 ounces bourbon   2 dashes bitters
½ ounce Southern
  Comfort

In a mixing glass half-filled with ice cubes, combine all of the ingredients. Stir well. Strain into a cocktail glass.

30 KENTUCKY B AND B

2 ounces bourbon   ½ ounce Bénédictine

Pour the bourbon and Bénédictine into a brandy snifter.

31 KENTUCKY COLONEL

3 ounces bourbon   1 lemon twist
½ ounce Bénédictine

In a shaker half-filled with ice cubes combine the bourbon and Bénédictine. Shake and strain into a cocktail glass. Garnish with the lemon twist.

32 MIDNIGHT COWBOY

2 ounces bourbon   ½ ounce heavy cream
1 ounce dark rum

In a shaker half-filled with ice cubes, combine all of the ingredients. Shake well. Strain into a cocktail glass.

33 MINT JULEP

Juleps, although not mint juleps, have been with us for far longer than Kentucky has, probably since the seventeenth century. The word was also used by pharmacists to describe a sweet-tasting liquid that disguised the taste of an unpleasant medicine. I imagine that the first mint juleps could easily have been made to mask the flavor of a rough whiskey before the bourbon distillers, as we know them, had honed their craft.

Unlike most drinks, the mint julep has a traditional serving day: the same as the Kentucky Derby. Every year on the first Saturday in May, the mint julep is served nationwide at parties celebrating the great race. There is some controversy, however, over whether or not to muddle the mint. Any drink that is served every year on the same day and can provoke a fight must be a classic.

The drink should really be served in a special silver julep cup, which is shaped like a small tankard, but a highball or collins glass will do just fine, as long as the drink is served with style. Although someone is bound to argue with me, I contend that traditionally the mint is used only for bouquet, so make sure the leaves spill over the top of the glass, and use short straws so the drinker has to really bury his or her nose in the drink.

1 teaspoon superfine sugar	6 fresh mint sprigs, stems
Crushed ice	cut short immediately
3 ounces bourbon	before use

In a silver julep cup, highball glass, or collins glass, dissolve the sugar in a few drops of water. Almost fill the glass with crushed ice. Add the bourbon and some short straws. Garnish with the sprigs of mint on top.

34 MINT JULEP #2

6 fresh mint sprigs	Crushed ice
1 teaspoon superfine sugar	3 ounces bourbon

Lightly muddle 4 of the mint sprigs with the sugar and a few drops of water in the bottom of the glass. Almost fill the glass with crushed ice. Add the bourbon and some short straws. Garnish with the remaining 2 mint sprigs.

35 MINT JULEP #3

6 fresh mint sprigs
1 teaspoon superfine
  sugar

Crushed ice
3 ounces bourbon

Lightly muddle 4 of the mint sprigs with the sugar and a few drops of water in the bottom of the glass. Now smear the leaves all around the inside of the glass to coat it with the mixture; discard the leaves. Almost fill the glass with crushed ice. Add the bourbon and some short straws. Garnish with the remaining 2 mint sprigs.

36 NARRAGANSETT

2 ounces bourbon
1 ounce sweet vermouth

½ teaspoon anisette
1 lemon twist

In an old-fashioned glass almost filled with ice cubes, combine the bourbon, vermouth, and anisette. Stir well and garnish with the lemon twist.

37 NEVINS

2 ounces bourbon
½ ounce apricot brandy
½ ounce grapefruit juice

½ ounce lemon juice
1 dash bitters

In a shaker half-filled with ice cubes, combine all of the ingredients. Shake well. Strain into a cocktail glass.

38 PENDENNIS

½ teaspoon superfine
  sugar
Crushed ice

2 ounces bourbon
1 lemon slice

In an old-fashioned glass, dissolve the sugar in a few drops of water. Almost fill the glass with crushed ice. Add the bourbon. Stir well and garnish with the lemon slice.

39 RAGGED COMPANY

2 ounces bourbon
½ ounce sweet vermouth
1 teaspoon Bénédictine

2 dashes bitters
1 lemon twist

In a mixing glass half-filled with ice cubes, combine the bourbon, vermouth, Bénédictine, and bitters. Stir well. Strain into a cocktail glass and garnish with the lemon twist.

40 REBEL YELL

2 ounces bourbon
½ ounce Cointreau or
triple sec

1 ounce lemon juice
1 egg white
1 orange slice

In a shaker half-filled with ice cubes, combine the bourbon, Cointreau, lemon juice, and egg white. Shake well. Pour into an old-fashioned glass and garnish with the orange slice.

41 SAZERAC

1 teaspoon Ricard
½ teaspoon superfine
sugar
2 dashes Peychaud bitters

1 teaspoon water
2 ounces bourbon
1 lemon twist

Pour the Ricard into an old-fashioned glass and swirl it around to coat the glass; discard any excess. Place the sugar, Peychaud bitters, and water into the glass and muddle thoroughly with the back of a teaspoon. Almost fill the glass with ice cubes. Pour the bourbon over the ice cubes. Garnish with the lemon twist.

3 · BRANDY

"The thoroughbred in a field of nags" would adequately describe a fine brandy compared to most other liquors. In the realm of cocktails, brandy is found in such classics as the Sidecar, the Brandy Alexander, and the Stinger. There is much controversy about what constitutes a brandy. I should tell you that the recipes in this chapter use as their base the generally accepted brandy made from fermented wine. Drinks made from the much-debated fruit brandies appear in the Cordials chapter (page 238).

There are many tales told about the "invention" of brandy, and its true origin may never be known. Undoubtedly, though, it is the French who have refined and perfected the art of making this spirit.

One story tells of brandy being brought from Italy in 1533 to help celebrate the marriage of Catherine de Médicis. Mention of brandy from the Armagnac region of France, however, dates to 1411. In my mind, when the origin of anything is so unsure, credit should be given to the best story. The best story about the development of brandy involves a Dutchman.

This particular Dutchman, who was a shipmaster in the sixteenth century, was in the business of transporting wine from France to Holland. Being a wily sort, the man thought that by removing most of the water from the wine by means of distillation, he could concentrate it and thus ship much more wine per trip. He would make his fortune by adding the water back to the concentrate when it arrived in Holland.

Unfortunately for the poor soul, his friends tried the concentrated wine before he added the water to it and decided that to adulterate it would be a sin. They called it *brandewijn,* "burned wine," and through the years the name became shortened to brandy.

HOW TO SERVE BRANDY

A practice I abhor is that of warming brandy over a flame before serving it. This ritual actually burns off alcohol and contributes an artificially intense bouquet. Good brandy should be served at room temperature, in decent measure, in a snifter, preferably made from quality crystal. The snifter should be held with the stem slotted between two fingers of the upturned palm, which cups the bottom of the glass. In this way the heat of the hand will warm the brandy, the aroma will gently lift from the surface, and the vapors will be captured at the lip of the glass. When drinking brandy, one's nose or mouth should never be too far from the rim of the glass, lest that delectable mist be wasted on the fairies.

PRODUCTION

As described above, grape brandy is the product of the distillation of wine. It is made in just about every country that produces wine, so rules and regulations about its production differ from place to place. Both pot stills and continuous stills can be used, although the pot still produces the better, albeit more expensive, distillation. Sometimes brandy from both methods is "married" to produce a medium-price blend. The word *brandy* does not tell you where the product is from. Other more specific names are often applied, such as Cognac and Armagnac, to describe the place of origin. These premium brandies are often governed by strict standards of production (see page 35).

FRUIT BRANDY

There are many different types of fruit brandies and exacting definitions can be tedious. I will endeavor to be brief.

The biggest controversy concerns products such as apricot brandy, which, for some reason, caused so much of an uproar with the U.S. legal authorities that they created a special category for them. These brandies must be made with a wine-brandy base, be over 70° proof, and contain a specified amount of sugar. In other countries, sweetened spirits made from fruits can be called brandies without containing any wine brandy at all. When you buy fruit brandies, you may want to check the label; if there is no mention of the word *brandy,* then it probably is a fruit liqueur, but not necessarily an inferior product. It is all a matter of taste and government regulations.

Eau-de-vie, a French phrase that means, literally, "water of life," generally refers to a distillation of any fruit other than the grape that has an alcohol content of around 100° proof. This spirit is almost always colorless, since it is either bottled immediately after distillation, or stored in glass-lined casks or earthenware containers. This method of storage retains the intense fruit flavor and maintains the high alcohol content.

Applejack, strictly an American product, was known in Prohibition times as "Jersey Lightning." It is made from fermented apple cider, must be aged for a minimum of two years, and can be bottled as is or blended with neutral grain spirits.

Calvados, the French equivalent of applejack, is distilled from good-quality apple cider fermented for a minimum of one month (by which time all of the sugar has gone) and then aged, often as long as 20 to 40 years.

Other well-known fruit brandies and *eaux-de-vie* are kirsch or kirschwasser, made from cherries, Poire William from pears, Slivovitz from plums, framboise from raspberries, and fraise from strawberries.

BRANDY-PRODUCING COUNTRIES AND REGIONS

Good brandies are produced in France, Spain, Greece, Germany, Italy, Australia, Portugal, Peru, Israel, Yugoslavia, and South Africa. In fact, one could safely say that wherever grapes are grown, wine and brandy are made.

COGNAC

Only brandy made from grapes grown in the delimited district of France in the Charente known as Cognac may be named Cognac. The boundaries of this area were set down in 1909 and have since been subdivided into seven divisions of varying quality. In order of preference they are: *Grande Champagne, Petite Champagne, Borderies, Fins Bois, Bons Bois, Bois Ordinaires,* and *Bois à Terroir.*

All Cognac is made from wine that is fermented from whole grapes—skins, seeds, and all. The resulting wine is double-distilled in pot stills, and the heart of the second distillation is destined to become Cognac. It is aged in new oak casks for one year, and then is transferred to used oak casks, lest it take on too much tannin from the virgin oak. (Tannin is what helps color spirits and imparts that dry, puckery feeling in your mouth.)

Labels on Cognac bottles use special abbreviations that are designed to denote the quality of the spirit inside. Here is how it works:

V = Very
S = Special
O = Old
P = Pale
F = Fine
X = Extra
C = Cognac
E = Especial

When we put the letters together, however, they take on additional meanings. V.O. and V.S.O.P. both mean that the Cognac has been aged for at least four and a half years. V.S.O.P., however, is usually aged for at least eight years. If the label is printed with the words *Extra, Napoléon, or Vieille Réserve,* the French government warrants that the Cognac in that bottle has been aged for a minimum of five and a half years, not, as one may be tempted to believe, since the Battle of Waterloo.

Stars found on Cognac labels came from a superstitious shipper of brandy who put a star on his bottles to pay homage to a comet that appeared in 1811, a great year for Cognac. These days, French law states that three-star Cognac, the youngest, must be aged for a minimum of 18 months.

ARMAGNAC

This spirit, distilled mainly in Gascony in the southwest of France, is recognized as being the only brandy to come close to the quality of Cognac. Indeed, some connoisseurs actually prefer the more pungent taste of Armagnac. It is distilled once, in a continuous copper still that was invented in the Armagnac region in the nineteenth century. Frequently, small farmers use a portable still, which is wheeled from farm to farm. It is then aged in black oak, which gives tannin and deep color to the brandy. The aging and labeling of Armagnac is done in much the same way as Cognac.

The region known as Armagnac is divided into three areas (in order of descending quality): *Bas-Armagnac, Ténarèze,* and *Haut-Armagnac.* Any bottle bearing only the word *Armagnac,* without mention of any of the regions, is a blend of two or all three regions.

AMERICAN BRANDY

Brandy was first made in the New World by the Spanish missions in California, and California is still the major producer in the United States. By law, American brandy must be aged in wood, usually oak, for a minimum of two years, although it may be made in either a pot still or the more economical continuous still. American brandy is generally fruitier and somewhat lighter than European brandies.

GREEK BRANDY

Called *koniak* in Greece (pretty sneaky), most Greek brandy is distilled in Piraeus and Cyprus. The grapes used give this brandy a distinctive flavor, which usually is then sweetened with caramel.

SPANISH BRANDY

This rich, dark, sweet brandy is produced mainly in Jerez and Valdepeñas. Although some are distilled from sherry, most Spanish brandies are made from other Spanish wines.

42 ALL DRESSED UP LIKE A DOG'S DINNER

1½ ounces brandy   1 ounce sweet vermouth
1 ounce applejack

In a mixing glass half-filled with ice cubes, combine all of the ingredients. Stir well. Strain into a cocktail glass.

43 AMERICAN BEAUTY

1 ounce brandy   1 ounce orange juice
½ ounce dry vermouth   1 teaspoon grenadine
¼ teaspoon white crème   ½ ounce tawny port
  de menthe

In a shaker half-filled with ice cubes, combine the brandy, vermouth, crème de menthe, orange juice, and grenadine. Shake well. Strain into a cocktail glass. Pouring slowly and carefully, float the port on top.

44 BALTIMORE BRACER

1½ ounces brandy   1 egg white
1 ounce anisette

In a shaker half-filled with ice cubes, combine all of the ingredients. Shake well. Strain into a cocktail glass.

45 BENGAL

1½ ounces brandy   1 ounce pineapple juice
½ ounce maraschino   2 dashes bitters
  liqueur
½ ounce Cointreau or
  triple sec

In a shaker half-filled with ice cubes, combine all of the ingredients. Shake well. Strain into a cocktail glass.

46 BETSY ROSS 1

Crushed ice   ½ teaspoon Cointreau or
2 ounces brandy   triple sec
1½ ounces tawny port

In a mixing glass half-filled with crushed ice, combine all of the ingredients. Stir well. Strain into a cocktail glass.

47 BETWEEN THE SHEETS

1 ounce brandy   1 ounce lemon juice
1 ounce light rum
1 ounce Cointreau or
  triple sec

In a shaker half-filled with ice cubes, combine all of the ingredients. Shake well. Strain into a cocktail glass.

48 BLACK BALTIMORE

2 ounces brandy   1 egg white
1 ounce black Sambuca
  (Opal Nera)

In a shaker half-filled with ice cubes, combine all of the ingredients. Shake well. Strain into a cocktail glass.

49 BLACK PAGODA

1½ ounces brandy
½ ounce sweet vermouth
½ ounce dry vermouth

2 teaspoons Cointreau or
triple sec

In a mixing glass half-filled with ice cubes, combine all of the ingredients. Stir well. Strain into a cocktail glass.

50 BOSOM CARESSER

Crushed ice
1½ ounces brandy
1 ounce Madeira

½ ounce Cointreau or
triple sec

In a mixing glass half-filled with crushed ice, combine all of the ingredients. Stir well. Strain into a cocktail glass.

51 BRANDIED EGG SOUR

1 egg
2 ounces brandy
½ ounce Cointreau or
triple sec

1 ounce lemon juice
1 teaspoon superfine
sugar

In a shaker half-filled with ice cubes, crack the egg and add the rest of the ingredients. Shake well. Strain into a cocktail glass.

52 BRANDY AND SODA

2 ounces brandy

5 ounces club soda

Pour the brandy and club soda into a highball glass almost filled with ice cubes. Stir well.

53 BRANDY ALEXANDER

1½ ounces brandy
1 ounce dark crème de
cacao

1 ounce half-and-half
¼ teaspoon grated
nutmeg

In a shaker half-filled with ice cubes, combine the brandy, crème de cacao, and half-and-half. Shake well. Strain into a cocktail glass and garnish with the nutmeg.

54 BRANDY ALEXANDER #2

1½ ounces brandy
1 ounce white crème de
  cacao

1 ounce heavy cream
¼ teaspoon grated
  nutmeg

In a shaker half-filled with ice cubes, combine the brandy, crème de cacao, and cream. Shake well. Strain into a cocktail glass and garnish with the nutmeg.

55 BRANDY BLAZER

1 teaspoon granulated
  sugar
2 ounces brandy

1 slice orange
1 lemon twist

In an old-fashioned glass, dissolve the sugar in the brandy. Add the orange slice. Tilt the glass and carefully ignite the drink with a match. Stir with a long spoon until the flame is extinguished. Strain into a punch cup and garnish with the lemon twist.

56 BRANDY CLASSIC

1 lemon wedge
1 tablespoon powdered
  sugar
Crushed ice
1½ ounces brandy

½ ounce Cointreau or
  triple sec
2 teaspoons maraschino
  liqueur
½ ounce lemon juice

Moisten the rim of a cocktail glass using the lemon wedge; discard the lemon. Roll the outside edge of the rim in a saucer containing the sugar. In a shaker almost filled with crushed ice, combine the brandy, Cointreau, maraschino liqueur, and lemon juice. Shake well. Strain into the cocktail glass.

57 BRANDY COBBLER

1 teaspoon superfine
  sugar
3 ounces club soda
Crushed ice

2 ounces brandy
1 maraschino cherry
1 orange slice
1 lemon slice

In an old-fashioned glass, dissolve the sugar in the club soda. Add crushed ice until the glass is almost full. Add the brandy. Stir well. Garnish with the cherry and the orange and lemon slices.

58 BRANDY COLLINS

2 ounces brandy
1 ounce lemon juice
1 teaspoon superfine
  sugar

3 ounces club soda
1 maraschino cherry
1 orange slice

In a shaker half-filled with ice cubes, combine the brandy, lemon juice, and sugar. Shake well. Strain into a collins glass almost filled with ice cubes. Add the club soda. Stir and garnish with the cherry and the orange slice.

59 BRANDY COOLER

2 ounces brandy
4 ounces lemon-lime
  soda

1 lemon wedge

Pour the brandy and the soda into a highball glass almost filled with ice cubes. Stir well. Garnish with the lemon wedge.

60 BRANDY CRUSTA

1 tablespoon superfine
  sugar
1 lemon wedge
Peel of 1 orange, cut into
  a spiral
Crushed ice

1½ ounces brandy
½ ounce Cointreau or
  triple sec
2 teaspoons maraschino
  liqueur
½ ounce lemon juice

Place the sugar in a saucer. Rub the rim of a wine goblet with the lemon wedge and dip it into the sugar to coat the rim thoroughly; discard the lemon. Place the orange peel spiral in the goblet and drape one end of it over the rim of the glass. Fill the glass with crushed ice. In a shaker half-filled with ice cubes, combine the brandy, Cointreau, maraschino liqueur, and lemon juice. Shake well. Strain into the goblet.

61 BRANDY DAISY

2 ounces brandy
1 ounce lemon juice
½ teaspoon superfine
  sugar

½ teaspoon grenadine
1 maraschino cherry
1 orange slice

In a shaker half-filled with ice cubes, combine the brandy, lemon juice, sugar, and grenadine. Shake well. Pour into an old-fashioned glass and garnish with the cherry and the orange slice.

62 BRANDY FIX

1 teaspoon superfine
  sugar
1 ounce lemon juice
2 teaspoons water

Crushed ice
2 ounces brandy
1 maraschino cherry
1 lemon slice

In a shaker half-filled with ice cubes, combine the sugar, lemon juice, and water. Shake well. Strain into a highball glass almost filled with crushed ice. Add the brandy. Stir well and garnish with the cherry and the lemon slice.

63 BRANDY FIZZ

2½ ounces brandy
1 ounce lemon juice
1 teaspoon superfine
  sugar

4 ounces club soda

In a shaker half-filled with ice cubes, combine the brandy, lemon juice, and sugar. Shake well. Strain into a collins glass almost filled with ice cubes. Add the club soda. Stir well.

64 BRANDY FLIP

2 ounces brandy
1 whole egg
1 teaspoon superfine
  sugar

½ ounce light cream
⅛ teaspoon grated
  nutmeg

In a shaker half-filled with ice cubes, combine the brandy, egg, sugar, and cream. Shake well. Strain into a sour glass and garnish with the nutmeg.

65 BRANDY SANGAREE

1 teaspoon superfine sugar	½ ounce tawny port
2 teaspoons water	1 lemon twist
1½ ounces brandy	⅛ teaspoon grated nutmeg
Crushed ice	⅛ teaspoon ground cinnamon
2½ ounces club soda	

In a highball glass, dissolve the sugar in the water and brandy. Almost fill the glass with crushed ice and add the club soda. Float the port on top. Garnish with the lemon twist and sprinkle on the nutmeg and cinnamon.

66 BRANDY SLING

1 teaspoon superfine sugar	1 ounce lemon juice
2 teaspoons water	2 ounces brandy
	1 lemon twist

In a shaker half-filled with ice cubes, combine the sugar, water, lemon juice, and brandy. Shake well. Strain into a highball glass. Garnish with the lemon twist.

67 BRANDY SMASH

4 fresh mint sprigs	2½ ounces brandy
1 teaspoon superfine sugar	1 orange slice
1 ounce club soda	1 maraschino cherry

In an old-fashioned glass, muddle the mint sprigs lightly with the sugar and club soda. Fill the glass with ice cubes. Add the brandy. Stir well and garnish with the orange slice and the cherry.

68 BRANDY SOUR

2 ounces brandy	1 slice orange
1 ounce lemon juice	1 maraschino cherry
½ teaspoon superfine sugar	

In a shaker half-filled with ice cubes, combine the brandy, lemon juice, and sugar. Shake well. Strain into a whiskey sour glass and garnish with the orange slice and the cherry.

69 BRANDY SWIZZLE

1½ ounces lime juice
1 teaspoon superfine
  sugar
2 ounces brandy

1 dash bitters
Crushed ice
3 ounces club soda

In a shaker half-filled with ice cubes, combine the lime juice, sugar, brandy, and bitters. Shake well. Almost fill a collins glass with crushed ice and stir until the glass is frosted. Strain the mixture in the shaker into the glass and add the club soda. Serve with a swizzle stick.

70 CHAMPS ELYSEES

2 ounces brandy
½ ounce yellow
  Chartreuse
½ ounce lemon juice

½ teaspoon superfine
  sugar
2 dashes bitters

In a shaker half-filled with ice cubes, combine all of the ingredients. Shake well. Strain into a cocktail glass.

71 CHARLES COCKTAIL

2 ounces brandy
½ ounce sweet vermouth

2 dashes bitters

In a mixing glass half-filled with ice cubes, combine all of the ingredients. Stir well. Strain into a cocktail glass.

72 CITY SLICKER

2 ounces brandy
½ ounce Cointreau or
  triple sec

1 tablespoon lemon juice

In a shaker half-filled with ice cubes, combine all of the ingredients. Shake well. Strain into a cocktail glass.

73 COMFORTING TIGER

Crushed ice
2 ounces brandy
½ ounce Southern
  Comfort

1 teaspoon sweet
  vermouth
1 lemon twist

In a mixing glass, half-filled with crushed ice, combine the brandy, Southern Comfort, and vermouth. Stir well. Strain into a cocktail glass and garnish with the lemon twist.

74 CORPSE REVIVER

1½ ounces brandy
½ ounce Fernet Branca

1 ounce white crème de
menthe

In a mixing glass half-filled with ice cubes, combine all of the ingredients. Stir well. Strain into a cocktail glass.

75 DANCE WITH A DREAM COCKTAIL

2 ounces brandy
½ ounce Cointreau or
triple sec

1 teaspoon anisette

In a shaker half-filled with ice cubes, combine all of the ingredients. Shake well. Strain into a cocktail glass.

76 FANCY BRANDY

2 ounces brandy
½ teaspoon Cointreau or
triple sec
¼ teaspoon superfine
sugar

2 dashes bitters
1 lemon twist

In a shaker half-filled with ice cubes, combine the brandy, Cointreau, sugar, and bitters. Shake well. Strain into a cocktail glass and garnish with the lemon twist.

FRENCH REVOLUTION

See Wine Drinks, page 267.

77 HORSE'S NECK

Peel of 1 lemon, cut into
a spiral
2 ounces brandy

5 ounces ginger ale
2 dashes bitters

Place the lemon peel spiral in a highball glass and drape one end of it over the rim of the glass. Fill the glass with ice cubes. Pour the brandy, ginger ale, and bitters into the glass. Stir well.

78 JAPANESE

2 ounces brandy
1 teaspoon orgeat syrup
½ ounce lime juice

1 dash bitters
1 lime twist

In a shaker half-filled with ice cubes, combine the brandy, orgeat syrup, lime juice, and bitters. Shake well. Strain into a cocktail glass and garnish with the lime twist.

79 LA JOLLA

2 ounces brandy
½ ounce crème de
bananes

1 teaspoon orange juice
½ ounce lemon juice

In a shaker half-filled with ice cubes, combine all of the ingredients. Shake well. Strain into a cocktail glass.

80 METROPOLITAN

Crushed ice
1 teaspon superfine sugar
2 ounces brandy

½ ounce sweet vermouth
1 dash bitters

In a shaker half-filled with crushed ice, combine all of the ingredients. Shake well. Strain into a cocktail glass.

81 MIKADO

1½ ounces brandy
½ ounce Cointreau or
triple sec
1 teaspoon crème de
noyaux

1 teaspoon grenadine
1 dash bitters

In an old-fashioned glass almost filled with ice cubes, combine all of the ingredients. Stir well.

PHOEBE SNOW

See Aperitifs, page 233.

82 SIDECAR

2 ounces brandy
½ ounce Cointreau or
triple sec

1 ounce lemon juice

In a shaker half-filled with ice cubes, combine all of the ingredients. Shake well. Strain into a cocktail glass.

83 SOUTHERN BELLE

½ ounce brandy
½ ounce white crème de
cacao

½ ounce Bènèdictine

Pour the brandy into a pousse café glass. Tilt the glass to a 45-degree angle and slowly pour the crème de cacao down the side of the glass so that it floats on the brandy. Repeat this procedure with the Bènèdictine.

84 STINGER

2 ounces brandy
½ ounce white crème de
menthe

In a mixing glass half-filled with ice cubes, combine both ingredients. Stir well. Strain into a cocktail glass.

4 · GIN

The word *gin* is merely a corruption of the Dutch for juniper—*jenever*—or from the French word for juniper—*genièvre*. Gin is a versatile yet distinctive beverage, the main ingredient in a Tom Collins, a Martini, and a Singapore Sling. Gin, a wonderfully perfumed potion, is probably the most notorious of liquors, and, for some reason, gin drinkers are seen as serious drinkers, people who like the taste of alcohol and do not try to disguise it. This attitude is much appreciated by gin distillers, who go to great lengths to make their gin distinctive and jealously guard their recipes.

Gin was first developed in the seventeenth century by a Dutch doctor, who combined alcohol with the juniper berry to concoct a remedy for kidney complaints. Apparently, although it did nothing for the kidneys, the "tonic" was very popular due to its amnesia-inducing qualities. It made the patient forget or, at the very least, not care about his complaint.

Then came William III, another Dutchman, who married Mary II and became King of England in 1689. William had a personal grudge against the French because they were threatening his native Holland. Vengefully he raised excise duties on all French wines and brandies. This action

made gin, the cheaper Dutch liquor, more accessible to the English public, thus hurting the French and benefiting Holland in one fell swoop.

His adopted country took to the gin very quickly. They were soon making it themselves, and for a large part of the eighteenth century, gin became the solace of the English poor. Soldiers drank it before going into battle, and their drunken bravery came to be known as "Dutch Courage." Juniper berries were erroneously believed to have the power to induce abortion, and thus gin earned the name "Mother's Ruin." If a person was living a debauched life, he was said to be on "Gin Lane."

All things considered, it is quite amazing that such a maligned drink is still with us, but gradually, gin became more socially acceptable, and today we have available to us a wide variety of distinctive gins. The next time you have a Martini, you may consider raising your glass to William III. Without him, you might be drinking straight vermouth.

PRODUCTION

1. Generally speaking, today's gin is made by infusing juniper and other flavorings into a high-quality, neutral grain spirit.
2. This spirit is made in a continuous still from wort, a liquid made, in the case of gin, by boiling and fermenting corn with malted barley and a small amount of another grain.
3. The infusion is usually achieved by means of distilling the spirit along with the flavorings in a pot still.

DRY GIN

If you order any standard gin drink, the gin that's poured will be dry gin, unquestionably the most popular type of gin. All distillers use juniper berries and coriander seed in their dry gin recipes, but other flavorings may include fennel, calamus root, orris root, angelica root, almond, cardamom, cassia, ginger, cinnamon, licorice, caraway seeds, orange and lemon peels, and perhaps some other secret ingredients that the distillers just won't talk about. This collection of flavorings is known as the "botanicals."

The botanicals either are added to the neutral spirit in a pot still before the spirit is redistilled, or they may be suspended in the tower of the still so that the spirit vapors absorb their flavors. The "two-shot" method of distilling dry gin calls for a much larger proportion of botanicals, and the resulting, highly flavored liquor is then mixed with unflavored neutral grain spirit to produce the correct strength.

In America, dry gin may be made by adding the botanicals to the original distillation of the wort or even by adding oils or extracts from juniper and other botanicals to neutral grain spirits. The second method produces compound gin, which cannot be called distilled gin.

DUTCH GIN

Dutch gin, also known as "Hollands gin" or "Genever gin," is made by infusing juniper and some, but not many, other botanicals into malt wine. Malt wine is a neutral grain spirit made from equal amounts of malted barley, corn, and rye. These products are boiled, and the resulting wort is allowed to ferment for a few days before being distilled in a pot still. The resulting liquor may be redistilled once or twice before finally being distilled in another pot still with the botanicals. Sometimes this liquor is then diluted with grain spirit from a continuous still to make the product less expensive.

The two main types of Dutch gin are *oude* and *jonge,* old and young. *Jonge* contains much less malt wine and much more continuous still grain spirit. The slight golden color found in many Dutch gins comes from a small amount of coloring added to the final product.

OLD TOM

Old Tom, rarely produced anymore, is a sweet gin that is made in England. It is said to have been the gin used to make the original Tom Collins. In addition to that lovely bit of trivia, Old Tom comes equipped with a wonderful legend. The tale told is that Old Tom gin was first distilled by Captain Dudley Broadsheet in eighteenth-century London. The captain used a carving of a tomcat as his shop sign and, I was amazed to hear, as his dispenser. The buyer would put his money into the cat's mouth and hold a receptacle under one of the cat's paws. Broadsheet would watch how much money was being spent and pour the appropriate amount of gin into a pipe that ran through the leg of his cat and into the buyer's glass. Personally, I would buy the dear captain's gin just to see the show.

PLYMOUTH GIN

Plymouth gin is made by only one distiller and is completely unsweetened. It was rumored that a small amount of sulfuric acid was added to Plymouth gin before it was distilled, but I cannot find any corroboration for this allegation. Plymouth gin is the traditional gin of the British Navy, and it is the gin of preference for an authentic Pink Gin.

85 ABBEY COCKTAIL

2 ounces gin	2 dashes orange bitters
1½ ounces orange juice	1 maraschino cherry

In a shaker half-filled with ice cubes, combine the gin, orange juice, and orange bitters. Shake well. Strain into a cocktail glass and garnish with the cherry.

86 ALASKA

2 ounces gin   1 dash orange bitters
½ ounce yellow
   Chartreuse

In a mixing glass half-filled with crushed ice, combine all of the ingredients. Stir well. Strain into a cocktail glass.

87 ALEXANDER

1½ ounces gin   1 ounce light cream
1 ounce white crème de   ⅛ teaspoon grated
   cacao   nutmeg

In a shaker half-filled with ice cubes, combine the gin, crème de cacao, and cream. Shake well. Strain into a cocktail glass and garnish with the nutmeg.

88 ALEXANDER'S SISTER

1 ½ ounces gin   1 ounce heavy cream
1 ounce green crème de   ⅛ teaspoon grated
   menthe   nutmeg

In a shaker half-filled with ice cubes, combine the gin, crème de menthe, and heavy cream. Shake well. Strain into a cocktail glass and garnish with the nutmeg.

89 ALEXANDER'S BIG BROTHER

2 ounces gin   ½ ounce heavy cream
½ ounce blue Curaçao

In a shaker half-filled with ice cubes, combine all of the ingredients. Shake well. Strain into a cocktail glass.

90 ARCADIA

1½ ounces gin   ½ ounce grapefruit juice
½ ounce Galliano
½ ounce crème de
   bananes

In a shaker half-filled with ice cubes, combine all of the ingredients. Shake well. Strain into a cocktail glass.

91 ARCHBISHOP

2 ounces gin
1 ounce green ginger wine

1 teaspoon Bènèdictine
1 lime wedge

In an old-fashioned glass almost filled with ice cubes, combine all of the ingredients. Stir well.

92 ARTHUR TOMPKINS

2 ounces gin
½ ounce Grand Marnier

2 teaspoons lemon juice
1 lemon twist

In a shaker half-filled with ice cubes, combine the gin, Grand Marnier, and lemon juice. Shake well. Strain into a sour glass and garnish with the lemon twist.

93 ARTILLERY

2 ounces gin
½ ounce sweet vermouth

2 dashes bitters

In a mixing glass half-filled with ice cubes, combine all of the ingredients. Stir well. Strain into a cocktail glass.

94 BANNISTER

Crushed ice
1½ ounces gin
1 ounce applejack

1 teaspoon Pernod
½ teaspoon grenadine

In a mixing glass half-filled with crushed ice, combine all of the ingredients. Stir well. Strain into a cocktail glass.

95 BARBARY COAST

1 ounce gin
½ ounce Scotch
½ ounce light rum

½ ounce dark crème de cacao
1 ounce light cream

In a shaker half-filled with ice cubes, combine all of the ingredients. Shake well. Strain into a cocktail glass.

96 BEAUTY SPOT

1½ ounces gin
2 teaspoons white crème
de cacao

1 egg white
½ teaspoon grenadine

In a shaker half-filled with ice cubes, combine the gin, crème de cacao, and egg white. Shake well. Strain into a cocktail glass. Drop the grenadine into the center of the drink.

97 BELLES OF ST. MARY'S

1½ ounces gin
1 ounce Cointreau or
triple sec

1 ounce apricot brandy
2 teaspoons lemon juice

In a shaker half-filled with ice cubes, combine all of the ingredients. Shake well. Strain into a cocktail glass.

98 BENNET COCKTAIL

1½ ounces gin
½ ounce lime juice
½ teaspoon superfine
sugar

1 dash orange bitters

In a shaker half-filled with ice cubes, combine all of the ingredients. Shake well. Strain into a cocktail glass.

99 BERMUDA ROSE

Crushed ice
2 ounces gin

½ ounce apricot brandy
1 teaspoon grenadine

In a mixing glass half-filled with crushed ice, combine all of the ingredients. Stir well. Strain into a cocktail glass.

100 BERNARD'S BEVIE

1½ ounces gin
½ ounce sweet vermouth

½ ounce dry vermouth
1 teaspoon B & B

In a mixing glass half-filled with ice cubes, combine all of the ingredients. Stir well. Strain into a cocktail glass.

101 BERNARDO

2 ounces gin
½ ounce Cointreau or
  triple sec

2 teaspoons lemon juice
2 dashes bitters
1 lemon twist

In a shaker half-filled with ice cubes, combine the gin, Cointreau, lemon juice, and bitters. Shake well. Strain into a cocktail glass and garnish with the lemon twist.

102 BITCH-ON-WHEELS

2 ounces gin
½ ounce dry vermouth
½ ounce white crème de
  menthe

1 teaspoon Pernod

In a mixing glass half-filled with ice cubes, combine all of the ingredients. Stir well. Strain into a cocktail glass.

103 BLUEBIRD

Crushed ice
1½ ounces gin
½ ounce Cointreau or
  triple sec

½ ounce blue Curaçao
2 dashes bitters
1 lemon twist
1 maraschino cherry

In a mixing glass half-filled with crushed ice, combine the gin, Cointreau, Curaçao, and bitters. Stir well. Strain into a cocktail glass and garnish with the lemon twist and the cherry.

104 BLUE COWBOY

Crushed ice
1½ ounces gin

½ ounce blue Curaçao

In a mixing glass half-filled with crushed ice, combine both of the ingredients. Stir well. Strain into a cocktail glass.

105 BOOMERANG

2 ounces gin
½ ounce dry vermouth
2 dashes bitters

½ teaspoon maraschino
 liqueur
1 maraschino cherry

In a mixing glass half-filled with ice cubes, combine the gin, vermouth, bitters, and maraschino liqueur. Stir well. Strain into a cocktail glass and garnish with the cherry.

106 BOXCAR

1½ ounces gin
1 ounce Cointreau or
 triple sec

1 teaspoon lemon juice
½ teaspon grenadine
1 egg white

In a shaker half-filled with ice cubes, combine all of the ingredients. Shake well. Strain into a sour glass.

107 THE BRONX AIN'T SO SWEET

1½ ounces gin
1 teaspoon dry vermouth

½ ounce orange juice

In a shaker half-filled with ice cubes, combine all of the ingredients. Shake well. Strain into a cocktail glass.

108 BRONX COCKTAIL

2 ounces gin
1 teaspoon dry vermouth
1 teaspoon sweet
 vermouth

½ ounce orange juice

In a shaker half-filled with ice cubes, combine all of the ingredients. Shake well. Strain into a cocktail glass.

109 CABARET

1 ounce gin
½ ounce dry vermouth
½ ounce Bènèdictine

2 dashes bitters
1 maraschino cherry

In a shaker half-filled with ice cubes, combine the gin, vermouth, Bènèdictine, and bitters. Shake well. Strain into a cocktail glass and garnish with the cherry.

110 CAFÉ DE PARIS

2 ounces gin
½ ounce anisette

1 egg white
1 ounce heavy cream

In a shaker half-filled with ice cubes, combine all of the ingredients. Shake well. Strain into a sour glass.

111 CAPTAIN COOK

1½ ounces gin
½ ounce maraschino
  liqueur

1 ounce orange juice

In a shaker half-filled with ice cubes, combine all of the ingredients. Shake well. Strain into a cocktail glass.

112 CAPTAIN'S TABLE

2 ounces gin
½ ounce Campari
1 teaspoon grenadine

1 ounce orange juice
4 ounces ginger ale
1 maraschino cherry

In a shaker half-filled with ice cubes, combine the gin, Campari, grenadine, and orange juice. Shake well. Pour into a collins glass almost filled with ice cubes. Top with the ginger ale. Garnish with the cherry.

113 CAROLI

Crushed ice
2 ounces gin

½ ounce apricot brandy
1 dash orange bitters

In a mixing glass half-filled with crushed ice, combine all of the ingredients. Stir well. Strain into a cocktail glass.

114 CARUSO

1½ ounces gin
1 ounce dry vermouth

1 ounce green crème de
  menthe

In a mixing glass half-filled with ice cubes, combine all of the ingredients. Stir well. Strain into a cocktail glass.

115 CARUSO BLANCO

1½ ounces gin
1 ounce dry vermouth

1 ounce white crème de
menthe

In a mixing glass half-filled with ice cubes, combine all of the ingredients. Stir well. Strain into a cocktail glass.

116 CASINO

2 ounces gin
½ ounce lemon juice
1 teaspoon maraschino
liqueur

2 dashes orange bitters

In a shaker half-filled with ice cubes, combine all of the ingredients. Shake well. Strain into a cocktail glass.

117 CASINO ROYALE

2 ounces gin
½ ounce lemon juice
1 teaspoon maraschino
liqueur

1 dash orange bitters
1 egg yolk

In a shaker half-filled with ice cubes, combine all of the ingredients. Shake well. Strain into a sour glass.

118 CHELSEA HOTEL

1½ ounces gin
½ ounce Cointreau or
triple sec

2 teaspoons lemon juice

In a shaker half-filled with ice cubes, combine all of the ingredients. Shake well. Strain into a cocktail glass.

119 CONFIRMED BACHELOR

Crushed ice
1½ ounces gin
1 teaspoon grenadine

½ teaspoon Rose's lime
juice
1 egg white

In a shaker half-filled with crushed ice, combine all of the ingredients. Shake well. Strain into a cocktail glass.

120 CRIMSON SUNSET

2 ounces gin   ½ teaspoon grenadine
2 teaspoons lemon juice   ½ ounce tawny port

In a shaker half-filled with ice cubes, combine the gin and lemon juice. Shake well. Strain into a cocktail glass. Drop the grenadine into the center of the drink and float the port on the top.

121 DELMONICO COCKTAIL

1 ounce gin   ½ ounce dry vermouth
½ ounce brandy   1 dash bitters
½ ounce sweet vermouth   1 lemon twist

In a mixing glass half-filled with ice cubes, combine the gin, brandy, sweet vermouth, dry vermouth, and bitters. Stir well. Strain into a cocktail glass and garnish with the lemon twist.

122 DIRTY DICK'S DOWNFALL

2 ounces gin   ½ ounce Campari
½ ounce dry vermouth   1 lemon twist

In a mixing glass half-filled with ice cubes, combine the gin, vermouth, and Campari. Stir well. Strain into a cocktail glass and garnish with the lemon twist.

123 DRAGONFLY

1½ ounces gin   1 lime wedge
4 ounces ginger ale

In a highball glass almost filled with ice cubes, combine the gin and ginger ale. Stir well. Garnish with the lime wedge.

124 EMERALD FOREST

Crushed ice   1 teaspoon white crème
1½ ounces gin   de menthe
1 teaspoon green crème
  de menthe

In a mixing glass half-filled with crushed ice, combine all of the ingredients. Stir well. Strain into a cocktail glass.

125 EMERALD ISLE

Crushed ice
2 ounces gin
2 teaspoons green crème
de menthe

1 dash bitters

In a mixing glass half-filled with crushed ice, combine all of the ingredients. Stir well. Strain into a cocktail glass.

126 EMERSON

2 ounces gin
1 ounce sweet vermouth
1 teaspoon maraschino
liqueur

2 teaspoons lemon juice

In a shaker half-filled with ice cubes, combine all of the ingredients. Shake well. Strain into a cocktail glass.

127 EUROPEAN

1 ounce gin
½ ounce cream sherry
½ ounce Dubonnet
Rouge

½ ounce dry vermouth
½ teaspoon Grand
Marnier
1 maraschino cherry

In an old-fashioned glass almost filled with ice cubes, combine the gin, sherry, Dubonnet, vermouth, and Grand Marnier. Stir well. Garnish with the cherry.

128 FARMER GILES

2 ounces gin
½ ounce dry vermouth
½ ounce sweet vermouth

2 dashes bitters
1 lemon twist

In a mixing glass half-filled with ice cubes, combine the gin, dry vermouth, sweet vermouth, and bitters. Stir well. Strain into a cocktail glass and garnish with the lemon twist.

129 FASTLAP

2 ounces gin
½ ounce Pernod

1 ounce orange juice
½ teaspoon grenadine

In a shaker half-filled with ice cubes, combine all of the ingredients. Shake well. Pour into an old-fashioned glass.

130 FAT FACE

1½ ounces gin
½ ounce apricot brandy

1 teaspoon grenadine
1 egg white

In a shaker half-filled with ice cubes, combine all of the ingredients. Shake well. Strain into a sour glass.

131 FIFTY-FIFTY

1½ ounces gin
1½ ounces dry vermouth

1 cocktail olive

In a mixing glass half-filled with ice cubes, combine the gin and vermouth. Stir well. Strain into a cocktail glass and garnish with the olive.

132 FINO MARTINI

2½ ounces gin or vodka
1½ teaspoons fino sherry

1 lemon twist

In a mixing glass half-filled with ice cubes, combine the gin or vodka and the sherry. Stir well. Strain into a cocktail glass. Garnish with the lemon twist.

133 FLEET STREET

1½ ounces gin
½ ounce sweet vermouth
1 teaspoon dry vermouth

1 teaspoon Cointreau or
   triple sec
1 teaspoon lemon juice

In a shaker half-filled with ice cubes, combine all of the ingredients. Shake well. Strain into a cocktail glass.

134 FLYING DUTCHMAN

2 ounces gin
½ ounce Cointreau or
   triple sec

In an old-fashioned glass almost filled with ice cubes, combine the gin and Cointreau. Stir well.

135 FRENCH "75"

1½ ounces gin
2 teaspoons superfine
  sugar
1½ ounces lemon juice
4 ounces chilled
  Champagne or sparkling
  wine

1 orange slice
1 maraschino cherry

In a shaker half-filled with ice cubes, combine the gin, sugar, and lemon juice. Shake well. Pour into a collins glass. Top with the Champagne. Stir well and garnish with the orange slice and the cherry.

136 GENTLEMAN'S CLUB

1½ ounces gin
1 ounce brandy

1 ounce sweet vermouth
1 ounce club soda

In an old-fashioned glass almost filled with ice cubes, combine all of the ingredients. Stir well.

137 GENT OF THE JURY

2 ounces gin
½ ounce cherry brandy
3 ounces pineapple juice

½ ounce lemon juice
1 dash bitters

In a shaker half-filled with ice cubes, combine all of the ingredients. Shake well. Strain into a highball glass almost filled with ice cubes.

138 GIBSON

2½ ounces gin
1½ teaspoons dry
  vermouth

3 cocktail onions

In a mixing glass half-filled with ice cubes, combine the gin and vermouth. Stir well. Strain into a cocktail glass. Garnish with the onions.

139 GIMLET

Originally a British concoction from the Far East, the gimlet combines two ingredients that probably spring immediately to mind with the very mention of the word British: gin and lime. Was it first made with fresh lime juice or Rose's lime juice, which is concentrated and sweetened? We shall probably never know, but since the Rose's product has had such a long and impressive history (which predates the gimlet), I am inclined to think that Rose's was the ingredient that invented the drink.

Rose's lime juice was first concocted by Lauchlin Rose of Scotland in 1867 and was sold to shipping companies as a preventative remedy for scurvy. This helpful and profitable sale of his product also served to introduce Rose's lime juice wherever the ships were headed throughout the world. It was first exported to America in 1901.

Variations on the gimlet include the Rum Gimlet (page 113), Tequila Gimlet (page 153), and Vodka Gimlet (page 177).

2 ounces gin	1 lime wedge
½ ounce Rose's lime juice	

Pour the gin and lime juice into a mixing glass half-filled with ice cubes. Stir well. Strain into a cocktail glass and garnish with the lime wedge.

140 GIN AND BITTER LEMON

1½ ounces gin	4 ounces tonic water
½ ounce lemon juice	
½ teaspoon superfine sugar	

In a shaker half-filled with ice cubes, combine the gin, lemon juice, and sugar. Shake well. Strain into a highball glass almost filled with ice cubes. Top with the tonic water.

141 GIN AND PINK

2 ounces gin	2 dashes bitters
5 ounces tonic water	1 lemon twist

In a highball glass almost filled with ice cubes, combine the gin, tonic, and bitters. Stir well and garnish with the lemon twist.

142 GIN AND SIN

1½ ounces gin
1 ounce orange juice

1 ounce lemon juice
½ teaspoon grenadine

In a shaker half-filled with ice cubes, combine all of the ingredients. Shake well. Strain into a cocktail glass.

143 GIN AND TONIC

2 ounces gin
5 ounces tonic water

1 lime wedge

Pour the gin and the tonic water into a highball glass almost filled with ice cubes. Stir well. Garnish with the lime wedge.

144 GIN BLOODY MARY

2½ ounces gin
5 ounces tomato juice
½ ounce lemon juice
⅛ teaspoon salt
⅛ teaspoon black pepper

3 dashes Worcestershire
sauce
1 dash Tabasco sauce
1 lime wedge

In a shaker half-filled with ice cubes, combine the gin, tomato juice, lemon juice, salt, pepper, Worcestershire, and Tabasco sauce. Shake well. Strain into a highball glass almost filled with ice cubes. Garnish with the lime wedge.

145 GIN-CASSIS FIZZ

2½ ounces gin
1½ ounces lemon juice
1 teaspoon superfine
sugar

4 ounces club soda
½ ounce crème de cassis

In a shaker half-filled with ice cubes, combine the gin, lemon juice, and sugar. Shake well. Strain into a collins glass almost filled with ice cubes. Add the club soda. Stir well. Drop the cassis into the center of the drink.

146 GIN COBBLER

1 teaspoon superfine
  sugar
3 ounces club soda
Crushed ice

2 ounces gin
1 maraschino cherry
1 orange slice
1 lemon slice

In an old-fashioned glass, dissolve the sugar in the club soda. Add crushed ice until the glass is almost full. Add the gin. Stir well. Garnish with the cherry and the orange and lemon slices.

147 GIN COOLER

2 ounces gin
4 ounces lemon-lime
  soda

1 lemon wedge

Pour the gin and soda into a highball glass almost filled with ice cubes. Stir well. Garnish with the lemon wedge.

148 GIN DAISY

2 ounces gin
1 ounce lemon juice
½ teaspoon superfine
  sugar

½ teaspoon grenadine
1 maraschino cherry
1 orange slice

In a shaker half-filled with ice cubes, combine the gin, lemon juice, sugar, and grenadine. Shake well. Pour into an old-fashioned glass and garnish with the cherry and the orange slice.

149 GIN FIX

1 teaspoon superfine
  sugar
1 ounce lemon juice
2 teaspoons water

Crushed ice
2 ounces gin
1 maraschino cherry
1 lemon slice

In a shaker half-filled with ice cubes, combine the sugar, lemon juice, and water. Shake well. Strain into a highball glass almost filled with crushed ice. Add the gin. Stir well and garnish with the cherry and the lemon slice.

150 GIN FIZZ

2½ ounces gin   4 ounces club soda
1 ounce lemon juice
1 teaspoon superfine
  sugar

In a shaker half-filled with ice cubes, combine the gin, lemon juice, and sugar. Shake well. Strain into a collins glass almost filled with ice cubes. Add the club soda. Stir well.

151 GIN SANGAREE

1 teaspoon superfine   ½ ounce tawny port
  sugar   1 lemon twist
2 teaspoons water   ⅛ teaspoon grated
1½ ounces gin   nutmeg
Crushed ice   ⅛ teaspoon ground
2½ ounces club soda   cinnamon

In a highball glass, dissolve the sugar in the water and gin. Almost fill the glass with crushed ice and add the club soda. Float the port on top. Garnish with the lemon twist and a sprinkling of nutmeg and cinnamon.

152 GIN SLING

1 teaspoon superfine   1 ounce lemon juice
  sugar   2 ounces gin
2 teaspoons water   1 lemon twist

In a shaker half-filled with ice cubes, combine the sugar, water, lemon juice, and gin. Shake well. Strain into an old-fashioned glass almost filled with ice cubes. Garnish with the lemon twist.

153 GIN SMASH

4 fresh mint sprigs   1 ounce club soda
1 teaspoon superfine   2½ ounces gin
  sugar   1 lemon twist

In an old-fashioned glass, muddle the mint sprigs lightly with the sugar and club soda. Fill the glass with ice cubes. Add the gin. Stir well and garnish with the lemon twist.

154 GIN SOUR

2 ounces gin
1 ounce lemon juice
½ teaspoon superfine
   sugar

1 orange slice
1 maraschino cherry

In a shaker half-filled with ice cubes, combine the gin, lemon juice, and sugar. Shake well. Strain into a sour glass and garnish with the orange slice and the cherry.

155 GIN SWIZZLE

1½ ounces lime juice
1 teaspoon superfine
   sugar

2 ounces gin
1 dash bitters
3 ounces club soda

In a shaker half-filled with ice cubes, combine the lime juice, sugar, gin, and bitters. Shake well. Almost fill a collins glass with ice cubes. Stir until the glass is frosted. Strain the mixture in the shaker into the glass and add the club soda. Serve with a swizzle stick.

156 GOLDEN BRONX

2 ounces gin
1 teaspoon dry vermouth
1 teaspoon sweet
   vermouth

½ ounce orange juice
1 egg yolk

In a shaker half-filled with ice cubes, combine all of the ingredients. Shake well. Strain into a sour glass.

157 GRASS SKIRT

1½ ounces gin
1 ounce Cointreau or
   triple sec

1 ounce pineapple juice
½ teaspoon grenadine
1 pineapple slice

In a shaker half-filled with ice cubes, combine the gin, Cointreau, pineapple juice, and grenadine. Shake well. Pour into an old-fashioned glass and garnish with the pineapple slice.

158 GREENHAM'S GROTTO

2 ounces gin
1 ounce brandy

2 teaspoons orgeat syrup
2 teaspoons lemon juice

In a shaker half-filled with ice cubes, combine all of the ingredients. Shake well. Pour into an old-fashioned glass.

159 GUMBO FIZZ

2 ounces gin
1 ounce lemon juice
1 teaspoon superfine
   sugar
1 egg white

1 teaspoon Cointreau or
   triple sec
1 ounce heavy cream
3 ounces club soda

In a shaker half-filled with ice cubes, combine the gin, lemon juice, sugar, egg white, Cointreau, and heavy cream. Shake well. Strain into a collins glass almost filled with ice cubes. Add the club soda. Stir well.

160 GYPSY

1½ ounces gin
1 ounce sweet vermouth

1 maraschino cherry

In a mixing glass half-filled with ice cubes, combine the gin and vermouth. Stir well. Strain into a cocktail glass and garnish with the cherry.

161 HORNPIPE

1½ ounces gin
2 teaspoons cherry
   brandy

1 egg white

In a shaker half-filled with ice cubes, combine all of the ingredients. Shake well. Strain into a cocktail glass.

162 HORSLEY'S HONOR

1½ ounces gin
½ ounce dry vermouth
½ ounce applejack

½ ounce Cointreau or
   triple sec
1 orange slice

In an old-fashioned glass almost filled with ice cubes, combine the gin, vermouth, applejack, and Cointreau. Stir well and garnish with the orange slice.

163 JET BLACK

1½ ounces gin
2 teaspoons sweet
vermouth

1 teaspoon black
Sambuca (Opal Nera)

In a mixing glass half-filled with ice cubes, combine all of
the ingredients. Stir well. Strain into a cocktail glass.

164 JEWEL OF THE NILE

1½ ounces gin
½ ounce green
Chartreuse

½ ounce yellow
Chartreuse

In a mixing glass half-filled with ice cubes, combine all of
the ingredients. Stir well. Strain into a cocktail glass.

165 JOCKEY CLUB

2 ounces gin
2 teaspoons crème de
noyaux
2 teaspoons white crème
de cacao

2 teaspoons lemon juice
1 dash orange bitters

In a shaker half-filled with ice cubes, combine all of the
ingredients. Shake well. Strain into a cocktail glass.

166 K.G.B.

1½ ounces gin
½ ounce kirsch
2 teaspoons apricot
brandy

½ ounce lemon juice
½ teaspoon superfine
sugar
1 lemon twist

In a shaker half-filled with ice cubes, combine the gin,
kirsch, apricot brandy, and lemon juice. Shake well. Strain
into a highball glass almost filled with ice cubes. Garnish
with the lemon twist.

167 LADYFINGER

1½ ounces gin
2 tablespoons kirsch
½ ounce cherry brandy

1 ounce lemon juice
½ teaspoon superfine
  sugar

In a shaker half-filled with ice cubes, combine all of the ingredients. Shake well. Strain into a cocktail glass.

168 LA STEPHANIQUE

1½ ounces gin
½ ounce Cointreau or
  triple sec

½ ounce sweet vermouth
1 dash bitters

In a shaker half-filled with ice cubes, combine all of the ingredients. Shake well. Strain into a cocktail glass.

169 LEANING TOWER

Crushed ice
2 ounces gin

1 teaspoon dry vermouth
2 dashes orange bitters

In a mixing glass half-filled with crushed ice, combine all of the ingredients. Stir well. Strain into a cocktail glass.

170 LONDON TOWN

1½ ounces gin
½ ounce maraschino
  liqueur

2 dashes orange bitters

In a mixing glass half-filled with ice cubes, combine all of the ingredients. Stir well. Strain into a cocktail glass.

171 MAIDEN-NO-MORE

1½ ounces gin
½ ounce Cointreau or
  triple sec

1 teaspoon brandy
1 ounce lemon juice

In a shaker half-filled with ice cubes, combine all of the ingredients. Shake well. Strain into a cocktail glass.

172 MAIDEN'S BLUSH

1½ ounces gin
½ ounce Cointreau or
   triple sec

1 teaspoon cherry brandy
1 ounce lemon juice
1 maraschino cherry

In a shaker half-filled with ice cubes, combine the gin, Cointreau, cherry brandy, and lemon juice. Shake well. Strain into a cocktail glass. Garnish with the cherry.

173 MARTINI

The martini is one of the simplest of drinks—smooth, dry, lightly perfumed (depending on which gin you prefer)—and it is a classic aperitif. The martini bespeaks an air of sophistication; it is an acquired taste that can be altered to suit the individual. It may be the classic cocktail.

However, the martini also seems to give a drinker a chance to boast of his or her individuality. Some say that one should merely introduce the bottle of vermouth to the gin, very politely of course: "Mr. Gin, allow me to introduce Mr. Vermouth. Don't shake hands now; you will never mix." Showman bartenders will keep the vermouth in an atomizer and merely spray the glass lightly before adding chilled gin. Others will keep their olives soaking in the vermouth, negating the need for any extra in the mixing glass. James Bond preferred his martini shaken, not stirred, but that can "bruise" the gin. Bruise the gin? I imagine that one can bruise an olive, but, personally, I don't believe that gin can be bruised. There seems to be no end of special treatments required for some people's martinis. They'll easily choose between straight up or on the rocks, and generally the choice between a twist and an olive won't challenge them too much. But then the peculiarities begin: They'll want the martini straight up with a glass of ice cubes on the side, two olives put in the glass before the drink is poured in, or the twist must be rubbed around the rim of the glass, waved twice over the top, and then thrown away. No request is too bizarre.

Of course, these days, you can make a martini with any white liquor at all—rum, tequila, gin, or vodka. The martini offers true freedom of choice: It might just be the very symbol of America. Put three cocktail onions into the drink, instead of the olive or twist, and it becomes a Gibson. Use a dash of

Scotch instead of the vermouth, and you have a Silver Bullet. Use saké, and you have a Sakétini, and, of course, if you make a martini with Scotch instead of gin and sweet vermouth instead of dry, the drink becomes a Rob Roy.

Variations on the Martini include the Fino Martini (page 61), Rum Martini (page 114), Sakétini (page 79), Silver Bullet (page 79), Tequila Martini (page 153), Vodka Martini (page 178), Rob Roy (page 133), and the Gibson (page 62).

2½ ounces gin	1 lemon twist or 1
1 teaspoon dry vermouth	cocktail olive

In a mixing glass half-filled with ice cubes, combine the gin and vermouth. Stir well. Strain into a cocktail glass. Garnish with the lemon twist or the olive.

174 MARTINI #2

2½ ounces gin	1 lemon twist or 1
1½ teaspoons dry vermouth	cocktail olive

In a mixing glass half-filled with ice cubes, combine the gin and vermouth. Stir well. Strain into a cocktail glass. Garnish with the lemon twist or the olive.

175 MARTINI #3

2½ ounces gin	1 lemon twist or 1
½ ounce dry vermouth	cocktail olive

In a mixing glass half-filled with ice cubes, combine the gin and vermouth. Stir well. Strain into a cocktail glass. Garnish with the lemon twist or the olive.

176 MARTINI #4

1½ ounces gin	1 lemon twist or 1
½ ounce dry vermouth	cocktail olive

In a mixing glass half-filled with ice cubes, combine the gin and vermouth. Stir well. Strain into a cocktail glass. Garnish with the lemon twist or the olive.

177 MARTINI COOLER

1½ ounces gin
1 teaspoon dry vermouth
4 ounces lemon-lime
  soda

1 lemon twist

Combine the gin, vermouth, and soda in a highball glass almost filled with ice cubes. Stir well. Garnish with the lemon twist.

178 MERRY WIDOW

1½ ounces gin
1 ounce dry vermouth
1 teaspoon Bénédictine

1 teaspoon Pernod
2 dashes orange bitters
1 lemon wedge

In a shaker half-filled with ice cubes, combine the gin, vermouth, Bénédictine, Pernod, and orange bitters. Shake well. Strain into a cocktail glass. Garnish with the lemon wedge.

179 MONKEY GLAND COCKTAIL

2 ounces gin
1 teaspoon Bénédictine

½ ounce orange juice
1 teaspoon grenadine

In a shaker half-filled with ice cubes, combine all of the ingredients. Shake well. Strain into a cocktail glass.

180 NAPOLEON

2 ounces gin
½ ounce Dubonnet
  Rouge

½ ounce Grand Marnier

In a mixing glass, combine all of the ingredients. Stir well. Strain into a cocktail glass.

NEGRONI

See Aperitifs, page 233.

181 OAXACA JIM

2 ounces gin
1 ounce orange juice
1 ounce grapefruit juice

2 dashes bitters
1 lemon twist
1 maraschino cherry

In a shaker half-filled with ice cubes, combine the gin, orange juice, grapefruit juice, and bitters. Shake well. Strain into an old-fashioned glass almost filled with ice cubes. Garnish with the lemon twist and the cherry.

182 ONCE-UPON-A-TIME

Crushed ice
1½ ounces gin

½ ounce apricot brandy
½ ounce Lillet

In a mixing glass half-filled with crushed ice, combine all of the ingredients. Stir well. Strain into a cocktail glass.

183 OPAL COCKTAIL

1½ ounces gin
½ ounce Cointreau or
triple sec

1 ounce orange juice
2 dashes orange bitters

In a shaker half-filled with ice cubes, combine all of the ingredients. Shake well. Strain into a cocktail glass.

184 OPERA COCKTAIL

1½ ounces gin
½ ounce Dubonnet
Rouge
½ ounce maraschino
liqueur

1 dash bitters
1 maraschino cherry

In a mixing glass, combine the gin, Dubonnet, maraschino liqueur, and bitters. Stir well. Strain into a cocktail glass. Garnish with the cherry.

185 ORANGE BLOSSOM

2 ounces gin
1 ounce orange juice
1 teaspoon superfine
sugar

1 orange slice

In a shaker half-filled with ice cubes, combine the gin,

orange juice, and sugar. Shake well. Strain into a cocktail glass. Garnish with the orange slice.

186 THE ORIGINAL SINGAPORE SLING

1 ounce gin	1 ounce cherry brandy
1 ounce Bénédictine	4 ounces club soda

In a mixing glass half-filled with ice cubes, combine the gin, Bénédictine, and cherry brandy. Stir well. Strain into a collins glass almost filled with ice cubes. Top with the club soda and stir well.

187 THE OTHER ORIGINAL SINGAPORE SLING

2 ounces gin	1/4 teaspoon Bénédictine
1 ounce cherry brandy	1/4 teaspoon brandy
1 ounce lime juice	

In a shaker half-filled with ice cubes, combine the gin, cherry brandy, and lime juice. Shake well. Strain into a collins glass almost filled with ice cubes. Drop the Bénédictine and brandy into the center of the drink.

188 PETTICOAT LANE

2 ounces gin	1/2 ounce Campari
1/2 ounce sweet vermouth	1 lemon twist

In a mixing glass half-filled with ice cubes, combine the gin, vermouth, and Campari. Stir well. Strain into a cocktail glass and garnish with the lemon twist.

189 PINK CREAM FIZZ

2 ounces gin	1 ounce light cream
1 ounce lemon juice	1 teaspoon grenadine
1 teaspoon superfine sugar	4 ounces club soda

In a shaker half-filled with ice cubes, combine the gin, lemon juice, sugar, cream, and grenadine. Shake well. Strain into a collins glass almost filled with ice cubes. Add the club soda. Stir well.

190 PINK GIN

3 dashes bitters
2 ounces gin, preferably
  Plymouth

Pour the bitters into a wine glass. Swirl the glass to coat the inside with the bitters; shake out the excess. Pour the gin into the glass. Do not add ice.

191 PINK LADY

2 ounces gin
1 teaspoon grenadine
½ teaspoon cherry
  brandy

½ ounce heavy cream
1 egg white

In a shaker half-filled with ice cubes, combine all of the ingredients. Shake well. Strain into a cocktail glass.

192 PINK PUSSYCAT

2 ounces gin
4 ounces pineapple juice

1 teaspoon cherry brandy

In an old-fashioned glass almost filled with ice cubes, combine the gin and pineapple juice. Stir well. Drop the cherry brandy into the center of the drink.

193 PRINCETON COCKTAIL

1½ ounces gin
1 ounce dry vermouth

1 ounce lime juice

In a shaker half-filled with ice cubes, combine all of the ingredients. Shake well. Strain into a cocktail glass.

194 RAMOS FIZZ

2 ounces gin
1 ounce lemon juice
1 teaspoon superfine
  sugar
1 egg white

1 teaspoon Cointreau or
  triple sec
½ ounce light cream
3 ounces club soda

In a shaker half-filled with ice cubes, combine the gin, lemon juice, sugar, egg white, Cointreau, and cream. Shake well. Strain into a collins glass almost filled with ice cubes. Add the club soda. Stir well.

195 RED GIN

Crushed ice
2 ounces gin
1 teaspoon Cherry
   Heering

1 maraschino cherry

In a mixing glass half-filled with crushed ice, combine the gin and Cherry Heering. Stir well. Strain into a cocktail glass. Garnish with the cherry.

196 RED RUBY

1½ ounces gin
½ ounce cherry brandy

½ ounce dry vermouth

In a mixing glass half-filled with ice cubes, combine all of the ingredients. Stir well. Strain into a cocktail glass.

197 ROLLS-ROYCE

1½ ounces gin
½ ounce sweet vermouth

½ ounce dry vermouth
1 teaspoon Bénédictine

In a mixing glass half-filled with ice cubes, combine all of the ingredients. Stir well. Strain into a cocktail glass.

198 ROOT BEER FIZZ

2 ounces gin
1 ounce lemon juice
1 teaspoon superfine
   sugar

4 ounces root beer
1 maraschino cherry

In a shaker half-filled with ice cubes, combine the gin, lemon juice, and sugar. Shake well. Strain into a collins glass almost filled with ice cubes. Add the root beer. Stir well. Garnish with the cherry.

199 ROSE COCKTAIL

2 teaspoons powdered
  sugar
1 lime wedge
1½ ounces gin
½ ounce apricot brandy

½ ounce dry vermouth
½ ounce lemon juice
½ ounce lime juice
1 teaspoon grenadine

Place the sugar in a saucer. Rub the rim of a cocktail glass with the lime wedge and dip it into the sugar to coat thoroughly; discard the lime. In a shaker half-filled with ice cubes, combine the gin, apricot brandy, vermouth, lemon juice, lime juice, and grenadine. Shake well. Strain into the cocktail glass.

200 ROUGE MARTINI

2 ounces gin   1 teaspoon Chambord

In a mixing glass half-filled with ice cubes, combine the gin and Chambord. Stir well. Strain into a cocktail glass.

201 ROYALTY FIZZ

2 ounces gin
1 ounce lemon juice
½ teaspoon blue Curaçao
1 teaspoon superfine
  sugar

1 whole egg
3 ounces club soda

In a shaker half-filled with ice cubes, combine the gin, lemon juice, Curaçao, sugar, and egg. Shake well. Strain into a collins glass almost filled with ice cubes. Add the club soda. Stir well.

202 RUBY IN THE ROUGH

1½ ounces gin
½ ounce cherry brandy

1 teaspoon sweet
  vermouth

In a mixing glass half-filled with ice cubes, combine all of the ingredients. Stir well. Strain into a cocktail glass.

203 SAKÉTINI

2½ ounces gin or vodka   1 cocktail olive
1½ teaspoons saké

In a mixing glass half-filled with ice cubes, combine the gin or vodka with the saké. Stir well. Strain into a cocktail glass. Garnish with the olive.

204 SHADY LADY

2 ounces gin   2 dashes bitters
½ ounce dry vermouth   1 lemon twist

In a mixing glass half-filled with ice cubes, combine the gin, vermouth, and bitters. Stir well. Strain into a cocktail glass. Garnish with the lemon twist.

205 SILVER BRONX

2 ounces gin   1 teaspoon orange juice
½ ounce dry vermouth   1 egg white
½ ounce sweet vermouth

In a shaker half-filled with ice cubes, combine all of the ingredients. Shake well. Strain into a sour glass.

206 SILVER BULLET

2½ ounces gin   1 lemon twist
1½ teaspoons Scotch

In a mixing glass half-filled with ice cubes, combine the gin and Scotch. Stir well. Strain into a cocktail glass. Garnish with the lemon twist.

207 SINGAPORE SLING

A drink that has changed enormously over the years, the original Singapore Sling was concocted at the Raffles Hotel in Singapore. It had equal amounts of gin, Bénédictine, and cherry brandy added to some club soda. Some folks, however, claim that it was first made with a few drops of brandy and Bénédictine, together with two parts gin to one part of cherry brandy and one part lime juice. These are indeed superb drinks, and they deserve mention alongside the recipe for what is now commonly accepted as a true Singapore Sling. See recipes for The Original Singapore Sling and The Other Original Singapore Sling on page 75.

1 teaspoon superfine sugar	½ ounce cherry brandy
1 ounce lemon juice	1 maraschino cherry
2½ ounces gin	1 orange slice
4 ounces club soda	1 lemon twist

In a shaker half-filled with ice cubes, combine the sugar, lemon juice, and gin. Shake well. Strain into a collins glass almost filled with ice cubes. Add the club soda. Stir well. Float the cherry brandy on top. Garnish with the cherry, the orange slice, and the lemon twist.

208 SMART CHRISTINE

2 ounces gin	2 ounces orange juice
½ ounce Bénédictine	1 maraschino cherry

In a shaker half-filled with ice cubes, combine the gin, Bénédictine, and orange juice. Shake well. Strain into an old-fashioned glass almost filled with ice cubes. Garnish with the cherry.

209 SUGAR DADDY

2 ounces gin	1 ounce pineapple juice
2 teaspoons maraschino liqueur	1 dash bitters

In a shaker half-filled with ice cubes, combine all of the ingredients. Shake well. Strain into a cocktail glass.

210 TEN QUIDDER

1½ ounces gin
1 ounce Cointreau or
triple sec

1 dash bitters
1 teaspoon blue Curaçao

In an old-fashioned glass almost filled with ice cubes, combine the gin, Cointreau, and bitters. Stir well. Pour the Curaçao into the center of the drink.

211 TOM COLLINS

Which came first, Tom Collins or John? I don't really know, although I suspect that it was actually John. Here is my reasoning: A Tom Collins is named after Old Tom Gin, which has been around since the early eighteenth century (see Gin, page 51). A John Collins was probably named after some bartender during the Civil War. It is made with bourbon, which has been around only since the late eighteenth century (see Bourbon, page 19). Since Americans are largely responsible for "inventing" cocktails in the first place, I choose to believe that the first "Collins" was a John Collins, concocted during the Civil War and later copied using Old Tom Gin. This drink was, of course, known as a Tom Collins in a reference to the gin.

Variations on the Tom Collins include the John Collins (page 27) and the Vodka Collins (page 176).

2 ounces gin
1 ounce lemon juice
1 teaspoon superfine
sugar

3 ounces club soda
1 maraschino cherry
1 orange slice

In a shaker half-filled with ice cubes, combine the gin, lemon juice, and sugar. Shake well. Strain into a collins glass almost filled with ice cubes. Add the club soda. Stir and garnish with the cherry and the orange slice.

212 TWENTY THOUSAND LEAGUES

Crushed ice
1½ ounces gin
1 ounce dry vermouth

1 teaspoon Pernod
2 dashes orange bitters

In a mixing glass half-filled with crushed ice, combine all of the ingredients. Stir well. Strain into a cocktail glass.

213 UNION JACK

1½ ounces gin   1 teaspoon grenadine
½ ounce sloe gin

In a shaker half-filled with ice cubes, combine all of the ingredients. Shake well. Strain into a cocktail glass.

214 WHITE LADY

2 ounces gin   1 teaspoon superfine
1 egg white   sugar
1 ounce light cream

In a shaker half-filled with ice cubes, combine all of the ingredients. Shake well. Strain into a cocktail glass.

215 WIDOW WITH A SECRET

1½ ounces gin   1 teaspoon Campari
1 ounce sweet vermouth   2 dashes orange bitters
1 teaspoon Bénédictine   1 maraschino cherry
1 teaspoon Pernod

In a shaker half-filled with ice cubes, combine the gin, vermouth, Bénédictine, Pernod, Campari, and orange bitters. Shake well. Strain into a cocktail glass. Garnish with the cherry.

216 YALE COCKTAIL

2 ounces gin   1 teaspoon blue Curaçao
½ ounce dry vermouth   1 dash bitters

In a mixing glass half-filled with ice cubes, combine all of the ingredients. Stir well. Strain into a cocktail glass.

5 · RUM

Christopher Columbus did much more than discover the Americas; he also brought sugar cane to the West Indies. This gave all of those pirates of yesteryear a darned good base from which to make some liquor and, ultimately, gave us cocktails such as the Cuba Libré, the Bacardi Cocktail, and the Daiquiri. For trade purposes, rum was the best way for the Spanish settlers to store their sugar cane, since, when distilled, it would not deteriorate with age as would the fresh product.

The derivation of the word *rum* is unknown. It may have come from *saccharum,* Latin for "sugar," but personally, I find that explanation a little mundane. I think the drink took on the word British sailors originally used to describe it—rum. Rum is a word still used in parts of England as an adjective. A "rum lad" is a man known for being a good sort of a chap, if somewhat of a daredevil or prankster, and this word dates back to the seventeenth century. In the early part of the eighteenth century, British sailors were given Barbados Water to combat scurvy. Naming the drink "rum" would seem to make sense when the drink was a good, if somewhat daring, way of combating a fatal disease.

PRODUCTION

Raw sugar cane is pressed between rollers to extract juice. The juice is boiled down, clarified, and put into machines that spin around at a ferocious rate, crystallizing the sugar and separating it from the residue, which is molasses. The molasses is reboiled, yielding a low-grade sugar, and the residue is then mixed with water and yeast, allowed to ferment, and then distilled to produce rum.

Rums are divided into four main categories: light, medium, full-bodied, and aromatic. Rum bottles must, by law, state their country of origin, and, although each country is usually connected to a certain type of rum, Jamaican rum does not *have* to be full-bodied, and Puerto Rican rum is not necessarily light. Añejo rum simply means "aged" rum; it usually has a tawny color and more mellow flavor.

PUERTO RICAN RUM

During the distillation process, small amounts of the "mash" from the previous distillation are added to the new batch, similar to the method employed in making sour mash whiskey. After the mash has fermented for a few days, it is distilled in a continuous still and then aged in oak casks. The casks may or may not be charred depending on the type of rum desired.

The rum must be aged for at least a year to produce a light-bodied, dry rum. Amber or golden rums from Puerto Rico are aged for a minimum of three years and have caramel added to enhance the color gained from the casks. If the rum is aged for over six years, it may be designated as *vieux* or *liqueur* rum.

VIRGIN ISLANDS RUM

The Virgin Islands generally produce a dry, light-bodied rum similar to Puerto Rican light rum.

DEMERARAN RUM

From Guyana, this rum is very dark and yet has only medium body. It is often bottled with a very high alcohol content (151° proof), and is the rum traditionally used in a Zombie (see Tropical Drinks, page 218).

JAMAICAN RUM

The molasses used to make a good, full-bodied Jamaican rum is naturally fermented for about three weeks. Natural fermentation means that yeast from the air, as opposed to cultured yeast, settles on the surface of the mash, which is supplemented by mash from previous distillations. It is double-distilled in pot stills and aged in oak casks for a minimum of five years. The color of Jamaican rum, however, comes more from the amount of caramel added than from the cask.

MARTINIQUE AND HAITIAN RUM

These rums are distilled from the juice of the sugar cane rather than from molasses. The juice is concentrated and distilled in pot stills; the rum is then aged in oak casks from which it takes its color. The final product is medium-bodied.

BATAVIA ARAK

The production of this aromatic rum from the island of Java is absolutely intriguing. Small cakes are made from Javanese red rice; these are put into the molasses, which then ferments naturally (see Jamaican rum). The distilled rum is aged for around three years in Java and then shipped to Holland, where it is further aged for up to six years before being blended and bottled. Batavia refers to the town where the *arak* (rum) is made.

AGUARDIENTE DE CAÑA

This is the name given to most rums from South America. The best known among them in America is cachaça, from Brazil. Cachaça is the main ingredient of a Caipirinha, a wonderful sweet-and-sour Brazilian cocktail.

217 ABILENE

1½ ounces dark rum   3 ounces orange juice
2 ounces peach nectar

Pour all of the ingredients into a highball glass almost filled with ice cubes. Stir well.

218 ACAPULCO

2 ounces light rum   1 teaspoon superfine
½ ounce Cointreau or   sugar
   triple sec   1 egg white
½ ounce lime juice   1 mint sprig

In a shaker half-filled with ice cubes, combine the rum, Cointreau, lime juice, sugar, and egg white. Shake well. Strain into an old-fashioned glass almost filled with ice cubes. Garnish with the mint sprig.

219 ADAM

2 ounces dark rum   1 teaspoon grenadine
1 ounce lemon juice

In a shaker half-filled with ice cubes, combine all of the ingredients. Shake well. Strain into a cocktail glass.

220 A FURLONG TOO LATE

2 ounces light rum   1 lemon twist
4 ounces ginger beer

Pour the rum and ginger beer into a highball glass almost

filled with ice cubes. Stir well. Garnish with the lemon twist.

221 ALMERIA

2 ounces dark rum	1 egg white
1 ounce Kahlúa	

In a shaker half-filled with ice cubes, combine all of the ingredients. Shake well. Strain into a cocktail glass.

222 A NIGHT IN OLD MANDALAY

1 ounce light rum	1/2 ounce lemon juice
1 ounce añejo rum	3 ounces ginger ale
1 ounce orange juice	1 lemon twist

In a shaker half-filled with ice cubes, combine the light rum, añejo rum, orange juice, and lemon juice. Shake well. Strain into a highball glass almost filled with ice cubes. Top with the ginger ale. Garnish with the lemon twist.

223 APPLED RUM COOLER

1 1/2 ounces añejo rum	2 teaspoons lime juice
1/2 ounce applejack	2 ounces club soda

In a shaker half-filled with ice cubes, combine the rum, applejack, and lime juice. Shake well. Strain into an old-fashioned glass almost filled with ice cubes. Top with the club soda.

224 APPLE PIE

1 ounce light rum	1 teaspoon lemon juice
1/2 ounce sweet vermouth	1/2 teaspoon grenadine
1 teaspoon applejack	

In a shaker half-filled with ice cubes, combine all of the ingredients. Shake well. Strain into a cocktail glass.

225 APRICOT LADY

1½ ounces light rum
1 ounce apricot brandy
1 teaspoon Cointreau or
 triple sec

½ ounce lemon juice
1 egg white
1 orange slice

In a shaker half-filled with ice cubes, combine the rum, apricot brandy, Cointreau, lemon juice, and egg white. Shake well. Strain into an old-fashioned glass almost filled with ice cubes. Garnish with the orange slice.

226 BACARDI COCKTAIL

1½ ounces Bacardi light
 rum

1 ounce lime juice
1 teaspoon grenadine

In a shaker half-filled with ice cubes, combine all of the ingredients. Shake well. Strain into a cocktail glass.

227 BANANA RUM CREAM

1½ ounces dark rum
½ ounce crème de
 bananes

1 ounce light cream

In a shaker half-filled with ice cubes, combine all of the ingredients. Shake well. Strain into a cocktail glass.

228 BARKIS IS WILLING

1½ ounces light rum
1 ounce lime juice
1 teaspoon grenadine
½ teaspoon superfine
 sugar

2 ounces club soda
2 ounces ginger ale
1 orange slice

In a shaker half-filled with ice cubes, combine the rum, lime juice, grenadine, and sugar. Shake well. Strain into a collins glass almost filled with ice cubes. Top with the club soda and ginger ale. Stir well and garnish with the orange slice.

229 BARRIER BREAKER

1½ ounces dark rum
½ ounce Galliano
2 teaspoons dark crème
  de cacao

4 ounces cold coffee
Crushed ice

Pour all of the ingredients into an Irish coffee glass filled with crushed ice. Stir well.

230 BASIC BILL

1½ ounces añejo rum
½ ounce Dubonnet
  Rouge

½ ounce Grand Marnier
2 dashes bitters

In a mixing glass half-filled with ice cubes, combine all of the ingredients. Stir well. Strain into a cocktail glass.

231 BATIDA ABACI

2 ounces cachaça
4 ounces fresh pineapple,
  cut into chunks
  (about 1 cup)

½ teaspoon granulated
  sugar
1 cup crushed ice

Place all of the ingredients into a blender. Blend well. Pour into a wine glass.

232 BATIDA LIMAO

2 ounces cachaça
1 ounce lime juice
2 teaspoons granulated
  sugar

1 cup crushed ice

Place all of the ingredients into a blender. Blend well. Pour into a wine glass.

233 BATIDA MANGO

2 ounces cachaça
4 ounces chopped fresh
  mango (about 1 cup)

2 teaspoons granulated
  sugar
1 cup crushed ice

Place all of the ingredients into a blender. Blend well. Pour into a wine glass.

234 BATIDA MORANGO

2 ounces cachaça
5 very ripe strawberries
½ teaspoon granulated
   sugar

1 cup crushed ice

Place all of the ingredients into a blender. Blend well. Pour into a wine glass.

235 BEACHCOMBER

2 teaspoons superfine
   sugar
1 lime wedge
2 ounces light rum

1 teaspoon maraschino
   liqueur
1 teaspoon cherry brandy
½ ounce lime juice

Place the sugar in a saucer. Rub the rim of a cocktail glass with the lime wedge and dip the glass into the sugar to coat the rim thoroughly; reserve the lime. In a shaker half-filled with ice cubes, combine the rum, maraschino liqueur, cherry brandy, and lime juice. Shake well. Strain into the cocktail glass. Garnish with the lime wedge.

236 BEADLER TO THE FRONT

1 ounce dark rum
½ ounce Pernod
½ ounce crème de
   bananes

2 dashes bitters

In a mixing glass half-filled with ice cubes, combine all of the ingredients. Stir well. Strain into a cocktail glass.

237 BIG BAND CHARLIE

1½ ounces dark rum
½ ounce melon liqueur
½ ounce Cointreau or
   triple sec

½ ounce lime juice

In a shaker half-filled with crushed ice, combine all of the ingredients. Shake well. Strain into a sour glass.

238 THE BIGWOOD GIRLS

3/4 ounce light rum   ½ ounce lemon juice
½ ounce brandy
½ ounce Cointreau or
   triple sec

In a shaker half-filled with ice cubes, combine all of the ingredients. Shake well. Strain into a cocktail glass.

239 BLACK DEVIL

2 ounces light rum   1 pitted black olive
½ ounce dry vermouth

In a mixing glass half-filled with ice cubes, combine the rum and vermouth. Stir well. Strain into a cocktail glass and garnish with the olive.

240 BLACK MONDAY

1 ounce dark rum   1 teaspoon cherry brandy
½ ounce black Sambuca   ½ ounce lemon juice
   (Opal Nera)

In a shaker half-filled with ice cubes, combine all of the ingredients. Shake well. Strain into a cocktail glass.

241 BLACK STRIPE COLD

2 ounces dark rum   1 ounce boiling water
½ ounce molasses   Crushed ice
1 teaspoon honey

Pour all of the ingredients into a mixing glass and stir well to dissolve the honey and molasses. Pour into an old-fashioned glass filled with crushed ice. Stir well.

242 BLIGHTER BOB

1 ounce light rum   2 dashes orange bitters
½ ounce dark rum   2 ounces ginger ale
½ ounce crème de cassis   1 lemon twist
1 ounce orange juice

Pour light rum, dark rum, cassis, orange juice, orange bitters, and ginger ale into a highball glass almost filled with ice cubes. Stir well and garnish with the lemon twist.

243 BLUE MOUNTAIN

1½ ounces añejo rum
½ ounce Tia Maria
½ ounce vodka

1 ounce orange juice
1 teaspoon lemon juice

In a shaker half-filled with ice cubes, combine all of the ingredients. Shake well. Strain into an old-fashioned glass almost filled with ice cubes.

244 BOLERO

1½ ounces añejo rum
½ ounce Calvados
2 teaspoons sweet
  vermouth

1 dash bitters

In a mixing glass half-filled with ice cubes, combine all of the ingredients. Stir well. Strain into an old-fashioned glass almost filled with ice cubes.

245 BOSTON SIDECAR

1 ounce light rum
½ ounce brandy
½ ounce Cointreau or
  triple sec

½ ounce lemon juice

In a shaker half-filled with ice cubes, combine all of the ingredients. Shake well. Strain into a cocktail glass.

246 BOWTON NELL

1½ ounces light rum
½ ounce brandy
½ ounce gin
1½ ounces orange juice

1 ounce lemon juice
1 teaspoon grenadine
1 ounce club soda
1 maraschino cherry

In a shaker half-filled with ice cubes, combine the rum, brandy, gin, orange juice, lemon juice, and grenadine. Shake well. Strain into a collins glass almost filled with ice cubes. Top with the club soda. Stir well and garnish with the cherry.

247 BRIAN'S BELIEF

1½ ounces añejo rum
½ ounce dark crème de
   cacao
½ ounce lemon juice
2 teaspoons superfine
   sugar
4 ounces cold tea

In a shaker half-filled with ice cubes, combine the rum, crème de cacao, lemon juice, and sugar. Shake well. Strain into a highball glass almost filled with ice cubes. Top with the tea and stir well.

248 BROWN COCKTAIL

1 ounce dark rum
1 ounce gin
½ ounce dry vermouth

In a mixing glass half-filled with ice cubes, combine all of the ingredients. Stir well. Strain into a cocktail glass.

249 BURNT EMBERS

1½ ounces añejo rum
½ ounce apricot brandy
1 ounce pineapple juice

In a shaker half-filled with ice cubes, combine all of the ingredients. Shake well. Strain into a cocktail glass.

250 BUMBO

2 ounces dark rum
1 ounce lemon juice
½ teaspoon grenadine
¼ teaspoon grated
   nutmeg

In a shaker half-filled with ice cubes, combine all of the ingredients. Shake well. Strain into a cocktail glass.

251 BUSHRANGER

1½ ounces light rum
½ ounce Dubonnet
   Rouge
1 dash bitters
1 lemon twist

In a mixing glass half-filled with ice cubes, combine the rum, Dubonnet, and bitters. Stir well. Strain into a cocktail glass and garnish with the lemon twist.

252 CAIPIRINHA

2 teaspoons granulated
  sugar

1 lime, cut into 8 wedges
2½ ounces cachaça

Muddle the sugar into the lime wedges in an old-fashioned glass. Fill the glass with ice cubes. Pour the cachaça into the glass. Stir well.

253 CAPE OF GOOD WILL

1½ ounces light rum
½ ounce apricot brandy
½ ounce lime juice

1 ounce orange juice
2 dashes orange bitters

In a shaker half-filled with ice cubes, combine all of the ingredients. Shake well. Strain into a cocktail glass.

254 CARDINAL

1½ ounces añejo rum
½ ounce maraschino
  liqueur

1 teaspoon Cointreau or
  triple sec
1 teaspoon grenadine

In a mixing glass half-filled with ice cubes, combine all of the ingredients. Stir well. Strain into a cocktail glass.

255 CASA BLANCA

1½ ounces light rum
½ ounce Grand Marnier
1 teaspoon maraschino
  liqueur

½ ounce lime juice

In a shaker half-filled with ice cubes, combine all of the ingredients. Shake well. Strain into a cocktail glass.

256 CATHERINE OF SHERIDAN SQUARE

1½ ounces dark rum
½ ounce Tia Maria
1 ounce light cream

4 ounces cold coffee
Crushed ice

Pour all of the ingredients into an Irish coffee glass filled with crushed ice. Stir well.

257 CHARGER

1½ ounces dark rum
½ ounce cherry brandy
½ ounce lemon juice

½ teaspoon superfine
sugar

In a shaker half-filled with ice cubes, combine all of the ingredients. Shake well. Strain into a cocktail glass.

258 CHERRIED CREAM RUM

1½ ounces light rum
½ ounce cherry brandy

½ ounce light cream

In a shaker half-filled with ice cubes, combine all of the ingredients. Shake well. Strain into a cocktail glass.

259 CHOCOLATE MINT RUM

1 ounce dark rum
½ ounce 151° proof rum
½ ounce dark crème de
cacao

2 teaspoons white crème
de menthe
½ ounce light cream

In a shaker half-filled with ice cubes, combine all of the ingredients. Shake well. Strain into a cocktail glass.

260 COMMUNICATOR

1½ ounces dark rum
½ ounce Galliano

2 teaspoons dark crème
de cacao

Pour all of the ingredients into an old-fashioned glass almost filled with ice cubes. Stir well.

261 CONTINENTAL

1½ ounces light rum
½ ounce green crème de
menthe
½ ounce lime juice

1 teaspoon lemon juice
½ teaspoon superfine
sugar
1 lemon twist

In a shaker half-filled with ice cubes, combine the rum, crème de menthe, lime juice, lemon juice, and sugar. Shake well. Strain into a cocktail glass and garnish with the lemon twist.

262 CORKSCREW

1½ ounces light rum
½ ounce peach schnapps

½ ounce dry vermouth
1 lemon twist

In a mixing glass half-filled with ice cubes, combine the rum, peach schnapps, and vermouth. Stir well. Strain into a cocktail glass and garnish with the lemon twist.

263 CORNWALL-NASH

1½ ounces light rum
½ ounce gin
½ ounce Cointreau or
triple sec

2 ounces grapefruit juice
1 teaspoon cherry brandy
1 maraschino cherry

Pour the rum, gin, Cointreau, and grapefruit juice into a highball glass almost filled with ice cubes. Stir well. Drop the cherry brandy into the center of the drink. Garnish with the cherry.

264 COSMOS

Crushed ice
2 ounces light rum
1 ounce lime juice

1 teaspoon superfine
sugar

In a shaker half-filled with crushed ice, combine all of the ingredients. Shake well. Strain into a cocktail glass.

265 CREOLE

2 ounces light rum
4 ounces beef bouillon
1 dash Tabasco sauce
1 dash Worcestershire
sauce

1 teaspoon lemon juice
⅛ teaspoon salt
⅛ teaspoon black pepper
1 lemon wedge

In a shaker half-filled with ice cubes, combine the rum, bouillon, Tabasco, Worcestershire, lemon juice, salt, and pepper. Shake well. Strain into a highball glass almost filled with ice cubes. Garnish with the lemon wedge.

266 CUBA LIBRE

2 ounces light rum   1 lime wedge
5 ounces cola

Pour the rum and cola into a highball glass almost filled
with ice cubes. Stir well. Garnish with the lime wedge.

267 CUBAN COCKTAIL

2 ounces light rum   ½ teaspoon superfine
2 teaspoons lime juice   sugar
2 teaspoons lemon juice

In a shaker half-filled with ice cubes, combine all of the
ingredients. Shake well. Strain into a cocktail glass.

268 CUL-DE-SAC

2½ ounces añejo rum   ½ ounce Ricard

In a mixing glass half-filled with ice cubes, combine both
of the ingredients. Stir well. Strain into a cocktail glass.

269 DAIQUIRI

*The town of Daiquiri, Cuba, gave its name to the popular and
refreshing rum cocktail that originated there in 1898. The
town's doctors were at a loss as to how to combat an outbreak
of malaria. The only "medicine" available to them was the
local rum, which they hoped would help ward off the fever.
American engineers who were working for the local mining
company added lime juice and sugar to the rum to make it
more palatable. They added ice cubes from distilled water,
shook it up, and enjoyed their medicine, as much then as
people do today.*

1½ ounces light rum   1 teaspoon superfine sugar
1 ounce lime juice

In a shaker half-filled with ice cubes, combine the rum,
lime juice, and sugar. Shake well. Strain into a cocktail
glass.

270 DAMN-YOUR-EYES

1½ ounces añejo rum	1 teaspoon dry vermouth
½ ounce Dubonnet Blonde	1 lemon twist

In a mixing glass half-filled with ice cubes, combine the rum, Dubonnet, and vermouth. Stir well. Strain into a cocktail glass and garnish with the lemon twist.

271 DAVID BAREFACE

1½ ounces light rum	1 ounce heavy cream
½ ounce white crème de cacao	

In a shaker half-filled with ice cubes, combine all of the ingredients. Shake well. Strain into a cocktail glass.

272 DEEP, DARK SECRET

1½ ounces dark rum	½ ounce Kahlúa
½ ounce añejo rum	½ ounce heavy cream

In a shaker half-filled with ice cubes, combine all of the ingredients. Shake well. Strain into a cocktail glass.

273 DeROSIER

1 ounce añejo rum	½ ounce cherry brandy
½ ounce bourbon	1 ounce heavy cream
½ ounce dark crème de cacao	

In a shaker half-filled with ice cubes, combine all of the ingredients. Shake well. Strain into a cocktail glass.

274 DIANNE-ON-THE-TOWER

2 ounces light rum	1 teaspoon cherry brandy
½ ounce bourbon	
1 teaspoon dark crème de cacao	

In a mixing glass half-filled with ice cubes, combine all of the ingredients. Stir well. Strain into a cocktail glass.

275 DROOG'S DATE COCKTAIL

1½ ounces light rum
2 teaspoons cherry
  brandy

2 teaspoons Cointreau or
  triple sec
½ ounce lime juice

In a shaker half-filled with ice cubes, combine all of the ingredients. Shake well. Strain into a cocktail glass.

276 ELEPHANT LIPS

1½ ounces dark rum
½ ounce crème de
  bananes
½ ounce lemon juice

In a shaker half-filled with ice cubes, combine all of the ingredients. Shake well. Strain into a cocktail glass.

277 EL PRESIDENTE

2 ounces light rum
1 ounce lime juice

½ ounce pineapple juice
1 teaspoon grenadine

In a shaker half-filled with ice cubes, combine all of the ingredients. Shake well. Strain into a cocktail glass.

278 ENTWISTLE'S ERROR

2 ounces dark rum
½ ounce lemon juice

4 ounces tonic water

Pour all of the ingredients into a highball glass almost filled with ice cubes. Stir well.

279 EYE-OPENER

1½ ounces light rum
½ ounce Cointreau or
  triple sec
2 teaspoons Pernod
1 teaspoon white crème
  de cacao

1 egg yolk
1 teaspoon superfine
  sugar

In a shaker half-filled with ice cubes, combine all of the ingredients. Shake well. Strain into a sour glass.

280 FELL JUICE

1 ounce light rum
½ ounce dark rum
2 ounces cranberry juice
2 teaspoons lemon juice
2 teaspoons lime juice

1 teaspoon superfine
    sugar
1 egg white
Crushed ice

In a shaker half-filled with ice cubes, combine all of the ingredients. Shake well. Strain into an old-fashioned glass almost filled with crushed ice.

281 FIREMAN'S SOUR

1½ ounces light rum
1½ ounces lime juice
½ ounce grenadine

2 ounces club soda
1 orange slice
1 maraschino cherry

In a shaker half-filled with ice cubes, combine the rum, lime juice, and grenadine. Shake well. Strain into a highball glass almost filled with ice cubes. Top with the club soda. Stir well. Garnish with the orange slice and the cherry.

282 FLIRTING WITH THE SANDPIPER

1½ ounces light rum
½ ounce cherry brandy

3 ounces orange juice
2 dashes orange bitters

Pour all of the ingredients into a highball glass almost filled with ice cubes. Stir well.

283 GARETH GLOWWORM

1½ ounces light rum
½ ounce white crème de
  cacao

1 ounce heavy cream
1 teaspoon cherry brandy

In a shaker half-filled with ice cubes, combine the rum, crème de cacao, and heavy cream. Shake well. Strain into a cocktail glass. Drop the cherry brandy into the center of the drink.

284 GROG

2 ounces dark rum   3 ounces water

Pour the rum and the water into an old-fashioned glass with no ice cubes. Stir well. Praise the gods that you weren't in the British Navy!

285 HAIDIN-HAIDIN

2 ounces light rum   1 dash bitters
1/2 ounce dry vermouth   1 lemon twist

In a mixing glass half-filled with ice cubes, combine the rum, vermouth, and bitters. Stir well. Strain into a cocktail glass and garnish with the lemon twist.

286 HAT TRICK

1/2 ounce dark rum   1/2 ounce sweet vermouth
1/2 ounce light rum

In a mixing glass half-filled with ice cubes, combine the dark rum, light rum, and vermouth. Stir well. Strain into a cocktail glass.

287 HAVANA COCKTAIL

1 ounce light rum   1 teaspoon lemon juice
1 ounce pineapple juice

In a shaker half-filled with ice cubes, combine all of the ingredients. Shake well. Strain into a cocktail glass.

288 HORSE AND JOCKEY

1 ounce añejo rum   1/2 ounce sweet vermouth
1 ounce Southern   2 dashes bitters
  Comfort

In a mixing glass half-filled with ice cubes, combine all of the ingredients. Stir well. Strain into a cocktail glass.

289 HOWELL SAYS SO

1½ ounces dark rum
½ ounce Cointreau or
   triple sec

½ ounce amaretto
½ ounce lemon juice
2 dashes orange bitters

In a shaker half-filled with ice cubes, combine all of the ingredients. Shake well. Strain into an old-fashioned glass almost filled with ice cubes.

290 IMMACULATA

1½ ounces light rum
½ ounce amaretto
½ ounce lime juice

1 teaspoon lemon juice
½ teaspoon superfine
   sugar

In a shaker half-filled with ice cubes, combine all of the ingredients. Shake well. Strain into a cocktail glass.

291 JONESEY

2 ounces dark rum
½ ounce dark crème de
   cacao

In a mixing glass half-filled with ice cubes, combine the rum and crème de cacao. Stir well. Strain into a cocktail glass.

292 JOY-TO-THE-WORLD

1½ ounces añejo rum
½ ounce bourbon

½ ounce dark crème de
   cacao

In a mixing glass half-filled with ices cubes, combine all of the ingredients. Stir well. Strain into a cocktail glass.

293 KRAZEE KEITH

1½ ounces light rum
2 teaspoons anisette
2 teaspoons cherry
   brandy

½ ounce lemon juice
4 ounces cola
1 lemon wedge

In a shaker half-filled with ice cubes, combine the rum, anisette, cherry brandy, and lemon juice. Shake well. Strain into a highball glass almost filled with ice cubes. Add the cola and stir well. Garnish with the lemon wedge.

294 LAMB BROTHERS

1½ ounces dark rum
½ ounce crème de cassis
2 ounces pineapple juice

In a shaker half-filled with ice cubes, combine all of the ingredients. Shake well. Strain into a cocktail glass.

295 LANDED GENTRY

1½ ounces dark rum
½ ounce Tia Maria
1 ounce heavy cream

In a shaker half-filled with ice cubes, combine all of the ingredients. Shake well. Strain into a cocktail glass.

296 LIFETIMER

1½ ounces light rum
½ ounce apricot brandy
½ ounce brandy
1 teaspoon Cointreau or triple sec
½ ounce lemon juice
½ teaspoon superfine sugar
4 ounces club soda
1 lime wedge

In a shaker half-filled with ice cubes, combine the rum, apricot brandy, brandy, Cointreau, lemon juice, and sugar. Shake well. Strain into a highball glass almost filled with ice cubes. Top with the club soda. Garnish with the lime wedge.

297 LITTLE PRINCESS COCKTAIL

1½ ounces light rum
1 ounce sweet vermouth

In a mixing glass half-filled with ice cubes, combine both of the ingredients. Stir well. Strain into a cocktail glass.

298 LORD AND LADY

1½ ounces dark rum
½ ounce Tia Maria

Pour the rum and Tia Maria into an old-fashioned glass almost filled with ice cubes. Stir well.

299 LOVE FOR TOBY

1½ ounces light rum   ½ ounce cherry brandy
½ ounce brandy   1 teaspoon lime juice

In a shaker half-filled with ice cubes, combine all of the ingredients. Shake well. Strain into a cocktail glass.

300 LUDWIG AND THE GANG

1 ounce añejo rum   1 dash bitters
1 ounce vodka   Crushed ice
½ ounce amaretto
½ ounce Southern
  Comfort

In a mixing glass half-filled with ice cubes, combine all of the ingredients. Stir well. Strain into an old-fashioned glass almost filled with crushed ice.

301 MAESTRO

1½ ounces añejo rum   Crushed ice
½ ounce cream sherry   4 ounces ginger ale
½ ounce lime juice   1 lemon twist

In a shaker half-filled with ice cubes, combine the rum, sherry, and lime juice. Shake well. Strain into a collins glass almost filled with crushed ice. Top with the ginger ale. Garnish with the lemon twist.

MAI TAI

See Tropical Drinks, page 214.

302 MALLELIEU

1½ ounces light rum   2 ounces orange juice
½ ounce Grand Marnier

Pour the rum, Grand Marnier, and orange juice into an old-fashioned glass almost filled with ice cubes. Stir well.

303 MANDEVILLE

1 ounce light rum	$\frac{1}{2}$ ounce lemon juice
1 ounce dark rum	$\frac{1}{2}$ teaspoon grenadine
1 teaspoon anisette	1 ounce cola

In a shaker half-filled with ice cubes, combine the light rum, dark rum, anisette, lemon juice, and grenadine. Shake well. Strain into an old-fashioned glass almost filled with ice cubes. Top with the cola. Stir well.

304 MARDEE MINE

$1\frac{1}{2}$ ounces dark rum	1 lemon twist
$\frac{1}{2}$ ounce sweet vermouth	

In a mixing glass half-filled with ice cubes, combine the rum and vermouth. Stir well. Strain into a cocktail glass. Garnish with the lemon twist.

305 MARGARET IN THE MARKETPLACE

2 ounces añejo rum	1 teaspoon grenadine
2 teaspoons lime juice	$\frac{1}{2}$ ounce light cream
2 teaspoons lemon juice	

In a shaker half-filled with ice cubes, combine all of the ingredients. Shake well. Strain into a cocktail glass.

306 MARY PICKFORD COCKTAIL

$1\frac{1}{2}$ ounces light rum	$\frac{1}{2}$ teaspoon grenadine
1 ounce pineapple juice	1 maraschino cherry
$\frac{1}{2}$ teaspoon maraschino liqueur	

In a shaker half-filled with ice cubes, combine the rum, pineapple juice, maraschino liqueur, and grenadine. Shake well. Strain into a cocktail glass. Garnish with the cherry.

307 MARY'S DREAM

2 ounces light rum
½ ounce Cointreau or
   triple sec

4 ounces orange juice
2 dashes orange bitters
1 orange slice

Pour the rum, Cointreau, orange juice, and orange bitters into a highball glass almost filled with ice cubes. Stir well and garnish with the orange slice.

308 MAX THE SILENT

1 ounce añejo rum
½ ounce brandy

½ ounce applejack
1 teaspoon anisette

In a mixing glass half-filled with ice cubes, combine all of the ingredients. Stir well. Strain into a cocktail glass.

309 MÉNAGE À TROIS

1 ounce dark rum
1 ounce Cointreau or
   triple sec

1 ounce light cream

In a shaker half-filled with ice cubes, combine all of the ingredients. Shake well. Strain into a cocktail glass.

310 MISS BELLE

1½ ounces dark rum
½ ounce Grand Marnier

2 teaspoons dark crème
   de cacao

In a mixing glass half-filled with ice cubes, combine all of the ingredients. Stir well. Strain into a cocktail glass.

311 MISTER CHRISTIAN

1½ ounces light rum
½ ounce brandy
1 ounce orange juice

½ ounce lemon juice
½ ounce lime juice
1 teaspoon grenadine

In a shaker half-filled with ice cubes, combine all of the ingredients. Shake well. Strain into a cocktail glass.

312 MONKEY WRENCH

1½ ounces light rum   1 dash bitters
3 ounces grapefruit juice

Pour all of the ingredients into an old-fashioned glass almost filled with ice cubes. Stir well.

313 MORGAN'S MOUNTAIN

1½ ounces light rum   1 ounce heavy cream
½ ounce white crème de   1 teaspoon Kahlúa
  cacao

In a shaker half-filled with ice cubes, combine the rum, crème de cacao, and cream. Shake well. Strain into a cocktail glass. Drop the Kahlúa into the center of the drink.

314 MOSTLY MAL

1½ ounces añejo rum   ½ teaspoon grenadine
½ ounce dry vermouth   1 maraschino cherry
½ ounce Cointreau or
  triple sec

In a shaker half-filled with ice cubes, combine the rum, vermouth, Cointreau, and grenadine. Shake well. Strain into a cocktail glass and garnish with the cherry.

315 MOZART

1½ ounces añejo rum   2 dashes orange bitters
½ ounce sweet vermouth   1 lemon twist
1 teaspoon Cointreau or
  triple sec

In a mixing glass half-filled with ice cubes, combine the rum, vermouth, Cointreau, and orange bitters. Stir well. Strain into a cocktail glass and garnish with the lemon twist.

316 MUMBO JUMBO

1½ ounces dark rum
½ ounce applejack
½ ounce lemon juice
½ teaspoon superfine
  sugar

⅛ teaspoon ground
  cinnamon
⅛ teaspoon grated
  nutmeg

In a shaker half-filled with ice cubes, combine all of the ingredients. Shake well. Strain into an old-fashioned glass almost filled with ice cubes.

317 MUMSICLE

1½ ounces dark rum
½ ounce bourbon

1 dash bitters
1 maraschino cherry

In a mixing glass half-filled with ice cubes, combine the rum, bourbon, and bitters. Stir well. Strain into a cocktail glass and garnish with the cherry.

318 MUTINY

1½ ounces dark rum
½ ounce Dubonnet
  Rouge

2 dashes bitters
1 maraschino cherry

In a mixing glass half-filled with ice cubes, combine the rum, Dubonnet, and bitters. Stir well. Strain into a cocktail glass and garnish with the cherry.

319 NEVADA COCKTAIL

1½ ounces light rum
1½ ounces grapefruit
  juice
1 dash bitters

1 ounce lime juice
2 teaspoons superfine
  sugar

In a shaker half-filled with ice cubes, combine all of the ingredients. Shake well. Strain into a cocktail glass.

320 OLYMPIA

2½ ounces dark rum
½ ounce cherry brandy

½ ounce lime juice

In a shaker half-filled with ice cubes, combine all of the ingredients. Shake well. Strain into a cocktail glass.

321 OWEN MOORE

1½ ounces light rum
½ ounce white crème de cacao

1 ounce heavy cream
1 teaspoon blue Curaçao

In a shaker half-filled with ice cubes, combine the rum, crème de cacao, and heavy cream. Shake well. Strain into a cocktail glass. Drop the Curaçao into the center of the drink.

322 PEREGRINE'S PERIL

1 ounce dark rum
½ ounce crème de bananes
½ ounce Southern Comfort

1 teaspoon lime juice
1 teaspoon lemon juice

In a shaker half-filled with ice cubes, combine all of the ingredients. Shake well. Strain into a cocktail glass.

PIÑA COLADA

See Tropical Drinks, page 214.

323 PLANTER'S PUNCH

1 ounce dark rum
1 ounce light rum
1 ounce añejo rum
1 ounce lime juice
½ ounce lemon juice
2 teaspoons superfine sugar

3 ounces club soda
1 maraschino cherry
1 orange slice
1 pineapple wedge
1 lime wedge

In a shaker half-filled with ice cubes, combine the dark rum, light rum, añejo rum, lime juice, lemon juice, and sugar. Shake well. Strain into a collins glass almost filled with ice cubes. Top with the club soda and garnish with the cherry, orange slice, and pineapple and lime wedges.

324 PLANTER'S PUNCH #2

1 ounce dark rum	½ ounce grapefruit juice
1 ounce light rum	1 teaspoon grenadine
1 ounce añejo rum	1 maraschino cherry
1 teaspoon lime juice	1 orange slice
1 teaspoon lemon juice	1 pineapple wedge
1 ounce orange juice	1 lime wedge
1 ounce pineapple juice	

In a shaker half-filled with ice cubes, combine the dark rum, light rum, añejo rum, lime juice, lemon juice, orange juice, pineapple juice, grapefruit juice, and grenadine. Shake well. Strain into a collins glass almost filled with ice cubes. Garnish with the cherry, orange slice, and pineapple and lime wedges.

325 PLANTER'S PUNCH #3

2 ounces dark rum	1 teaspoon lemon juice
½ ounce light rum	2 ounces orange juice
½ ounce añejo rum	1 ounce pineapple juice
2 teaspoons bourbon	2 dashes bitters
1 teaspoon crème de cassis	1 maraschino cherry
1 teaspoon Rose's lime juice	1 orange slice
	1 pineapple wedge
	1 lime wedge

In a shaker half-filled with ice cubes, combine the dark rum, light rum, añejo rum, bourbon, cassis, Rose's lime juice, lemon juice, orange juice, pineapple juice, and bitters. Shake well. Strain into a collins glass almost filled with ice cubes. Garnish with the cherry, orange slice, and pineapple and lime wedges.

326 P.T.O.

1½ ounces dark rum	2 ounces orange juice
½ ounce vodka	1 orange slice
½ ounce Cointreau or triple sec	

Pour the rum, vodka, Cointreau, and orange juice into a highball glass almost filled with ice cubes. Stir well and garnish with the orange slice.

327 PUFFER

2 ounces light rum
2 ounces orange juice

2 ounces grapefruit juice
1 teaspoon grenadine

Pour the rum, orange juice, and grapefruit juice into a highball glass almost filled with ice cubes. Stir well. Drop the grenadine into the center of the drink.

328 QUARTER DECK

1 ounce light rum
½ ounce dark rum

½ ounce cream sherry
½ ounce lime juice

In a shaker half-filled with ice cubes, combine all of the ingredients. Shake well. Strain into a cocktail glass.

329 QUENTIN

1½ ounces dark rum
½ ounce Kahlúa
1 ounce light cream

⅛ teaspoon grated nutmeg

In a shaker half-filled with ice cubes, combine the rum, Kahlúa, and cream. Shake well. Strain into a cocktail glass and garnish with the nutmeg.

330 REDCOAT

1½ ounces light rum
½ ounce vodka
½ ounce apricot brandy

½ ounce lime juice
1 teaspoon grenadine

In a shaker half-filled with ice cubes, combine all of the ingredients. Shake well. Strain into a cocktail glass.

331 RILEY'S SPARROW

1½ ounces dark rum
½ ounce Southern Comfort

2 dashes bitters

In a mixing glass half-filled with ice cubes, combine all of the ingredients. Stir well. Strain into a cocktail glass.

332 RUM COBBLER

1 teaspoon superfine
  sugar
3 ounces club soda
Crushed ice

2 ounces dark rum
1 maraschino cherry
1 orange slice
1 lemon slice

In an old-fashioned glass, dissolve the sugar in the club
soda. Add crushed ice until the glass is almost full. Add
the rum. Stir well. Garnish with the cherry and the orange
and lemon slices.

333 RUM COLLINS

2 ounces dark or light
  rum
1 ounce lemon juice
1 teaspoon superfine
  sugar

3 ounces club soda
1 maraschino cherry
1 orange slice

In a shaker half-filled with ice cubes, combine the rum,
lemon juice, and sugar. Shake well. Strain into a collins
glass almost filled with ice cubes. Add the club soda. Stir
and garnish with the cherry and the orange slice.

334 RUM COOLER

2 ounces dark or light
  rum
4 ounces lemon-lime
  soda

1 lemon wedge

Pour the rum and soda into a highball glass almost filled
with ice cubes. Stir well and garnish with the lemon
wedge.

335 RUM CRUSTA

1 tablespoon superfine
  sugar
1 lemon wedge
Peel of 1 orange, cut into
  a spiral
Crushed ice

1½ ounces dark rum
½ ounce Cointreau or
  triple sec
2 teaspoons maraschino
  liqueur
½ ounce lemon juice

Place the sugar in a saucer. Rub the rim of a wine goblet
with the lemon wedge and dip the glass into the sugar to

coat the rim thoroughly; discard the lemon. Place the orange peel spiral in the goblet and drape one end of it over the rim of the glass. Fill the glass with crushed ice. In a shaker half-filled with ice cubes, combine the rum, Cointreau, maraschino liqueur, and lemon juice. Shake well. Strain into the goblet.

336 RUM DAISY

2 ounces dark rum
1 ounce lemon juice
½ teaspoon superfine
  sugar

½ teaspoon grenadine
1 maraschino cherry
1 orange slice

In a shaker half-filled with ice cubes, combine the rum, lemon juice, sugar, and grenadine. Shake well. Pour into an old-fashioned glass and garnish with the cherry and the orange slice.

337 RUM FIX

1 teaspoon superfine
  sugar
1 ounce lemon juice
2 teaspoons water
Crushed ice

2 ounces light or dark
  rum
1 maraschino cherry
1 lemon slice

In a shaker half-filled with ice cubes, combine the sugar, lemon juice, and water. Shake well. Strain into a highball glass almost filled with crushed ice. Add the rum. Stir well and garnish with the cherry and the lemon slice.

338 RUM GIMLET

2 ounces light rum
½ ounce Rose's lime juice

1 lime wedge

Pour the rum and Rose's lime juice into a mixing glass half-filled with ice cubes. Stir well. Strain into a cocktail glass. Garnish with the lime wedge.

339 RUM MARTINI

2½ ounces light rum
1½ teaspoons dry
   vermouth

1 lemon twist or 1
   cocktail olive

In a mixing glass half-filled with ice cubes, combine the rum and vermouth. Stir well. Strain into a cocktail glass. Garnish with the lemon twist or the olive.

340 RUM SOUR

2 ounces light rum
1 ounce lemon juice
½ teaspoon superfine
   sugar

1 orange slice
1 maraschino cherry

In a shaker half-filled with ice cubes, combine the rum, lemon juice, and sugar. Shake well. Strain into a sour glass and garnish with the orange slice and the cherry.

341 RUM SWIZZLE

1½ ounces lime juice
1 teaspoon superfine
   sugar
2 ounces rum

1 dash bitters
Crushed ice
3 ounces club soda

In a shaker half-filled with ice cubes, combine the lime juice, sugar, rum, and bitters. Shake well. Almost fill a collins glass with crushed ice and stir until the glass is frosted. Strain the mixture in the shaker into the glass and add the club soda. Serve with a swizzle stick.

342 SAND-GROWN-UN

1½ ounces dark rum
½ ounce sweet vermouth
½ ounce cherry brandy

½ ounce lemon juice
½ teaspoon superfine
   sugar

In a shaker half-filled with ice cubes, combine all of the ingredients. Shake well. Strain into a cocktail glass.

343 SANDRA BUYS A DOG

1 ounce dark rum   1 ounce orange juice
1 ounce añejo rum   1 dash bitters
3 ounces cranberry juice

Pour all of the ingredients into a highball glass almost filled with ice cubes. Stir well.

344 SAXON COCKTAIL

1½ ounces light rum   ½ ounce lime juice
½ teaspoon grenadine   1 orange slice

In a shaker half-filled with ice cubes, combine the rum, grenadine, and lime juice. Shake well. Strain into a cocktail glass and garnish with the orange slice.

SCORPION

See Tropical Drinks, page 216.

345 SECRET PLACE

1½ ounces dark rum   4 ounces cold coffee
½ ounce cherry brandy   Crushed ice
2 teaspoons dark crème
  de cacao

Pour all of the ingredients into an Irish coffee glass filled with crushed ice. Stir well.

346 SEPTEMBER MORNING

1½ ounces light rum   ½ teaspoon grenadine
1 teaspoon cherry brandy   1 egg white
½ ounce lime juice

In a shaker half-filled with ice cubes, combine all of the ingredients. Shake well. Strain into a cocktail glass.

347 SERPENTINE

1 ounce light rum
½ ounce brandy
½ ounce sweet vermouth
½ ounce lemon juice

½ teaspoon superfine
  sugar
1 lemon twist

In a shaker half-filled with ice cubes, combine the rum, brandy, vermouth, lemon juice, and sugar. Shake well. Strain into a cocktail glass and garnish with the lemon twist.

348 SEVILLA COCKTAIL

1 ounce light rum
½ ounce tawny port
2 dashes orange bitters

½ teaspoon superfine
  sugar
1 egg

In a shaker half-filled with ice cubes, combine all of the ingredients. Shake well. Strain into a sour glass.

349 SEVILLA COCKTAIL #2

1½ ounces light rum
1 ounce tawny port
1 teaspoon superfine
  sugar

1 egg

In a shaker half-filled with ice cubes, combine all of the ingredients. Shake well. Strain into a sour glass.

350 SHANGHAI

1½ ounces light rum
½ ounce anisette

½ ounce lemon juice
½ teaspoon grenadine

In a shaker half-filled with ice cubes, combine all of the ingredients. Shake well. Strain into a cocktail glass.

351 SILENT BROADSIDER

1½ ounces light rum
2 teaspoons brandy
2 teaspoons Frangelico

2 teaspoons sweet
  vermouth
1 teaspoon grenadine

In a mixing glass half-filled with ice cubes, combine all of the ingredients. Stir well. Strain into a cocktail glass.

352 SISTER STARSEEKER

2 ounces light rum
1 ounce lemon juice
1 teaspoon grenadine

4 ounces tonic water
1 lemon wedge

Pour the rum, lemon juice, grenadine, and tonic water into a highball glass almost filled with ice cubes. Stir well and garnish with the lemon wedge.

353 SITARSKI

1½ ounces dark rum
½ ounce lime juice
1 teaspoon lemon juice

2 ounces grapefruit juice
1 teaspoon superfine
 sugar

In a shaker half-filled with ice cubes, combine all of the ingredients. Shake well. Strain into an old-fashioned glass almost filled with ice cubes.

354 SLEEPY LEMON CLEGG

1½ ounces dark rum
½ ounce crème de
 bananes
½ ounce lemon juice

1 ounce orange juice
1 ounce pineapple juice
Crushed ice
1 lemon wedge

Pour the rum, crème de bananes, lemon juice, orange juice, and pineapple juice into an old-fashioned glass almost filled with crushed ice. Stir well and garnish with the lemon wedge.

355 SLY GOES TO HAVANA

1½ ounces light rum
1 teaspoon white crème
 de cacao
1 teaspoon green
 Chartreuse

1 ounce pineapple juice
½ ounce lime juice
Crushed ice

In a shaker half-filled with ice cubes, combine all of the ingredients. Shake well. Strain into an old fashioned glass almost filled with crushed ice.

356 SONNY GETS KISSED

1½ ounces light rum
½ ounce apricot brandy
2 teaspoons lime juice
2 teaspoons lemon juice
½ teaspoon superfine
  sugar

In a shaker half-filled with ice cubes, combine all of the ingredients. Shake well. Strain into a cocktail glass.

357 SON OF ADAM

1½ ounces light rum
½ ounce apricot brandy
½ ounce lemon juice
½ teaspoon superfine
  sugar
1 teaspoon grenadine

In a shaker half-filled with ice cubes, combine all of the ingredients. Shake well. Strain into a cocktail glass.

358 SPARK IN THE NIGHT

1½ ounces dark rum
½ ounce Kahlúa
2 teaspoons lime juice

In a shaker half-filled with ice cubes, combine all of the ingredients. Shake well. Strain into a cocktail glass.

359 STANLEY SENIOR

2 ounces light rum
1 ounce grapefruit juice
½ ounce cranberry
  liqueur

In a shaker half-filled with ice cubes, combine all of the ingredients. Shake well. Strain into a cocktail glass.

360 STARSEEKER

2 ounces light rum
1 ounce orange juice
1 teaspoon grenadine
4 ounces tonic water

Pour all of the ingredients into a highball glass almost filled with ice cubes. Stir well and garnish with the lemon wedge.

361 STRAIN THE REIN

3 teaspoons superfine
  sugar
1 lime wedge
1½ ounces light rum
½ ounce raspberry
  liqueur

1 teaspoon Cointreau or
  triple sec
1 ounce lemon juice

Place 2 teaspoons of the sugar in a saucer. Rub the rim of
a cocktail glass with the lime wedge and dip the glass into
the sugar to coat the rim thoroughly; discard the lime. In
a shaker half-filled with ice cubes, combine the rum, raspberry liqueur, Cointreau, lemon juice, and remaining 1
teaspoon sugar. Shake well. Strain into the cocktail glass.

362 STRANGER-IN-TOWN

1½ ounces light rum
½ ounce sweet vermouth
½ ounce Calvados

½ ounce cherry brandy
1 maraschino cherry

In a mixing glass half-filled with ice cubes, combine the
rum, vermouth, Calvados, and cherry brandy. Stir well.
Strain into a cocktail glass and garnish with the cherry.

363 SUE RIDING HIGH

1½ ounces dark rum
½ ounce dark crème de
  cacao
2 ounces hot chocolate,
  cooled to room
  temperature

1 teaspoon heavy cream

In a shaker half-filled with ice cubes, combine the rum,
crème de cacao, and hot chocolate. Shake well. Strain into
a cocktail glass. Drop the cream into the center of the
drink.

364 SUFFRAGETTE CITY

1½ ounces light rum
½ ounce Grand Marnier

½ ounce lime juice
½ teaspoon grenadine

In a shaker half-filled with ice cubes, combine all of the
ingredients. Shake well. Strain into a cocktail glass.

365 SURREY SLIDER

1½ ounces añejo rum   4 ounces orange juice
½ ounce peach schnapps   1 orange slice

Pour the rum, peach schnapps, and orange juice into a highball glass almost filled with ice cubes. Stir well and garnish with the orange slice.

366 SUSAN LITTLER

1 ounce dark rum   1 teaspoon Galliano
½ ounce bourbon   2 ounces orange juice

Pour all of the ingredients into a highball glass almost filled with ice cubes. Stir well.

367 THREE-MILER COCKTAIL

1 ounce light rum   2 teaspoons lemon juice
1 ounce brandy   ½ teaspoon grenadine

In a shaker half-filled with ice cubes, combine all of the ingredients. Shake well. Strain into a cocktail glass.

368 TRIAD

½ ounce añejo rum   4 ounces ginger ale
½ ounce sweet vermouth   1 lemon twist
½ ounce amaretto

Pour the rum, vermouth, amaretto, and ginger ale into a highball glass almost filled with ice cubes. Stir well and garnish with the lemon twist.

369 TROUBLE FOR TINA

1½ ounces añejo rum   1 ounce heavy cream
½ ounce dark crème de   ¼ teaspoon ground
  cacao   cinnamon
½ ounce white crème de
  cacao
2 ounces brewed coffee,
  cooled to room
  temperature

In a shaker half-filled with ice cubes, combine the rum, dark crème de cacao, white crème de cacao, coffee, and cream. Shake well. Strain into an old-fashioned glass almost filled with ice cubes. Dust with the cinnamon.

370 VETERAN

2 ounces dark rum   ½ ounce cherry brandy

Pour the rum and cherry brandy into an old-fashioned glass almost filled with ice cubes. Stir well.

371 VICIOUS SID

1½ ounces light rum   1 ounce lemon juice
½ ounce Southern   1 dash bitters
  Comfort
½ ounce Cointreau or
  triple sec

In a shaker half-filled with ice cubes, combine all of the ingredients. Shake well. Strain into an old-fashioned glass almost filled with ice cubes.

372 WAKING TO THE CALL OF THE MOCKINGBIRD

1½ ounces light rum   1 teaspoon superfine
½ ounce sweet vermouth   sugar
½ ounce tawny port   1 egg white
1 ounce lemon juice

In a shaker half-filled with ice cubes, combine all of the ingredients. Shake well. Strain into an old-fashioned glass almost filled with ice cubes.

ZOMBIE

See Tropical Drinks, page 218.

6 · SCOTCH

Without Scotch, the peaty whisky from the land of swirling kilts and bellowing bagpipes, there would be no Rusty Nail, no Godfather, and no Rob Roy, and the world would be a sadder place. The word *Scotch* defines a whisky and cannot be applied to just any old object or person hailing from Scotland (known as Scottish).

The art of distillation probably was introduced to Scotland by Irish monks who themselves learned the process from the Spaniards. They brought it to the west coast of Scotland when seeking to convert the then "heathen" Scot. It probably went a long way to convincing the Scots that Christianity was a fine religion.

In 1643 excise taxes were introduced to Scotland, and many distillers fled to the hills to escape the grasp of the tax man. These distilleries were often protected by the local citizens and were still in widespread use up until the early 1800s, when another law was introduced prohibiting the use of any still with a capacity of less than 500 gallons. Using a little tact and diplomacy this time, the government managed to convince the illegal distillers that if their stills were legally recognized, then they could sell their product to a far larger audience.

The continuous still (also known as the Coffey or the

patent still; see page 20) was introduced in 1831, making the production of whisky much easier and far quicker. Competition between distilleries became rife, and Scotch was exported for the first time.

Prohibition played a large part in making Scotch popular in America. A certain Captain McCoy, a famous Prohibition-era smuggler, guaranteed that any Scotch bought from him was the real thing. That's how the term "the real McCoy" entered our language.

PRODUCTION

Blended Scotches have long been popular in America. "Single malt" Scotch gained much popularity in the late 1980s. In defining the production processes involved in making Scotch, it is easiest to describe each "category" separately, starting with the "single malt," the pure, unblended form.

SINGLE MALT SCOTCH

Single malt Scotch is made entirely from malted barley, that is, barley that has been germinated to release fermentable sugars and then heated to stop the germination process. The malt is then milled and "mashed," mixed with warm water in a "mashtun," to complete the conversion of starches to fermentable sugars. The liquid is strained and becomes known as "wort." Yeast is added to the wort, and the resulting fermentation yields alcohol. The fermented wort is distilled in pot stills to produce single malt Scotch. Finally it is poured into oak sherry or bourbon casks for aging.

It was not until the late nineteenth century that the Scots discovered that aging their single malts made a vast difference in the taste. Legally, single malt must be aged for at least three years, although it is rare that a distiller will offer it for sale under five years old. The popular standard is to give malt whisky 12 years of barrel aging, until it is mature and has soaked up the flavors from the casks. Many experts say that after 15 years the Scotch begins to take on the flavor of the wood rather than the sherry or bourbon. Wood flavors are not desirable. This group prefers single malts aged no more than 15 years. Others believe that some heartier distillations can withstand 18 to 25 years of aging without suffering any ill effects whatsoever.

Just like a fine Cognac or a vintage wine, the single malt Scotch offers bouquet, palate, and finish, and therefore, each one can be properly savored and judged on these aspects. The differences among single malt Scotches come from many variants within each distillery and its location. The deciding factors include:

1. The *water* from which they are made. Distilleries are located near the springs and wells that supply the water for the Scotch. They are built *because* of the quality of the nearby water, and that water is not treated before it is used in the distilling process. Ideally, the water used distilling single malts rises from granite and flows over peat.

2. The *peat,* a type of moss over which the water flows. In some cases, the peat also is used in the kilns to stop the malting process. The flavor of the peat differs from area to area, helping make each district and even each distillery produce a Scotch that is peculiar to itself.

3. The *air* surrounding the casks during maturation. Since the casks breathe the air, the atmospheric characteristics of the region are infused into the Scotch giving, for example, Islay Scotches an undertone of sea air or iodine.

4. The *shape of the pot still.* This factor is so important that when a still must be replaced, it is copied right down to the last dent that some careless welder may have put into the original one in 1824! Tall towers on the pot still tend to produce lighter Scotches, whereas short, squat towers produce a heavier, oilier Scotch.

5. The *casks in which they are aged.* Oak casks are always used, but since virgin oak imparts too much vanilla flavor, the casks used for aging single malts are bought from bourbon or sherry distillers. The single malt,

therefore, takes on some of the flavor of the previous occupant of the cask. Some malts are aged in bourbon casks, some in sherry casks, and some are started in bourbon and finished in sherry.

In addition to these influences, the heather or the seaweed in the peat, the microflora in the wood of the tunroom, and some say even the color of the distiller's tartan make a difference, too. Indeed, the possibilities are mind boggling, and these variants make the single malt intriguing to connoisseurs.

Single malt Scotches are usually divided into four regions: Highlands, Lowlands, Islay, and Cambeltown. The Highlands can be further broken down since the area is so large, and in addition to Islay, there are other Scotch-producing islands—Skye, Mull, Jura, and Orkney. Scotches from these small areas can be hard to find in the United States and, since they are few, are almost impossible to regionalize.

I give here a *generalization* of the characteristics of each area. Remember, these are not descriptions of the brand names used as examples; these brands serve only as a guideline to help you choose a Scotch representative of each area. Each individual single malt Scotch differs from the next.

The Lowlands yield soft, sweetish, fruity malts relying less on peat and granite springs and more on the flavor of the malt itself. Try Auchentoshen, Glenkinchie, or Ladyburn.

Cambeltown produces briny, salt-sweet Scotch, drawing on the sea air for much of its character. This Scotch usually imparts a light peatiness along with a fresh palate. Try Springbank or Longrow.

Islay delivers a very distinctive product drawing on the sea air that not only permeates the casks, but is also responsible for the flavor imparted from the peat. These malts are known for having an iodine and peaty flavor, some say almost medicinal. Try Bunnahabhain, Laphroaig, or Lagavulin.

Speyside is often referred to as the Rolls-Royce of Scotch-producing regions. A delimited area of the Highlands,

Speyside runs roughly between the cities of Iverness and Aberdeen. The whiskies from this region are diverse within themselves and actually can be divided into smaller areas within Speyside. Generally, however, they tend toward being smoky and full-bodied; many are aged totally in sherry casks and therefore impart sweetness from the sherry. Try The Macallan, The Singleton, or Glenlivet.

Western Highland Scotches are few and therefore hard to categorize. They are generally firm and dry with some peatiness. Try Oban or Glengoyne.

Northern Highland malts draw from the sea air and the heather-packed soil to produce Scotch that is both spicy and flowery. Try Glenmorangie, Dalmore, or Glenordie.

Eastern Highlands produce sweet, fruity single malts that are ideal after dinner. Try Lochnagar or Glen Garioch.

The Southern Highland or *Midland* region tends to be better known for its blended Scotches, such as Dewar's and Famous Grouse. Malts from this district tend to be fruity, medium sweet, and nutty. Try Edradour or Glenforres (vatted).

VATTED MALT SCOTCH

This is a blend of single malt Scotches from a variety of distilleries. No whisky from continuous stills is added. These Scotches tend to be more consistent than regular single malts, since the proportions used in the blending process can be fine-tuned to guarantee the exact same flavor as the previous bottling.

BLENDED SCOTCH

These Scotches use a proportion of several single malt Scotches that are blended with whisky distilled in continuous stills from unmalted barley or corn. The continuous still is more effective than the pot still, but the resulting liquor is correspondingly less flavorful.

373 AFFINITY

1½ ounces Scotch
1 ounce sweet vermouth

1 ounce dry vermouth
2 dashes orange bitters

In a mixing glass half-filled with ice cubes, combine all of the ingredients. Stir well. Strain into a cocktail glass.

374 BALMORAL

1½ ounces Scotch
½ ounce sweet vermouth
½ ounce dry vermouth
2 dashes bitters

In a mixing glass half-filled with ice cubes, combine all of the ingredients. Stir well. Strain into a cocktail glass.

375 BLACK JACK

1½ ounces Scotch
1 ounce Kahlúa
½ ounce Cointreau or
   triple sec

½ ounce lemon juice

In a shaker half-filled with ice cubes, combine all of the ingredients. Shake well. Strain into a cocktail glass.

376 BLIMEY

2 ounces Scotch
½ ounce lime juice

½ teaspoon superfine
   sugar

In a shaker half-filled with ice cubes, combine all of the ingredients. Shake well. Strain into a cocktail glass.

377 BLINDER

2 ounces Scotch
5 ounces grapefruit juice

1 teaspoon grenadine

Pour the Scotch and grapefruit juice into a highball glass almost filled with ice cubes. Drop the grenadine into the center of the drink.

378 BRAINSTORM

2 ounces Scotch
½ ounce Bénédictine

1 teaspoon sweet
vermouth

In a mixing glass half-filled with ice cubes, combine all of
the ingredients. Stir well. Strain into a cocktail glass.

379 CALEIGH

1½ ounces Scotch
½ ounce blue Curaçao

½ ounce white crème de
cacao

In a mixing glass half-filled with ice cubes, combine all of
the ingredients. Stir well. Strain into a cocktail glass.

380 CELTIC MIX COCKTAIL

1½ ounces Scotch
1 ounce Irish whiskey

½ ounce lemon juice
1 dash bitters

In a shaker half-filled with ice cubes, combine all of the
ingredients. Shake well. Strain into a cocktail glass.

381 CHOKER

2 ounces Scotch
2 teaspoons Pernod

2 dashes bitters

In a mixing glass half-filled with ice cubes, combine all of
the ingredients. Stir well. Strain into a cocktail glass.

382 DICKIE WARD

2 ounces Scotch
1 dash bitters

4 ounces ginger ale
1 lime wedge

Pour the Scotch, bitters, and ginger ale into a highball
glass almost filled with ice cubes. Stir well and garnish
with the lime wedge.

383 DRY ROB ROY

2½ ounces Scotch
1½ teaspoons dry
vermouth

1 lemon twist

In a mixing glass half-filled with ice cubes, combine the

Scotch and vermouth. Stir well. Strain into a cocktail glass. Garnish with the lemon twist.

384 FANCY SCOTCH

2 ounces Scotch
½ teaspoon Cointreau or
  triple sec
¼ teaspoon superfine
  sugar

2 dashes bitters
1 lemon twist

In a shaker half-filled with ice cubes combine the Scotch, Cointreau, sugar, and bitters. Shake well. Strain into a cocktail glass and garnish with the lemon twist.

385 GODFATHER

1½ ounces Scotch

½ ounce amaretto

Pour both of the ingredients into an old-fashioned glass almost filled with ice cubes. Stir well.

386 GRAND MASTER

2 ounces Scotch
½ ounce peppermint
  schnapps

3 ounces club soda
1 lemon twist

Pour the Scotch, schnapps, and soda into a highball glass almost filled with ice cubes. Stir well. Garnish with the lemon twist.

387 HIGHLAND FLING

2 ounces Scotch
½ ounce sweet vermouth

2 dashes orange bitters
1 maraschino cherry

In a mixing glass half-filled with ice cubes, combine the Scotch, vermouth, and orange bitters. Stir well. Strain into a cocktail glass. Garnish with the cherry.

388 HIGHLAND SLING

1 teaspoon superfine
  sugar
2 teaspoons water

1 ounce lemon juice
2 ounces Scotch
1 lemon twist

In a shaker half-filled with ice cubes, combine the sugar, water, lemon juice, and Scotch. Shake well. Strain into a highball glass. Garnish with the lemon twist.

389 HOOTS MON

1½ ounces Scotch
½ ounce Lillet

½ ounce sweet vermouth

In a mixing glass half-filled with ice cubes, combine all of the ingredients. Stir well. Strain into a cocktail glass.

390 ITALIAN HEATHER

1½ ounces Scotch
1 ounce Galliano

Crushed ice
1 lime wedge

Pour the Scotch and Galliano into an old-fashioned glass almost filled with crushed ice. Stir well. Garnish with the lime wedge.

391 JAMES THE SECOND COMES FIRST

2 ounces Scotch
½ ounce tawny port

½ ounce dry vermouth
1 dash bitters

In a mixing glass half-filled with ice cubes, combine all of the ingredients. Stir well. Strain into a cocktail glass.

392 JOCK COLLINS

2 ounces Scotch
1 ounce lemon juice
1 teaspoon superfine
  sugar

3 ounces club soda
1 maraschino cherry
1 orange slice

In a shaker half-filled with ice cubes, combine the Scotch, lemon juice, and sugar. Shake well. Strain into a collins glass almost filled with ice cubes. Add the club soda. Stir and garnish with the cherry and the orange slice.

393 JOCK-IN-A-BOX

1½ ounces Scotch
½ ounce sweet vermouth

½ ounce lemon juice
1 egg

In a shaker half-filled with ice cubes, combine all of the ingredients. Shake well. Strain into an old-fashioned glass half-filled with ice cubes.

394 L'AIRD OF SUMMER ISLE

1½ ounces Scotch
½ ounce Pernod

3 ounces pineapple juice

In a shaker half-filled with ice cubes, combine all of the ingredients. Shake well. Strain into an old-fashioned glass almost filled with ice cubes.

395 LOCH LOMOND

2 ounces Scotch
½ ounce Drambuie

½ ounce dry vermouth
1 lemon twist

In a mixing glass half-filled with ice cubes, combine the Scotch, Drambuie, and vermouth. Stir well. Strain into a cocktail glass. Garnish with the lemon twist.

396 MA BONNIE WEE HEN

1½ ounces Scotch
½ ounce cream sherry
½ ounce orange juice

½ ounce lemon juice
1 teaspoon grenadine

In a shaker half-filled with ice cubes, combine all of the ingredients. Shake well. Strain into a cocktail glass.

397 MACBETH'S DREAM

2 ounces Scotch
1 teaspoon white
  Curaçao
1 teaspoon amaretto

2 dashes orange bitters
½ ounce lemon juice
½ teaspoon superfine
  sugar

In a shaker half-filled with ice cubes, combine all of the ingredients. Shake well. Strain into a cocktail glass.

398 MAN OF THE MOMENT

1½ ounces Scotch
1 ounce Grand Marnier

1 ounce lemon juice
1 teaspoon grenadine

In a shaker half-filled with ice cubes, combine all of the ingredients. Shake well. Strain into a cocktail glass.

399 MA WEE HEN

1½ ounces Scotch
½ ounce dry sherry
½ ounce orange juice

½ ounce lemon juice
1 teaspoon grenadine

In a shaker half-filled with ice cubes, combine all of the ingredients. Shake well. Strain into a cocktail glass.

400 McDUFF

1½ ounces Scotch
½ ounce Cointreau or
   triple sec

2 dashes bitters
1 orange slice

In a mixing glass half-filled with ice cubes, combine the Scotch, Cointreau, and bitters. Stir well. Strain into a cocktail glass. Garnish with the orange slice.

401 MIAMI BEACH COCKTAIL

1 ounce Scotch
1 ounce dry vermouth

1 ounce grapefruit juice

In a shaker half-filled with ice cubes, combine all of the ingredients. Shake well. Strain into a cocktail glass.

402 MITHERING BASTARD

1½ ounces Scotch
½ ounce Cointreau or
   triple sec

1 ounce orange juice

In a shaker half-filled with ice cubes, combine all of the ingredients. Shake well. Strain into an old-fashioned glass almost filled with ice cubes.

403 MODERN COCKTAIL

1½ ounces Scotch
1 teaspoon dark rum
½ teaspoon Pernod
½ teaspoon lemon juice
2 dashes orange bitters

In a shaker half-filled with ice cubes, combine all of the ingredients. Shake well. Strain into a cocktail glass.

404 PERFECT ROB ROY

2½ ounces Scotch
1 teaspoon sweet
   vermouth
1 teaspoon dry vermouth
1 maraschino cherry or 1
   lemon twist

In a mixing glass half-filled with ice cubes, combine the Scotch, sweet vermouth, and dry vermouth. Stir well. Strain into a cocktail glass. Garnish with the cherry or the lemon twist.

405 PIPER AT THE GATES OF DAWN

1½ ounces Scotch
1 ounce Kahlúa
½ ounce maraschino
   liqueur
1 ounce heavy cream

In a mixing glass half-filled with ice cubes, combine the Scotch, Kahlúa, and maraschino liqueur. Stir well. Strain into an old-fashioned glass almost filled with ice cubes. Pour the cream slowly and carefully over the back of a teaspoon so that it floats on top of the drink.

406 PIPER AT ARMS

1½ ounces Scotch
1 ounce dry vermouth
1 lemon twist

In a mixing glass half-filled with ice cubes, combine the Scotch and vermouth. Stir well. Strain into a cocktail glass. Garnish with the lemon twist.

407 ROB ROY

Variations on the Rob Roy include the Dry Rob Roy (page 129) and the Perfect Rob Roy (page 133).

2½ ounces Scotch
1½ teaspoons sweet
  vermouth

1 maraschino cherry

In a mixing glass half-filled with ice cubes, combine the Scotch and vermouth. Stir well. Strain into a cocktail glass. Garnish with the cherry.

408 RUSTY NAIL

1½ ounces Scotch
½ ounce Drambuie

1 lemon twist

Pour the Scotch and Drambuie into an old-fashioned glass almost filled with ice cubes. Stir well. Garnish with the lemon twist.

409 SCOTCH AND WATER

2 ounces Scotch

5 ounces water

Pour the Scotch and the water into a highball glass almost filled with ice cubes. Stir well.

410 SCOTCH COBBLER

1 teaspoon superfine
  sugar
3 ounces club soda
Crushed ice

2 ounces Scotch
1 maraschino cherry
1 orange slice
1 lemon slice

In an old-fashioned glass, dissolve the sugar in the club soda. Add crushed ice until the glass is almost full. Add the Scotch. Stir well. Garnish with the cherry and the orange and lemon slices.

411 SCOTCH COOLER

2 ounces blended Scotch
4 ounces lemon-lime
   soda

1 lemon wedge

Pour the Scotch and soda into a highball glass almost filled with ice cubes. Stir well. Garnish with the lemon wedge.

412 SCOTCH DAISY

2 ounces Scotch
1 ounce lemon juice
1/2 teaspoon superfine
   sugar

1/2 teaspoon grenadine
1 maraschino cherry
1 orange slice

In a shaker half-filled with ice cubes, combine the Scotch, lemon juice, sugar, and grenadine. Shake well. Pour into an old-fashioned glass. Garnish with the cherry and the orange slice.

413 SCOTCH FIX

1 teaspoon superfine
   sugar
1 ounce lemon juice
2 teaspoons water

Crushed ice
2 ounces Scotch
1 maraschino cherry
1 lemon slice

In a shaker half-filled with ice cubes, combine the sugar, lemon juice, and water. Shake well. Strain into a highball glass almost filled with crushed ice. Add the Scotch. Stir well and garnish with the cherry and the lemon slice.

414 SCOTCH FLIP

2 ounces Scotch
1 egg
1 teaspoon superfine
   sugar

1/2 ounce light cream
1/8 teaspoon grated
   nutmeg

In a shaker half-filled with ice cubes, combine the Scotch, egg, sugar, and cream. Shake well. Strain into a sour glass and garnish with the nutmeg.

415 SCOTCH MIST

2½ ounces Scotch   1 lemon twist
Crushed ice

Pour the Scotch into a shaker half-filled with crushed ice.
Shake well. Pour, unstrained, into an old-fashioned glass.
Garnish with the lemon twist.

416 SCOTCH OLD-FASHIONED

3 dashes bitters   3 ounces Scotch
1 teaspoon water   1 orange slice
1 sugar cube   1 maraschino cherry

In an old-fashioned glass, muddle the bitters and water
into the sugar cube, using the back of a teaspoon. Almost
fill the glass with ice cubes and add the Scotch. Garnish
with the orange slice and the cherry. Serve with a swizzle
stick.

417 SCOTCH SANGAREE

1 teaspoon superfine   ½ ounce tawny port
  sugar   1 lemon twist
2 teaspoons water   ⅛ teaspoon grated
1½ ounces Scotch   nutmeg
Crushed ice   ⅛ teaspoon ground
2½ ounces club soda   cinnamon

In a highball glass, dissolve the sugar in the water and
Scotch. Almost fill the glass with crushed ice and add the
club soda. Float the port on top. Garnish with the lemon
twist and a dusting of nutmeg and cinnamon.

418 SCOTCH SOUR

2 ounces Scotch   1 orange slice
1 ounce lemon juice   1 maraschino cherry
½ teaspoon superfine
  sugar

In a shaker half-filled with ice cubes, combine the Scotch,
lemon juice, and sugar. Shake well. Strain into a sour glass.
Garnish with the orange slice and the cherry.

419 SWIRLING TO THE BEAT OF THE HAGGIS WINGS

1½ ounces Scotch
½ ounce Cointreau or
   triple sec

1 ounce lemon juice
1 teaspoon grenadine
1 teaspoon egg white

In a shaker half-filled with ice cubes, combine all of the ingredients. Shake well. Strain into a cocktail glass.

420 TARTAN SWIZZLE

1½ ounces lime juice
1 teaspoon superfine
   sugar
2 ounces Scotch

1 dash bitters
Crushed ice
3 ounces club soda

In a shaker half-filled with ice cubes, combine the lime juice, sugar, Scotch, and bitters. Shake well. Almost fill a collins glass with crushed ice. Stir until the glass is frosted. Strain the mixture in the shaker into the glass and add the club soda. Serve with a swizzle stick.

421 TARTANTULA

1½ ounces Scotch
1 ounce sweet vermouth

½ ounce Bénédictine
1 lemon twist

In a mixing glass half-filled with ice cubes, combine the Scotch, vermouth, and Bénédictine. Stir well. Strain into a cocktail glass. Garnish with the lemon twist.

422 THRILLER

1½ ounces Scotch
1 ounce green ginger
   wine

1 ounce orange juice

In a shaker half-filled with ice cubes, combine all of the ingredients. Shake well. Strain into a cocktail glass.

423 TO HELL WITH SWORDS AND GARTERS

1½ ounces Scotch
1 ounce dry vermouth

1½ ounces pineapple
juice

In a shaker half-filled with ice cubes, combine all of the ingredients. Shake well. Strain into an old-fashioned glass almost filled with ice cubes.

424 WHISKY MAC

1½ ounces Scotch
1 ounce green ginger
wine

Pour both of the ingredients into a wine goblet with no ice.

425 WIDOW WOODS' NIGHTCAP

2 ounces Scotch
½ ounce dark crème de
cacao

4 ounces milk

In a shaker half-filled with ice cubes, combine all of the ingredients. Shake well. Strain into a cocktail glass.

7 · TEQUILA

This unique briny liquor, made exclusively in Mexico from the *agave* plant, gives us the base for a Margarita, the Brave Bull, and, of course, the Tequila Sunrise. It is a romantic, daring drink, which bears a distinctive dry taste that lends itself to producing a strain of cocktails peculiar to tequila. Tequila acquired a cult status in the 1950s, when the erroneous rumor that it contained mescaline coupled with its romantic rituals made it a favorite with "hip" Californians. The drink was then incorporated into the aforementioned popular cocktails, as well as many others, and the demand for tequila extended throughout the States.

For at least one thousand years before Spain invaded Mexico, the Aztecs were drinking *pulque,* a low-alcohol wine made from the mezcal plant; it is still consumed in Mexico today. Along came the Spaniards in the early part of the sixteenth century, bringing with them the art of distillation, and tequila was born. *Pulque* was used by the Aztecs in many rituals, and, indeed, tequila is well known as a drink of ritual, being consumed straight with salt and lime in a ceremony seen in bars throughout the world. (The ritual is described in detail in this chapter under Tequila Cruda, page 152.)

Tequila was first imported legally to the United States

in the 1870s. It was further promoted by American soldiers defending Zapata's raids during the Mexican Revolution in 1916. Prohibition also helped tequila gain popularity in the States. Since it was distilled legally in Mexico, tequila only had to be smuggled over the border to quench the thirst of deprived Americans.

PRODUCTION

The base of a mature agave plant is steamed in order to extract the sap. The sap ferments for about 10 days, producing "mother pulque." This is then added to fresh sap and allowed to ferment, producing *pulque* (wine). The *pulque* is then double-distilled in pot stills, and the resultant *vino mezcal* can be exported immediately as a "white" liquor, or it may be aged in oak casks to produce an *añejo* or aged product.

For tequila aficionados, let's set the record straight on mezcal and tequila. Tequila is to mezcal what Cognac is to brandy; that is, tequila is a superior form of mezcal. Tequila is produced only in two designated regions of Mexico, one surrounding the town of Tequila, the other in the area of Tepatitlan. Mezcal is produced in numerous regions throughout Mexico.

While tequila is made only from a blue-colored agave plant, specifically *Agave tequilana weber,* mezcal can be made from different varieties of agave. Production of tequila is governed by stringent quality standards that are not applied to mezcal. Ordinary tequila is considered "white" tequila.

GOLD TEQUILA

There are no Mexican regulations governing the aging of this product, although most producers claim that it is aged in white oak casks for two to four years.

TEQUILA AÑEJO

This "aged" tequila *must* be aged for a minimum of one year in white oak casks.

SILVER TEQUILA

Wax-lined vats are used to age this product, which is mellower than ordinary (white) tequila but still has no color.

426 ALLELUIA

1½ ounces tequila
1 teaspoon blue Curaçao
1 teaspoon maraschino
  liqueur
½ ounce lemon juice

½ teaspoon superfine
  sugar
4 ounces tonic water
1 maraschino cherry
1 orange slice

In a shaker half-filled with ice cubes, combine the tequila, Curaçao, maraschino liqueur, lemon juice, and sugar. Shake well. Strain into a highball glass almost filled with ice cubes. Top with the tonic water and garnish with the cherry and the orange slice.

427 BLOODY MARIA

2½ ounces tequila
5 ounces tomato juice
½ ounce lemon juice

⅛ teaspoon black pepper
⅛ teaspoon celery salt
1 dash Tabasco sauce

In a shaker half-filled with ice cubes, combine all of the ingredients. Shake well. Strain into a highball glass almost filled with ice cubes.

428 BLUE MARGARITA

2 teaspoons coarse salt
1 lime wedge
1½ ounces tequila
½ ounce blue Curaçao

1½ teaspoons Cointreau
   or triple sec
1½ ounces lime juice

Place the salt in a saucer. Rub the rim of a cocktail glass with the lime wedge and dip the glass into the salt to coat the rim thoroughly; reserve the lime. In a shaker half-filled with ice cubes, combine the tequila, Curaçao, Cointreau, and lime juice. Shake well. Strain into the cocktail glass and garnish with the lime wedge.

429 BORDER CROSSING

1½ ounces tequila
2 teaspoons lime juice
1 teaspoon lemon juice

4 ounces cola
1 lime wedge

Pour the tequila, lime juice, lemon juice, and cola into a highball glass almost filled with ice cubes. Stir well and garnish with the lime wedge.

430 BRAVE BULL

2 ounces tequila

1 ounce Kahlúa

Pour the tequila and Kahlúa into an old-fashioned glass almost filled with ice cubes. Stir well.

431 CACTUS BITE

2 ounces tequila
2 teaspoons Cointreau or
   triple sec
2 teaspoons Drambuie

2 ounces lemon juice
½ teaspoon superfine
   sugar
1 dash bitters

In a shaker half-filled with ice cubes, combine all of the ingredients. Shake well. Strain into a cocktail glass.

432 CALIFORNIA DREAM

2 ounces tequila
1 ounce sweet vermouth

½ ounce dry vermouth
1 maraschino cherry

In a mixing glass half-filled with ice cubes, combine the

tequila, sweet vermouth, and dry vermouth. Stir well. Strain into a cocktail glass and garnish with the cherry.

433 CAMPBELL F. CRAIG

1½ ounces tequila
2 ounces orange juice

2 ounces pineapple juice
½ ounce Chambord

Pour the tequila, orange juice, and pineapple juice into a highball glass almost filled with ice cubes. Stir well. Drop the Chambord into the center of the drink.

434 COMPADRE

1½ ounces tequila
½ teaspoon maraschino liqueur

1 teaspoon grenadine
2 dashes orange bitters

In a mixing glass half-filled with ice cubes, combine all of the ingredients. Stir well. Strain into a cocktail glass.

435 DARING DYLAN

2 ounces tequila
1 ounce Kahlúa
4 ounces Mexican hot chocolate, cooled to room temperature

Crushed ice

Pour all of the ingredients into an Irish coffee glass almost filled with crushed ice. Stir well.

436 DOCTOR DAWSON

2 ounces tequila
½ ounce lemon juice
1 teaspoon superfine sugar

1 dash bitters
1 egg
3 ounces club soda

In a shaker half-filled with ice cubes, combine the tequila, lemon juice, sugar, bitters, and egg. Shake well. Strain into a highball glass almost filled with ice cubes. Top with the club soda.

437 DORALTO

1½ ounces tequila
½ ounce lemon juice
½ teaspoon superfine
  sugar

1 dash bitters
4 ounces tonic water
1 lime wedge

In a shaker half-filled with ice cubes, combine the tequila, lemon juice, sugar, and bitters. Shake well. Strain into a highball glass almost filled with ice cubes. Top with the tonic water and garnish with the lime wedge.

438 DOWNSIDER

1½ ounces tequila
½ ounce crème de
  bananes
½ ounce Galliano

½ ounce light cream
1 teaspoon lemon juice
1 dash bitters
1 teaspoon grenadine

In a shaker half-filled with ice cubes, combine all of the ingredients. Shake well. Strain into a cocktail glass.

439 EXECUTIVE SUNRISE

1½ ounces gold tequila
4 ounces freshly
  squeezed orange juice

2 teaspoons crème de
  cassis

Pour the tequila and the orange juice into a collins glass almost filled with ice cubes. Stir well. Drop the cassis into the center of the drink.

440 FREDDY FUDPUCKER

2 ounces tequila
4 ounces orange juice

½ ounce Galliano

Pour the tequila and orange juice into a highball glass almost filled with ice cubes. Pouring slowly and carefully over the back of a teaspoon, float the Galliano on top of the drink.

441 FROZEN MARGARITA

2 teaspoons coarse salt
1 lime wedge
3 ounces white tequila
1 ounce Cointreau or
    triple sec

2 ounces lime juice
1 cup crushed ice

Place the salt in a saucer. Rub the rim of a collins glass
with the lime wedge and dip the glass into the salt to coat
the rim thoroughly; reserve the lime. Pour the tequila,
Cointreau, lime juice, and crushed ice into a blender.
Blend well at high speed. Pour into the collins glass. Garnish with the reserved lime wedge.

442 GATES OF HELL

1½ ounces tequila
2 teaspoons lemon juice
2 teaspoons lime juice

Crushed ice
1 teaspoon cherry brandy

In a shaker half-filled with ice cubes, combine the tequila,
lemon juice, and lime juice. Shake well. Strain into an old-
fashioned glass almost filled with crushed ice. Drizzle the
cherry brandy over the top.

443 GENTLE BEN

1½ ounces tequila
½ ounce vodka

½ ounce gin
4 ounces orange juice

Pour all of the ingredients into a highball glass almost
filled with ice cubes. Stir well.

444 GOLD MARGARITA

2 teaspoons coarse salt
1 lime wedge
2 ounces gold tequila

½ ounce Cointreau
1½ ounces lime juice

Place the salt in a saucer. Rub the rim of a cocktail glass
with the lime wedge and dip the glass into the salt to coat
the rim thoroughly; reserve the lime. In a shaker half-filled
with ice cubes, combine the tequila, Cointreau, and lime
juice. Shake well. Strain into the cocktail glass and garnish
with the lime wedge.

445 GULL'S WING

Crushed ice
2 ounces tequila
½ ounce crème de
 bananes

½ ounce lemon juice

In a shaker half-filled with crushed ice, combine all of the ingredients. Shake well. Strain into an old-fashioned glass almost filled with crushed ice.

446 HOT PANTS

2 teaspoons salt
1 lime wedge
2 ounces tequila
½ ounce peppermint
 schnapps

½ ounce grapefruit juice
½ teaspoon superfine
 sugar

Place the salt in a saucer. Rub the rim of an old-fashioned glass with the lime wedge and dip the glass into the salt to coat the rim thoroughly; discard the lime. Almost fill the glass with ice cubes. In a shaker half-filled with ice cubes, combine the tequila, schnapps, grapefruit juice, and sugar. Shake well. Strain into the glass.

447 JOUMBABA

1½ ounces tequila
2 ounces grapefruit juice

3 ounces tonic water

Pour all of the ingredients into a highball glass almost filled with ice cubes. Stir well.

448 JUAN BLUE

1½ ounces tequila
2 ounces orange juice
1 ounce grapefruit juice

½ ounce lemon juice
1 dash bitters
2 teaspoons blue Curaçao

In a shaker half-filled with ice cubes, combine the tequila, orange juice, grapefruit juice, lemon juice, and bitters. Shake well. Strain into a highball glass almost filled with ice cubes. Pouring slowly and carefully over the back of a teaspoon, float the Curaçao on top of the drink.

449 JUBILEE

1 ounce tequila	½ teaspoon superfine
½ ounce gin	sugar
½ ounce vodka	4 ounces club soda
½ ounce blue Curaçao	1 maraschino cherry
½ ounce lemon juice	

In a shaker half-filled with ice cubes, combine the tequila, gin, vodka, Curaçao, lemon juice, and sugar. Shake well. Strain into a highball glass almost filled with ice cubes. Top with the club soda and garnish with the cherry.

450 JUMPING BEAN

1½ ounces tequila	3 coffee beans
½ ounce Sambuca	

In a mixing glass half-filled with ice cubes, combine the tequila and Sambuca. Stir well. Strain into a cocktail glass and garnish with the coffee beans.

451 LEAPFROG

1½ ounces tequila	1 teaspoon sweet
½ ounce sloe gin	vermouth
	1 lime wedge

Pour the tequila, sloe gin, and vermouth into an old-fashioned glass almost filled with ice cubes. Stir well and garnish with the lime wedge.

452 MARGARITA

These days Margaritas come in a variety of colors and flavors—blue, peach, mango—none of them bearing much resemblance to the pure, original cocktail that spread through California in the early part of the twentieth century. One thing certain about the Margarita is that it was named for a woman; exactly which woman and what she did to earn the accolade is arguable. One Mexico City–born señorita claims that she was the inspiration for the drink in the 1930s, while another lady claims it was first concocted for her in the 1950s in Acapulco. I think that both stories are absolutely true, and I wish both women, and any others out there who claim to be the Margarita, all the best and my heartfelt congratulations. The Margarita is indeed a wonderful creation.

Variations on the Margarita include the Blue Margarita (page 142), Frozen Margarita (page 145), Gold Margarita (page 145), Peach Margarita (page 149), and Strawberry Margarita (page 151).

2 teaspoons coarse salt	½ ounce Cointreau or
1 lime wedge	triple sec
2 ounces tequila	1½ ounces lime juice

Place the salt in a saucer. Rub the rim of a cocktail glass with the lime wedge and dip the glass into the salt to coat the rim thoroughly; reserve the lime wedge. In a shaker half-filled with ice cubes, combine the tequila, Cointreau, and lime juice. Shake well. Strain into the cocktail glass. Garnish with the reserved lime wedge.

453 MASSACRE

2 ounces tequila	4 ounces ginger ale
1 teaspoon Campari	

Pour all of the ingredients into a highball glass almost filled with ice cubes. Stir well.

454 MEXICANA

2 ounces tequila	1 ounce pineapple juice
½ ounce lemon juice	1 teaspoon grenadine

In a shaker half-filled with ice cubes, combine all of the ingredients. Shake well. Strain into a cocktail glass.

455 MOONRAKER

1½ ounces tequila	½ ounce blue Curaçao
4 ounces pineapple juice	

Pour the tequila and pineapple juice into a highball glass almost filled with ice cubes. Stir well. Drop the Curaçao into the center of the drink.

456 PEACH MARGARITA

2 teaspoons coarse salt
1 lime wedge
1½ ounces tequila
½ ounce peach liqueur
1½ teaspoons Contreau
  or triple sec
1½ ounces lime juice

Place the salt in a saucer. Rub the rim of a cocktail glass with the lime wedge and dip the glass into the salt to coat the rim thoroughly; reserve the lime. In a shaker half-filled with ice cubes, combine the tequila, peach liqueur, Cointreau, and lime juice. Shake well. Strain into the cocktail glass and garnish with the lime wedge.

457 PINK PARADISE

2 ounces tequila
3 dashes bitters

Pour the tequila into a mixing glass half-filled with ice cubes. Stir well. Put the bitters into a brandy snifter and swirl it around to coat the glass. Discard any extra bitters. Strain the tequila into the snifter.

458 PIPER

2 ounces tequila
½ ounce lemon juice
½ ounce dark crème de
  cacao
4 ounces strong coffee,
  cooled to room
  temperature
Crushed ice

Pour all of the ingredients into an Irish coffee glass almost filled with crushed ice. Stir well.

459 POKER FACE

1½ ounces tequila
½ ounce Cointreau or
  triple sec
4 ounces pineapple juice
1 lime wedge

Combine the tequila, Cointreau, and pineapple juice in a highball glass almost filled with ice cubes. Stir well. Garnish with the lime wedge.

460 RED FACE

1½ ounces tequila
1 teaspoon cranberry
  liqueur

4 ounces cranberry juice
1 lime wedge

Pour the tequila, cranberry liqueur, and cranberry juice in a highball glass almost filled with ice cubes. Stir well and garnish with the lime wedge.

461 ROSITA

1½ ounces tequila
1 ounce Campari
½ ounce sweet vermouth
½ ounce dry vermouth

1 dash bitters
Crushed ice
1 lemon twist

Pour the tequila, Campari, sweet vermouth, dry vermouth, and bitters into an old-fashioned glass almost filled with crushed ice. Stir well and garnish with the lemon twist.

462 SCOTTIE WAS BEAMED UP

2 ounces tequila   ½ ounce Galliano

In a mixing glass half-filled with ice cubes, combine the tequila and Galliano. Stir well. Strain into a cocktail glass.

463 SHADY LADY

1½ ounces tequila
½ ounce melon liqueur

5 ounces grapefruit juice

Pour all of the ingredients into a highball glass almost filled with ice cubes. Stir well.

464 SHAKER

1½ ounces tequila
3 ounces pineapple juice

½ ounce lemon juice
½ teaspoon grenadine

In a shaker half-filled with ice cubes, combine all of the ingredients. Shake well. Strain into a cocktail glass.

465 SILK STOCKING

1½ ounces tequila
½ ounce dark crème de
  cacao

1 ounce heavy cream
½ teaspoon Chambord

In a shaker half-filled with ice cubes, combine all of the ingredients. Shake well. Strain into a cocktail glass.

466 SMILER

1½ ounces tequila
½ ounce lemon juice
½ teaspoon superfine
  sugar

2 teaspoons ruby port
1 maraschino cherry

In a shaker half-filled with ice cubes, combine the tequila, lemon juice, sugar, and port. Shake well. Pour into a highball glass almost filled with ice cubes. Garnish with the cherry.

467 STELLA'S STINGER

1½ ounces tequila
1 teaspoon Pernod
1 teaspoon white crème
  de menthe

1 lemon twist

In a mixing glass half-filled with ice cubes, combine the tequila, Pernod, and crème de menthe. Stir well. Strain into a cocktail glass. Garnish with the lemon twist.

468 STRAWBERRY MARGARITA

2 teaspoons coarse salt
1 lime wedge
1½ ounces tequila
½ ounce strawberry
  liqueur

1½ teaspoons Cointreau
  or triple sec
1½ ounces lime juice
1 strawberry

Place the salt in a saucer. Rub the rim of a cocktail glass with the lime wedge and dip the glass into the salt to coat the rim thoroughly; discard the lime. In a shaker half-filled with ice cubes, combine the tequila, strawberry liqueur, Cointreau, and lime juice. Shake well. Strain into the cocktail glass and garnish with the strawberry.

469 TEQUILA COLLINS

2 ounces tequila
1 ounce lemon juice
1 teaspoon superfine
   sugar

3 ounces club soda
1 maraschino cherry
1 orange slice

In a shaker half-filled with ice cubes, combine the tequila, lemon juice, and sugar. Shake well. Strain into a collins glass almost filled with ice cubes. Add the club soda. Stir and garnish with the cherry and the orange slice.

470 TEQUILA COOLER

2 ounces tequila
4 ounces lemon-lime
   soda

1 lemon wedge

Pour the tequila and soda into a highball glass almost filled with ice cubes. Stir well. Garnish with the lemon wedge.

471 TEQUILA CRUDA

1½ ounces tequila
1 lime wedge

1 pinch salt

Pour the tequila into a shot glass. Take the lime wedge and rub it on your left hand where your thumb and index finger meet. Sprinkle the salt over the now wet part of your hand. Hold the lime wedge between your left thumb and index finger. Hold the shot glass in your right hand. Are you ready? Lick the salt off your hand. Wash it away with the tequila. Suck on the lime wedge. Scrunch up your eyes and shake your head as if involuntarily.

472 TEQUILA FIZZ

2½ ounces tequila
1 ounce lemon juice
1 teaspoon superfine
   sugar

4 ounces club soda

In a shaker half-filled with ice cubes combine the tequila, lemon juice, and sugar. Shake well. Strain into a collins glass almost filled with ice cubes. Add the club soda. Stir well.

473 TEQUILA GIMLET

2 ounces tequila ½ ounce Rose's lime juice

1 lime wedge

Pour the tequila and Rose's lime juice into a mixing glass half-filled with ice cubes. Stir well. Strain into a cocktail glass. Garnish with the lime wedge.

474 TEQUILA MARTINI

2½ ounces tequila
1½ teaspoons dry
  vermouth

1 lemon twist or 1
  cocktail olive

In a mixing glass half-filled with ice cubes, combine the tequila and vermouth. Stir well. Strain into a cocktail glass. Garnish with the lemon twist or the olive.

475 TEQUILA MOCKINGBIRD

2 ounces tequila
1 teaspoon white crème
  de menthe

½ ounce lemon juice

In a shaker half-filled with ice cubes, combine all of the ingredients. Shake well. Strain into a cocktail glass.

476 TEQUILA MOONRISE

3 ounces tequila
1 ounce light rum
1 ounce dark rum
½ ounce Rose's lime juice

½ ounce lemon juice
1 teaspoon sugar
2 ounces ale

In a shaker half-filled with ice cubes, combine the tequila, light rum, dark rum, Rose's lime juice, lemon juice, and sugar. Shake well. Strain into a collins glass almost filled with ice cubes. Top with the ale.

477 TEQUILA SOUR

2 ounces tequila
1 ounce lemon juice
½ teaspoon superfine
   sugar

1 orange slice
1 maraschino cherry

In a shaker half-filled with ice cubes, combine the tequila, lemon juice, and sugar. Shake well. Strain into a sour glass. Garnish with the orange slice and the cherry.

478 TEQUILA STINGER

2 ounces tequila
½ ounce white crème de
   menthe

In a mixing glass half-filled with ice cubes, combine the tequila and crème de menthe. Stir well. Strain into a cocktail glass.

479 TEQUILA SUAVE

1½ ounces tequila
½ ounce lemon juice
1 teaspoon white crème
   de cacao

1 teaspoon grenadine
1 dash bitters
1 orange slice
1 maraschino cherry

In a shaker half-filled with ice cubes, combine the tequila, lemon juice, crème de cacao, grenadine, and bitters. Shake well. Strain into a cocktail glass. Garnish with the orange slice and the cherry.

480 TEQUILA SUNRISE

Word has it that this drink was concocted by a befuddled bartender in San Francisco, who had stayed at the bar drinking with a few friends until the boss walked in at around 9:00 A.M. The bar owner demanded an explanation, and the drunken bartender explained that he had stayed to watch the sun rise so that he could create a drink that resembled the occurrence. Of course, he had to produce the drink in order to prove his story, and to his credit, he quickly built a Tequila Sunrise. Yes,

it sounds pretty unlikely to me, too. A variation on the Tequila
Sunrise is the Executive Sunrise (page 144).

1½ ounces tequila   2 teaspoons grenadine
4 ounces orange juice

Pour the tequila and orange juice into a collins glass almost
filled with ice cubes. Stir well. Drop the grenadine into
the center of the drink.

481 TIME KILLER

1½ ounces tequila   ½ teaspoon salt
5 ounces Mexican beer   1 lemon wedge

Pour the tequila and beer into a highball glass almost filled
with ice cubes. Stir well. Sprinkle the salt on top and
garnish with the lemon wedge.

482 TOREADOR

2 ounces tequila   1 ounce heavy cream
1 ounce dark crème de   ¼ teaspoon unsweetened
   cacao   cocoa powder

In a shaker half-filled with ice cubes, combine the tequila,
crème de cacao, and cream. Shake well. Strain into a cocktail glass and garnish with the cocoa.

483 VIVA VILLA

2 teaspoons superfine   2 ounces tequila
   sugar   1 ounce lime juice
1 lime wedge   1 teaspoon lemon juice

Place the sugar in a saucer. Rub the rim of a cocktail glass
with the lime wedge and dip the glass into the sugar to
coat the rim thoroughly; discard the lime. In a shaker half-
filled with ice cubes, combine the tequila, lime juice, and
lemon juice. Shake well. Strain into the cocktail glass.

484 ZULTRY ZOË

2 ounces tequila
½ ounce Galliano
4 ounces Mexican hot
  chocolate, cooled to
  room temperature

Crushed ice

Pour all of the ingredients into an Irish coffee glass almost filled with crushed ice. Stir well.

8 · VODKA

Once referred to as a "necklace of negatives," vodka, the base of the Screwdriver, Bloody Mary, and the Kamikaze, is immediately recognizable for its distinct lack of aroma, color, and taste. The word *vodka* comes from the diminutive of the Russian word *voda*, meaning "water," making it "little water." Little water with a big kick.

Vodka is mentioned in twelfth-century Russian literature, but at that time the name was used to refer to any spirit, no matter what it was distilled from or how highly flavored it was. The spirit, as we know it, was probably concocted in fourteenth-century Russia. It didn't come to America until the 1930s when the Smirnoff family arrived with their recipe and set up, once again, in the distillery business. The production of vodka in Russia was banned by the czar at the start of World War I, and, by the time it was once again legalized, the state had taken control of all industry.

There is a romantic Russian ritual of smashing glasses in the fireplace after consuming vodka to ensure that whatever toast has just been made will come true. A manager from the Russian Samovar Restaurant in New York City told me that a famous Russian poet was visiting Robert Kennedy and together they drank a toast to life with Rus-

sian vodka. Ethel Kennedy refused to let them smash the glasses, which were family heirlooms, but she brought, in their stead, some plastic glasses to break. The plastics merely bounced around the fireplace.

PRODUCTION

Vodka can almost be made from whatever happens to be lying around—beets are used in Turkey, while Britain tends to favor molasses—though most vodka is produced from potatoes, corn, and wheat. It is distilled at a very high alcohol content and then filtered through vegetable charcoal. The better ones are filtered through activated charcoal or very fine quartz sand.

GOLD VODKA

This spirit, referred to as *Stárka* or "old," is simply vodka that has been aged in wine casks for around 10 years.

PEPPER VODKA

Known as *Pertsovka,* this fiery hot Russian vodka is infused with cubeb, cayenne, and capsicum. This style of vodka is said to come from Czar Peter the Great, who added pepper to his vodka.

There are other classic flavored vodkas such as *Yubileyneya Osobaya,* containing honey and brandy, and *Okhotnichya,* which is infused with a collection of herbs. And, as I write this, there is probably some well-meaning entrepreneur about to infuse vodka with a mixture of Chinese tea leaves and banana peel. That is actually the beauty of vodka: It lends itself to being flavored with whatever the drinker wishes.

485 ABERFOYLE

1½ ounces vodka 1 ounce Drambuie

Pour both of the ingredients into an old-fashioned glass almost filled with ice. Stir well.

486 AQUEDUCT

1½ ounces vodka
1 teaspoon white
  Curaçao
1 teaspoon apricot
  brandy

1 teaspoon lime juice
1 teaspoon lemon juice
1 lemon twist

In a shaker half-filled with ice cubes, combine the vodka, Curaçao, apricot brandy, lime juice, and lemon juice. Shake well. Strain into a cocktail glass. Garnish with the lemon twist.

487 BERTRAND'S BLACK MAGIC

1½ ounces vodka ½ ounce black Sambuca
       (Opal Nera)

In a mixing glass combine both of the ingredients. Stir well. Strain into a cocktail glass.

488 BLACK EYE

1½ ounces vodka ½ ounce blackberry
       brandy

In a mixing glass half-filled with ice cubes, combine both of the ingredients. Stir well. Strain into a cocktail glass.

489 BLACK RUSSIAN

1½ ounces vodka ½ ounce Kahlúa

Pour both of the ingredients into an old-fashioned glass almost filled with ice cubes. Stir well.

490 BLOODY BULL

2½ ounces vodka
3 ounces tomato juice
2 ounces beef bouillon
½ ounce lemon juice
⅛ teaspoon black pepper

1 dash Worcestershire
  sauce
1 dash Tabasco sauce
1 lemon wedge

In a shaker half-filled with ice cubes, combine the vodka, tomato juice, bouillon, lemon juice, pepper, Worcestershire, and Tabasco. Shake well. Strain into a highball glass almost filled with ice cubes. Garnish with the lemon wedge.

491 BLOODY MARY

I have heard only two explanations for the name of this drink. One is that it was named after Mary I of England, a sixteenth-century queen who was nicknamed Bloody Mary because of the number of people that she had put to death. It is quite certain that nobody drank vodka and tomato juice before Mary got her epithet, so I prefer this explanation to the one that gives credit to the character in the 1949 musical South Pacific *who was designated bloody because her teeth were stained red from chewing betel nuts.*

Of course, given the way English royalty used to have people killed, it is somewhat surprising that we don't have a whole lineage of drinks named Bloody Ethelred, Bloody Henry, Bloody Richard, and Bloody Harold. I imagine that the Brits only gave the title to Mary because such behavior was unbecoming to a female.

As to who first concocted the Bloody Mary, well, many different people have taken credit, but it is usually credited to a bartender at Harry's New York Bar in Paris during the 1920s. His name was Fernand Petiot.

You may want to make a batch of Bloody Marys if you are throwing a brunch or a breakfast party. If so, make the tomato juice mixture without the vodka. That way the mix won't separate, and nondrinkers can help themselves to Virgin Marys.

Variations on the Bloody Mary include the Bloody Bull (above), Bloody Maria (page 141), and Clamato Cocktail (page 163).

2½ ounces vodka
5 ounces tomato juice
½ ounce lemon juice
⅛ teaspoon black pepper
⅛ teaspoon salt
⅛ teaspoon celery seed

3 dashes Worcestershire
  sauce
1 dash Tabasco sauce
1 celery rib
1 lime wedge

In a shaker half-filled with ice cubes, combine the vodka, tomato juice, lemon juice, pepper, salt, celery seed, Worcestershire, and Tabasco. Shake well. Strain into a highball glass almost filled with ice cubes. Garnish with the celery and the lime wedge.

492 BLOODY MARY #2

2 ounces pepper vodka
4 ounces V-8 juice

1 slice jalapeño pepper

In a shaker half-filled with ice cubes, combine the vodka and V-8 juice. Shake well. Strain into a highball glass almost filled with ice cubes. Float the jalapeño slice on top.

493 BLOODY MARY #3

2 ounces lemon-flavored
  vodka
4 ounces tomato juice

¼ teaspoon minced fresh
  dill or a dash of dried
1 lemon slice

In a shaker half-filled with ice cubes, combine the vodka, tomato juice, and dill. Shake well. Strain into a highball glass almost filled with ice cubes. Float the lemon slice on top.

494 BLUEBEARD

1½ ounces vodka

½ ounce blueberry
  brandy

In a mixing glass half-filled with ice cubes, combine both of the ingredients. Stir well. Strain into a cocktail glass.

495 BLUE LAGOON

1½ ounces vodka
½ ounce blue Curaçao
4 ounces lemonade

1 maraschino cherry
1 orange slice

In a highball glass almost filled with ice cubes, combine the vodka, Curaçao, and lemonade. Stir well. Garnish with the cherry and the orange slice.

496 BLUE MONDAY

1 ounce vodka
½ ounce Cointreau or
   triple sec

½ ounce blue Curaçao

In a mixing glass half-filled with ice cubes, combine all of the ingredients. Stir well. Strain into a cocktail glass.

497 BRAZEN HUSSY

1 ounce vodka
1 ounce Cointreau or
   triple sec

½ ounce lemon juice

In a shaker half-filled with ice cubes, combine all of the ingredients. Shake well. Strain into a cocktail glass.

498 BULLFROG

2 ounces vodka
1 teaspoon Cointreau or
   triple sec

4 ounces lemonade
1 lemon wedge

In a highball glass almost filled with ice cubes, combine the vodka, Cointreau, and lemonade. Stir well. Garnish with the lemon wedge.

499 BULLSHOT

2½ ounces vodka
5 ounces beef bouillon
⅛ teaspoon black pepper
1 dash Worcestershire
   sauce

1 dash Tabasco sauce
1 lemon wedge

In a shaker half-filled with ice cubes, combine the vodka, bouillon, pepper, Worcestershire, and Tabasco. Shake well.

Strain into a highball glass almost filled with ice cubes. Garnish with the lemon wedge.

500 CAPE CODDER

2 ounces vodka
5 ounces cranberry juice

1 lime wedge

In a highball glass almost filled with ice cubes, combine the vodka and cranberry juice. Stir well. Garnish with the lime wedge.

501 CHERRY RIPE

1½ ounces vodka
½ ounce cherry brandy

½ ounce brandy
1 maraschino cherry

In a mixing glass half-filled with ice cubes, combine the vodka, cherry brandy, and brandy. Stir well. Strain into a cocktail glass. Garnish with the cherry.

502 CLAMATO COCKTAIL

2½ ounces vodka
3 ounces tomato juice
2 ounces clam juice
⅛ teaspoon black pepper

1 dash Worcestershire sauce
1 dash Tabasco sauce
1 lemon wedge

In a shaker half-filled with ice cubes, combine the vodka, tomato juice, clam juice, pepper, Worcestershire, and Tabasco. Shake well. Strain into a highball glass almost filled with ice cubes. Garnish with the lemon wedge.

503 CZARINE

1 ounce vodka
½ ounce dry vermouth

½ ounce apricot brandy
1 dash bitters

In a mixing glass half-filled with ice cubes, combine all of the ingredients. Stir well. Strain into a cocktail glass.

504 DEANNE

1 ounce vodka
½ ounce sweet vermouth
½ ounce Cointreau or
  triple sec

1 lemon twist

In a mixing glass half-filled with ice cubes, combine the vodka, vermouth, and Cointreau. Stir well. Strain into a cocktail glass. Garnish with the lemon twist.

505 DESERT SHIELD

1½ ounces vodka
½ ounce cranberry
  liqueur

4 ounces cranberry juice

Combine all of the ingredients in a highball glass. Stir well.

506 DOYLES' DELIBERATION

1½ ounces vodka

½ ounce melon liqueur

In a mixing glass half-filled with ice cubes, combine both of the ingredients. Stir well. Strain into a cocktail glass.

507 DUKE'S A CHAMP

1½ ounces vodka
½ ounce blackberry
  brandy

In a mixing glass half-filled with ice cubes, combine the vodka and brandy. Strain into a cocktail glass.

508 DUSTY DOG

2 ounces vodka
½ ounce crème de cassis
1 teaspoon lemon juice

1 dash bitters
5 ounces ginger ale
1 lemon twist

In a shaker half-filled with ice cubes, combine the vodka, cassis, lemon juice, and bitters. Shake well. Strain into a highball glass almost filled with ice cubes. Top with the ginger ale. Stir well. Garnish with the lemon twist.

509 EXTERMINATOR

2½ ounces vodka   ½ ounce fino sherry

In a mixing glass half-filled with ice cubes, combine both of the ingredients. Stir well. Strain into a cocktail glass.

510 FIRE AND ICE

1½ ounces pepper vodka   1 teaspoon dry vermouth

In a mixing glass half-filled with ice cubes, combine both of the ingredients. Stir well. Strain into a cocktail glass.

511 FIREFLY

2 ounces vodka   1 teaspoon grenadine
4 ounces grapefruit juice

Pour the vodka and grapefruit juice into a highball glass almost filled with ice cubes. Drop the grenadine into the center of the drink.

512 FOGGY AFTERNOON

1 ounce vodka   1 teaspoon crème de
½ ounce apricot brandy   bananes
½ ounce Cointreau or   1 teaspoon lemon juice
  triple sec   1 maraschino cherry

In a shaker half-filled with ice cubes, combine the vodka, brandy, Cointreau, crème de bananes, and lemon juice. Shake well. Strain into a cocktail glass. Garnish with the cherry.

513 FRIGHTLEBERRY MURZENQUEST

1 ounce vodka   1 teaspoon maraschino
½ ounce Galliano   liqueur
½ ounce Cointreau or   1 dash bitters
  triple sec   1 maraschino cherry
½ ounce lime juice

In a shaker half-filled with ice cubes, combine the vodka, Galliano, Cointreau, lime juice, maraschino liqueur, and bitters. Shake well. Strain into a cocktail glass. Garnish with the cherry.

514 FUZZY NAVEL

1 ounce vodka   4 ounces orange juice
1 ounce peach schnapps

Pour all of the ingredients into a highball glass almost filled with ice cubes. Stir well.

515 GALE AT SEA

1½ ounces vodka   ½ ounce Galliano
½ ounce dry vermouth   ½ ounce blue Curaçao

In a mixing glass half-filled with ice cubes, combine all of the ingredients. Stir well. Strain into a cocktail glass.

516 GALWAY GREY

1 ounce vodka   1 ounce lime juice
½ ounce white crème de   1 ounce light cream
  cacao
½ ounce Cointreau or
  triple sec

In a shaker half-filled with ice cubes, combine all of the ingredients. Shake well. Strain into an old-fashioned glass almost filled with ice cubes.

517 GLACIER MINT

1½ ounces vodka   ½ ounce green crème de
½ ounce lemon-flavored   menthe
  vodka

In a mixing glass half-filled with ice cubes, combine all of the ingredients. Stir well. Strain into a cocktail glass.

518 GLASNOST

2 ounces vodka
½ ounce peppermint
  schnapps

In a mixing glass half-filled with ice cubes, combine both of the ingredients. Stir well. Strain into a cocktail glass.

519 GODMOTHER

1½ ounces vodka   ½ ounce amaretto

Pour both of the ingredients into an old-fashioned glass almost filled with ice cubes. Stir well.

520 GORKY PARK

1½ ounces vodka   1 ounce lemon juice
½ ounce cherry brandy   1 maraschino cherry

In a shaker half-filled with ice cubes, combine the vodka, cherry brandy, and lemon juice. Shake well. Strain into a cocktail glass. Garnish with the cherry.

521 GREEN MIRAGE

1 ounce vodka   1 teaspoon blue Curaçao
½ ounce Galliano
2 teaspoons dry
    vermouth

In a mixing glass half-filled with ice cubes, combine all of the ingredients. Stir well. Strain into a cocktail glass.

522 GREYHOUND

2 ounces vodka   5 ounces grapefruit juice

In a highball glass almost filled with ice cubes, combine the vodka and grapefruit juice. Stir well.

523 HARVEY WALLBANGER

1½ ounces vodka   ½ ounce Galliano
4 ounces orange juice

In a highball glass almost filled with ice cubes, combine the vodka and orange juice. Stir well. Float the Galliano on top.

524 HER NAME IN LIGHTS

1 ounce vodka
½ ounce yellow
   Chartreuse
2 teaspoons Galliano

2 teaspoons blue Curaçao
½ ounce lemon juice
1 maraschino cherry

In a shaker half-filled with ice cubes, combine the vodka, Chartreuse, Galliano, Curaçao, and lemon juice. Shake well. Strain into a cocktail glass. Garnish with the cherry.

525 HOSS'S HOLDUP

1½ ounces vodka
½ ounce Cointreau or
   triple sec

3 ounces orange juice
½ teaspoon grenadine

In a shaker half-filled with ice cubes, combine all of the ingredients. Shake well. Strain into a highball glass almost filled with ice cubes.

526 IDONIS

2 ounces vodka
½ ounce apricot brandy

1 ounce pineapple juice

In a shaker half-filled with ice cubes, combine all of the ingredients. Shake well. Strain into a cocktail glass.

527 JACKATH

1 ounce vodka
2 teaspoons brandy
1 teaspoon crème de cassis

1 teaspoon Cointreau or
   triple sec
2 dashes orange bitters

In a mixing glass half-filled with ice cubes, combine all of the ingredients. Stir well. Strain into a cocktail glass.

528 JOY JUMPER

1½ ounces vodka
2 teaspoons kümmel
1 teaspoon lime juice
1 teaspoon lemon juice

¼ teaspoon superfine
   sugar
1 lemon twist

In a shaker half-filled with ice cubes, combine the vodka, kümmel, lime juice, lemon juice, and sugar. Shake well. Strain into a cocktail glass. Garnish with the lemon twist.

529 KAMIKAZE

2 ounces Stolichnaya
  vodka

1 teaspoon Rose's lime
  juice

In a mixing glass half-filled with ice cubes, combine both of the ingredients. Stir well. Strain into a cocktail glass. Drink in one go.

530 KAMIKAZE #2

The Kamikaze described above was the original formula. It was designed to get a person drunk—quickly. Since then the drink below has been modified slightly and designed more for sipping than gulping—probably a very good idea.

1½ ounces vodka
½ ounce Cointreau or
  triple sec

2 teaspoons Rose's lime
  juice

In a mixing glass half-filled with ice cubes, combine all of the ingredients. Stir well. Strain into a cocktail glass.

531 KANGAROO COCKTAIL

2 ounces vodka
1 ounce dry vermouth

1 lemon twist

In a mixing glass half-filled with ice cubes, combine the vodka and vermouth. Stir well. Strain into a cocktail glass. Garnish with the lemon twist.

532 KAROFF

1½ ounces vodka
1 ounce cranberry juice

5 ounces club soda
1 lime wedge

Pour the vodka, cranberry juice, and club soda into a high-ball glass almost filled with ice cubes. Stir well. Garnish with the lime wedge.

533 KRETCHMA COCKTAIL

1 ounce vodka
½ ounce white crème de
  cacao

½ ounce lemon juice
1 dash grenadine

In a shaker half-filled with ice cubes, combine all of the ingredients. Shake well. Strain into a cocktail glass.

534 LA CARRÉ

1½ ounces vodka
2 teaspoons dry
  vermouth

2 teaspoons kümmel

In a mixing glass half-filled with ice cubes, combine all of the ingredients. Stir well. Strain into a cocktail glass.

535 LATHAM'S RULE

1½ ounces vodka
½ ounce Grand Marnier

3 ounces orange juice
2 dashes orange bitters

In a shaker half-filled with ice cubes, combine all of the ingredients. Shake well. Strain into an old-fashioned glass almost filled with ice cubes.

536 LAUGHING AT THE WAVES

1½ ounces vodka
½ ounce dry vermouth

½ ounce Campari
1 lemon twist

In a mixing glass half-filled with ice cubes, combine the vodka, vermouth, and Campari. Stir well. Strain into a cocktail glass. Garnish with the lemon twist.

537 LONG ISLAND ICED TEA

1 ounce vodka
1 ounce gin
1 ounce light rum
1 ounce tequila

1 ounce lemon juice
1 teaspoon superfine
  sugar
4 ounces cola

In a shaker half-filled with ice cubes, combine the vodka, gin, rum, tequila, lemon juice, and sugar. Shake well. Strain into a mixing glass almost filled with ice cubes. Add the cola and stir well. Sip this drink over a long period of time—two days isn't out of the question.

538 MADRAS

1½ ounces vodka
2 ounces cranberry juice
2 ounces orange juice

Pour all of the ingredients into a highball glass almost filled with ice cubes. Stir well.

539 MAJOR TOM

1½ ounces vodka
½ ounce Cointreau or triple sec
½ ounce kirsch
½ ounce grapefruit juice

In a shaker half-filled with ice cubes, combine all of the ingredients. Shake well. Strain into a cocktail glass.

540 MARC FELDINI

2 ounces vodka
½ teaspoon saké
1 cucumber rind sliver

In a mixing glass half-filled with ice cubes, combine the vodka and saké. Stir well. Strain into a cocktail glass. Garnish with the cucumber.

541 MAZRICK

1½ ounces vodka
½ ounce amaretto
½ ounce Cointreau or triple sec
2 teaspoons Galliano
1 ounce orange juice
1 ounce pineapple juice
2 dashes bitters

In a shaker half-filled with ice cubes, combine all of the ingredients. Shake well. Strain into a highball glass almost filled with ice cubes.

542 MORNING GLORY

1½ ounces vodka
½ ounce dark crème de cacao
2 ounces light cream
¼ teaspoon grated nutmeg

In a shaker half-filled with ice cubes, combine the vodka, crème de cacao, and cream. Shake well. Strain into a cocktail glass. Garnish with the nutmeg.

543 MOSCOW MULE

1½ ounces vodka
1 ounce lime juice

4 ounces ginger beer
1 lime wedge

Pour the vodka, lime juice, and ginger beer into a highball glass almost filled with ice cubes. Stir well and garnish with the lime wedge.

544 NINOTCHKA COCKTAIL

2 ounces vodka
½ ounce white crème de cacao

½ ounce lemon juice

In a shaker half-filled with ice cubes, combine all of the ingredients. Shake well. Strain into a cocktail glass.

545 ON-THE-TOWN

1 ounce vodka
½ ounce Campari

2 ounces orange juice
1 egg white

In a shaker half-filled with ice cubes, combine all of the ingredients. Shake well. Strain into an old-fashioned glass almost filled with ice cubes.

546 OUR STANLEY

1½ ounces vodka
½ ounce gin

½ ounce Cointreau or triple sec

In a mixing glass half-filled with ice cubes, combine all of the ingredients. Stir well. Strain into a cocktail glass.

547 OWDHAM EDGE

1 ounce vodka
½ ounce white crème de cacao

2 teaspoons Sambuca
1 ounce light cream

In a shaker half-filled with ice cubes, combine all of the ingredients. Shake well. Strain into a cocktail glass.

548 PIECE OF MIND

1½ ounces vodka   1 lemon twist
1 ounce kümmel

Pour the vodka and kümmel into an old-fashioned glass almost filled with ice cubes. Stir well. Garnish with the lemon twist.

549 PRETTY THING

1½ ounces vodka   ½ ounce coconut cream
½ ounce amaretto   ½ ounce heavy cream

In a shaker half-filled with ice cubes, combine all of the ingredients. Shake well. Strain into a cocktail glass.

550 PURPLE HAZE

½ ounce Chambord   1 ounce lemon-lime soda
1½ ounces lemon-
    flavored vodka

Pour the Chambord into a snifter. Pour the vodka into a mixing glass half-filled with ice cubes; stir well. Carefully strain the vodka on top of the Chambord. Top with the soda. Add a straw and drink through the straw from the bottom to the top.

551 PURPLE   PASSION

2 ounces vodka   2 teaspoons superfine
2 ounces grape juice   sugar
2 ounces grapefruit juice

In a shaker half-filled with ice cubes, combine all of the ingredients. Shake well. Strain into a highball glass almost filled with ice cubes.

552 QUIET BUT QUICK

1½ ounces vodka   1 ounce orange juice
½ ounce cherry brandy   1 dash orange bitters

In a shaker half-filled with ice cubes, combine all of the ingredients. Shake well. Strain into a cocktail glass.

553 ROCKY'S DILEMMA

1½ ounces vodka   ½ ounce Grand Marnier

In a mixing glass half-filled with ice cubes, combine both of the ingredients. Stir well. Strain into a cocktail glass.

554 RUSSIAN COCKTAIL

1 ounce vodka   ½ ounce gin
½ ounce white crème de
  cacao

In a mixing glass half-filled with ice cubes, combine all of the ingredients. Stir well. Strain into a cocktail glass.

555 RUSSIAN KAMIKAZE

2 ounces vodka   1 teaspoon Chambord

In a mixing glass half-filled with ice cubes, combine both of the ingredients. Stir well. Strain into a sour glass.

556 SALTY DOG

2 teaspoons salt   2 ounces vodka
1 lime wedge   5 ounces grapefruit juice

Place the salt in a saucer. Rub the rim of a highball glass with the lime wedge and dip the glass into the salt to coat the rim thoroughly; discard the lime. Almost fill the glass with ice cubes. Pour the vodka and grapefruit juice into the glass. Stir thoroughly.

557 SARAH

1 ounce vodka   1 teaspoon Campari
½ ounce cherry brandy   1 teaspoon crème de
½ ounce dry vermouth   bananes

In a mixing glass half-filled with ice cubes, combine all of the ingredients. Stir well. Strain into a cocktail glass.

558 SCREWDRIVER

2 ounces vodka   5 ounces orange juice

Pour the vodka and orange juice into a highball glass almost filled with ice cubes. Stir well.

559 SEA BREEZE

1½ ounces vodka   3 ounces cranberry juice
2 ounces grapefruit juice   1 lime wedge

Pour the vodka, grapefruit juice, and cranberry juice into a highball glass almost filled with ice cubes. Stir well. Garnish with the lime wedge.

560 SEX ON THE BEACH

1 ounce vodka   2 ounces orange juice
1 ounce peach schnapps   2 ounces cranberry juice

Pour all of the ingredients into a highball glass almost filled with ice cubes. Stir well.

561 SILVER SUNSET

1½ ounces vodka   2 ounces orange juice
½ ounce apricot brandy   1 egg white
½ ounce Campari   1 maraschino cherry
½ ounce lemon juice   1 orange slice

In a shaker half-filled with ice cubes, combine the vodka, apricot brandy, Campari, lemon juice, orange juice, and egg white. Shake well. Strain into a cocktail glass. Garnish with the cherry and the orange slice.

562 SLOW COMFORTABLE SCREW

1½ ounces vodka   4 ounces orange juice
½ ounce sloe gin
½ ounce Southern
  Comfort

Pour all of the ingredients into a highball glass almost filled with ice cubes. Stir well.

563 SPYMASTER

1½ ounces vodka
½ ounce crème de
  bananes

½ ounce lemon juice
1 egg white

In a shaker half-filled with ice cubes, combine all of the
ingredients. Shake well. Strain into an old-fashioned glass
almost filled with ice cubes.

564 STUFFY-IN-A-SUIT

1 ounce vodka
½ ounce Lillet
½ ounce Cointreau or
  triple sec

1 dash orange bitters
1 egg white
1 orange slice

In a shaker half-filled with ice cubes, combine the vodka,
Lillet, Cointreau, orange bitters, and egg white. Shake well.
Strain into an old-fashioned glass almost filled with ice
cubes. Garnish with the orange slice.

565 VICKER'S TREAT

1½ ounces vodka
4 ounces lemonade

2 dashes orange bitters

Pour all of the ingredients into a highball glass almost
filled with ice cubes. Stir well.

566 VODKA AND BITTER LEMON

1½ ounces vodka
½ ounce lemon juice
½ teaspoon superfine
  sugar

4 ounces tonic water

In a shaker half-filled with ice cubes, combine the vodka,
lemon juice, and sugar. Shake well. Strain into a highball
glass almost filled with ice cubes. Top with the tonic water.

567 VODKA COLLINS

2 ounces vodka
1 ounce lemon juice
1 teaspoons superfine
  sugar

3 ounces club soda
1 maraschino cherry
1 orange slice

In a shaker half-filled with ice cubes, combine the vodka,

lemon juice, and sugar. Shake well. Strain into a collins glass almost filled with ice cubes. Add the club soda and stir. Garnish with the cherry and the orange slice.

568 VODKA COOLER

2 ounces vodka	1 lemon wedge
4 ounces lemon-lime soda	

Pour the vodka and soda into a highball glass almost filled with ice cubes. Stir well. Garnish with the lemon wedge.

569 VODKA DAISY

2 ounces vodka	½ teaspoon grenadine
1 ounce lemon juice	1 maraschino cherry
½ teaspoon superfine sugar	1 orange slice

In a shaker half-filled with ice cubes, combine the vodka, lemon juice, sugar, and grenadine. Shake well. Pour into an old-fashioned glass. Garnish with the cherry and the orange slice.

570 VODKA DRY

1 teaspoon dry sherry	1 lemon twist
1½ ounces vodka	

Pour the sherry into a snifter. Swirl it around the glass and pour out the excess. Stir the vodka in a mixing glass half-filled with ice cubes. Strain into the snifter. Garnish with the lemon twist.

571 VODKA GIMLET

2 ounces vodka	1 lime wedge
½ ounce Rose's lime juice	

Pour the vodka and Rose's lime juice into a mixing glass half-filled with ice cubes. Stir well. Strain into a cocktail glass. Garnish with the lime wedge.

572 VODKA MARTINI

2½ ounces vodka
1½ teaspoons dry
  vermouth

1 lemon twist or 1
  cocktail olive

In a mixing glass half-filled with ice cubes, combine the vodka and vermouth. Stir well. Strain into a cocktail glass. Garnish with the lemon twist or the olive.

573 VODKA SLING

1 teaspoon superfine
  sugar
2 teaspoons water

1 ounce lemon juice
2 ounces vodka
1 lemon twist

In a shaker half-filled with ice cubes, combine the sugar, water, lemon juice, and vodka. Shake well. Strain into an old-fashioned glass almost filled with ice cubes. Garnish with the lemon twist.

574 VODKA SOUR

2 ounces vodka
1 ounce lemon juice
½ teaspoon superfine
  sugar

1 orange slice
1 maraschino cherry

In a shaker half-filled with ice cubes, combine the vodka, lemon juice, and sugar. Shake well. Strain into a sour glass. Garnish with the orange slice and the cherry.

575 VODKA SWIZZLE

1½ ounces lime juice
1 teaspoon superfine
  sugar
2 ounces vodka

1 dash bitters
Crushed ice
3 ounces club soda

In a shaker half-filled with ice cubes, combine the lime juice, sugar, vodka, and bitters. Shake well. Almost fill a collins glass with crushed ice and stir until the glass is frosted. Strain the mixture in the shaker into the glass and add the club soda. Serve with a swizzle stick.

576 WHITE RUSSIAN

1½ ounces vodka   1 ounce light cream
1 ounce Kahlúa

In a shaker half-filled with ice cubes, combine all of the ingredients. Shake well. Strain into an old-fashioned glass almost filled with ice cubes.

577 WHITE SPIDER

1½ ounces vodka
½ ounce white crème de
  menthe

In a mixing glass half-filled with ice cubes, combine both of the ingredients. Stir well. Strain into a cocktail glass.

578 WINDEX

2½ ounces vodka   ½ ounce blue Curaçao
½ ounce Cointreau or
  triple sec

In a mixing glass half-filled with ice cubes, combine all of the ingredients. Stir well. Strain into a cocktail glass.

579 WITCH OF VENICE

1½ ounces vodka   1 ounce orange juice
½ ounce Strega
2 teaspoons crème de
  bananes

In a shaker half-filled with ice cubes, combine all of the ingredients. Shake well. Strain into a cocktail glass.

580 WOO WOO

1½ ounces vodka   4 ounces cranberry juice
½ ounce peach schnapps

Pour all of the ingredients into a highball glass almost filled with ice cubes. Stir well.

9 · WHISKEY

The word *whiskey* comes from the Gaelic word *uisgebaugh,* which means "water of life." If you say *"uisgebaugh"* quickly (if you can say it at all), it comes out something like WYS-GER-BAW, which was shortened and Anglicized to "whiskey." Whiskey is made from grain; the types and proportion of grains together with the different aging processes determine each whiskey's style and flavor.

The cocktails in this chapter contain a base of either blended American whiskey, Canadian whisky, or Irish whiskey; they include cocktails like the Manhattan, the Old-Fashioned, and the Presbyterian. There are many different varieties of American whiskies—wheat, sour mash, Tennessee, rye, corn, malt, rye malt, and bourbon. All of them fall under one or more of the headings straight, blended, or light whiskies. Bourbon and sour mash are described in the Bourbon chapter; the rest are defined here.

WHISKEY AND WHISKY

Here's another wonderful bar discussion—the *e* in "whiskey." This *e* is used only in spelling the names of Irish

and American whiskies. There is, of course, an exception here, and it lies with a brand of bourbon known as Maker's Mark. The founder of the distillery, Mr. Samuels, was given special permission to drop the *e* from his whisky in order to pay homage to his Scottish heritage.

PRODUCTION

All whiskies undergo a similar basic distillation process:

Grain is ground into a product known as "grist" in a gristmill.

Water is added to the grist, and it is cooked to release starches.

Malt is added to convert the starches into sugar.

The grist is strained off, and the remaining liquid, "wort," is fed with cultured yeast and allowed to ferment, which results in an alcoholic liquid known as beer.

This beer is then distilled in either a pot still or a continuous still—often called a Coffey still, patent still, or double-column still—to produce whiskey.

The whiskey is then watered down to around 100° proof (50 percent alcohol) and aged in a variety of types of barrels, determined by the type of whiskey being made.

AMERICAN WHISKEY

As far as is known, the first whiskey in the New World was distilled in the Northeast during the Revolutionary War, during which the British set up naval blockades that stopped the supply of rum from the West Indies and Cuba—probably the cruelest move the British could have made.

Initially, American whiskey was made from the abundant rye and barley, and later on, as people moved westward, corn. The farmers of that era found that using their grain for the production of whiskey was the best way to make it a viable, transportable product for sale in the cities in the East.

American whiskey is usually aged in oak barrels that have been charred on the inside. Just how this method came about is unsure. Some say that it was the result of a fire in a cooperage, after which the charred barrels had to be used since no others were available. Others claim that it resulted from the practice of burning out barrels previously used for fish or molasses to rid the cask of the flavor and odor of the previous occupant.

STRAIGHT WHISKEY

This term simply means that the whiskey it describes—bourbon, Tennessee, corn, rye, malt, malted rye, or wheat—is a bottling of a distillation that has not been blended with any other whiskey or neutral grain spirit. Water, of course, is always added to a distillation to bring the proof down to the desired level. Any "straight" whiskey must be distilled from a 51 percent base of a single grain, the type of grain being dependent on the type of whiskey.

BLENDED WHISKEY

The word *blended* is applicable to about 47 percent of all American whiskies. Each blend contains a minimum of 20 percent straight whiskey, mixed with neutral grain spirit, grain spirit (aged in used oak barrels), or light whiskey. A blended whiskey may also contain a small amount of sherry, or peach or prune juice.

LIGHT WHISKEY

Usually made from a very high percentage of corn, light whiskey is aged in uncharred casks or previously used casks. This practice serves a great purpose. It gives the bourbon distillers someone other than the Scots to sell their used casks to (see Bourbon, page 20). This product may be bottled as light whiskey or blended light whiskey.

RYE WHISKEY

This term can be applied only to whiskies made from a mash containing a minimum of 51 percent rye. The category can be split into straight rye and blended rye, although blended rye can contain neutral grain spirit or whiskey made from grain other than rye.

TENNESSEE WHISKEY

This whiskey absolutely *must* be made in Tennessee. It must also be made from at least 51 percent of any one grain, usually corn.

CORN WHISKEY

As opposed to bourbon, which must use a minimum of 51 percent corn, corn whiskey must use at least 80 percent corn and is aged in previously used or uncharred oak casks.

WHEAT, MALT, AND RYE MALT WHISKEY

All of these whiskeys must contain, respectively, 51 percent wheat, barley malt, or rye malt grains.

CANADIAN WHISKY

Canadian whisky must be produced only from cereal grain, such as corn, rye, wheat, or barley. The actual percentages used by the individual distillers aren't specified by law as they are in the United States. The American government, however, insists that all imported Canadian whiskies be designated as "blended" as opposed to "straight."

IRISH WHISKEY

Ireland generally employs similar methods of distillation to Scotland (see Scotch, page 123) with one or two variations. The main difference is that Irish whiskey is normally distilled three times in a pot still, whereas Scotch is distilled only twice (except in a few cases in the Lowlands). Irish whiskey is sweeter and not as peaty as many Scotches, and it is usually blended with whiskey made from a continuous still, although there are single malt Irish whiskeys available.

The single malt Irish whiskies are made purely from malted barley, whereas, like Scotch, the whiskey used in blending can be made from unmalted barley, corn, rye, wheat, or oats. Irish whiskey is generally aged for a minimum of five years in used sherry casks.

POTEEN

Usually pronounced PO-CHEEN, this word comes from the Gaelic *poit'in,* meaning "in a pot." Poteen merely refers to any unlawfully distilled spirit, usually very high in alcohol, colorless, unaged, undistinctive but somehow very romantic to drink.

581 ALGONQUIN

1½ ounces blended
  whiskey

½ ounce dry vermouth
1 ounce pineapple juice

In a shaker half-filled with ice cubes, combine all of the ingredients. Shake well. Strain into a cocktail glass.

582 AVRIL

2 ounces Canadian
  whisky

½ ounce cranberry
  liqueur

In a mixing glass half-filled with ice cubes, combine both of the ingredients. Stir well. Strain into a cocktail glass.

583 BABY'S BOTTOM

1½ ounces blended
   whiskey
½ ounce white crème de
   menthe
½ ounce white crème de
   cacao

In a mixing glass half-filled with ice cubes, combine all of
the ingredients. Stir well. Strain into a cocktail glass.

584 BANFF COCKTAIL

1½ ounces Canadian
   whisky
½ ounce Grand Marnier
½ ounce kirsch
1 dash bitters
1 lemon twist

In a mixing glass half-filled with ice cubes, combine the
whisky, Grand Marnier, kirsch, and bitters. Stir well. Strain
into a cocktail glass. Garnish with the lemon twist.

585 BARNSTORMER

1½ ounces Canadian
   whisky
½ ounce peppermint
   schnapps
1 teaspoon dark crème de
   cacao
1 teaspoon white crème
   de cacao
½ ounce lemon juice

In a shaker half-filled with ice cubes, combine all of the
ingredients. Shake well. Strain into an old-fashioned glass
almost filled with ice cubes.

586 BAY HORSE

1½ ounces blended
   whiskey
½ ounce Pernod
½ ounce dark crème de
   cacao
1 ounce heavy cream
¼ teaspoon grated
   nutmeg

In a shaker half-filled with ice cubes, combine the whiskey,
Pernod, crème de cacao, and cream. Shake well. Strain
into an old-fashioned glass almost filled with ice cubes.
Garnish with the nutmeg.

587 BILL LEAVES TOWN

2 ounces blended
  whiskey
½ ounce sweet vermouth

1 teaspoon grenadine
1 maraschino cherry

In a mixing glass half-filled with ice cubes, combine the whiskey, vermouth, and grenadine. Stir well. Strain into a cocktail glass. Garnish with the cherry.

588 BLACK HAWK

2 ounces blended
  whiskey

1 ounce sloe gin

In a mixing glass half-filled with ice cubes, combine both of the ingredients. Stir well. Strain into a cocktail glass.

589 BLUE MONDAY

1½ ounces Canadian
  whisky
½ ounce blueberry
  brandy

1 teaspoon brandy

In a mixing glass half-filled with ice cubes, combine all of the ingredients. Stir well. Strain into a cocktail glass.

590 BOILERMAKER

1 ounce blended whiskey   12 ounces beer

Pour the whiskey into a shot glass. Pour the beer into a Pilsner or beer mug. Drink the whiskey in one go. Sip the beer. Drink a Boilermaker only if you are sober before you start and tough enough to drink whiskey in one go.

591 BOOT HILL

2 ounces blended
  whiskey
½ ounce applejack

½ ounce lemon juice
½ teaspoon superfine
  sugar

In a shaker half-filled with ice cubes, combine all of the ingredients. Shake well. Strain into a cocktail glass.

592 BORROWED TIME

1½ ounces Canadian
  whisky
½ ounce ruby port

1 egg yolk
1 teaspoon grenadine

In a shaker half-filled with ice cubes, combine all of the
ingredients. Shake well. Strain into a cocktail glass.

593 CABLEGRAM

1½ ounces blended
  whiskey
½ ounce lemon juice
½ teaspoon superfine
  sugar

4 ounces ginger ale
1 lemon twist

In a shaker half-filled with ice cubes, combine the whiskey,
lemon juice, and sugar. Shake well. Strain into a highball
glass almost filled with ice cubes. Top with the ginger ale.
Garnish with the lemon twist.

594 CALIFORNIA LEMONDADE

1½ ounces blended
  whiskey
1 ounce lemon juice
1 teaspoon superfine
  sugar

4 ounces club soda
1 maraschino cherry
1 orange slice

In a shaker half-filled with ice cubes, combine the whiskey,
lemon juice, and sugar. Shake well. Strain into a highball
glass almost filled with ice cubes. Top with the club soda.
Garnish with the cherry and the orange slice.

595 CANADIAN COCKTAIL

2 ounces blended
  whiskey
½ ounce Cointreau or
  triple sec

½ teaspoon superfine
  sugar
1 dash bitters

In a shaker half-filled with ice cubes, combine all of the
ingredients. Shake well. Strain into a cocktail glass.

596 CANADIAN SALAD

1 ounce Canadian whisky
½ ounce brandy
½ ounce Irish Mist
½ ounce Scotch
1 ounce orange juice
½ ounce lemon juice
½ teaspoon superfine sugar
1 orange slice
1 maraschino cherry

In a shaker half-filled with ice cubes, combine the whisky, brandy, Irish Mist, Scotch, orange juice, lemon juice, and sugar. Shake well. Strain into an old-fashioned glass almost filled with ice cubes. Garnish with the orange slice and the cherry.

597 CAT AND FIDDLE

1½ ounces Canadian whisky
½ ounce Cointreau or triple sec
1 teaspoon Pernod
1 teaspoon Dubonnet Blanc

In a mixing glass half-filled with ice cubes, combine all of the ingredients. Stir well. Strain into a cocktail glass.

598 COMMODORE

2 ounces Canadian whisky
1 ounce lime juice
1 dash bitters
½ teaspoon superfine sugar

In a shaker half-filled with ice cubes, combine all of the ingredients. Shake well. Strain into a cocktail glass.

599 DINAH COCKTAIL

2 ounces blended whiskey
½ ounce lemon juice
½ teaspoon superfine sugar

In a shaker half-filled with ice cubes, combine all of the ingredients. Shake well. Strain into a cocktail glass.

600 DOUBLE STANDARD SOUR

1 ounce blended whiskey
1 ounce gin
1 ounce lemon juice
½ teaspoon superfine
  sugar

½ teaspoon grenadine
1 maraschino cherry
1 orange slice

In a shaker half-filled with ice cubes, combine the whiskey, gin, lemon juice, sugar, and grenadine. Shake well. Strain into a sour glass. Garnish with the cherry and the orange slice.

601 DRY MANHATTAN

2 ounces blended
  whiskey

¾ ounce dry vermouth
1 lemon twist

In a mixing glass half-filled with ice cubes, combine the whiskey and vermouth. Stir well. Strain into a cocktail glass. Garnish with the lemon twist.

602 DUBONNET MANHATTAN

2 ounces blended
  whiskey
½ ounce Dubonnet
  Rouge

1 dash bitters
1 maraschino cherry

In a mixing glass half-filled with ice cubes, combine the whiskey, Dubonnet, and bitters. Stir well. Strain into a cocktail glass. Garnish with the cherry.

603 DUSTY BILL

1½ ounces Canadian
  whisky
½ ounce applejack
1 teaspoon brandy

2 teaspoons lemon juice
½ teaspoon superfine
  sugar
1 maraschino cherry

In a shaker half-filled with ice cubes, combine the whisky, applejack, brandy, lemon juice, and sugar. Shake well. Strain into an old-fashioned glass almost filled with ice cubes. Garnish with the cherry.

604 ERUPTION

2 ounces Canadian
  whisky

½ ounce crème de cassis
1 maraschino cherry

In a mixing glass half-filled with ice cubes, combine the whisky and cassis. Stir well. Strain into a cocktail glass. Garnish with the cherry.

605 EVERYBODY'S IRISH

2 ounces Irish whiskey
1 ounce green crème de
  menthe

1 ounce green Chartreuse

In a mixing glass half-filled with ice cubes, combine all of the ingredients. Stir well. Strain into a cocktail glass.

606 FANCY WHISKEY

2 ounces blended
  whiskey
½ teaspoon Cointreau or
  triple sec

¼ teaspoon superfine
  sugar
2 dashes bitters
1 lemon twist

In a shaker half-filled with ice cubes, combine the whiskey, Cointreau, sugar, and bitters. Shake well. Strain into a cocktail glass. Garnish with the lemon twist.

607 FAUX SCRUMPY

1½ ounces blended
  whiskey

6 ounces apple juice

Pour both of the ingredients into a highball glass almost filled with ice cubes. Stir well.

608 FINE AND DANDY

1½ ounces Canadian
  whisky
½ ounce Dubonnet
  Rouge

½ ounce Cointreau or
  triple sec
1 dash bitters
1 lemon twist

Combine the whisky, Dubonnet, Cointreau, and bitters in an old-fashioned glass almost filled with ice cubes. Garnish with the lemon twist.

609 GAULT'S GUMPTION

1½ ounces Canadian
  whisky
½ ounce peach schnapps

1 teaspoon sweet
vermouth

In a mixing glass half-filled with ice cubes, combine all of the ingredients. Stir well. Strain into a cocktail glass.

610 GERALDINE

1½ ounces Canadian
  whisky
½ ounce yellow
  Chartreuse
½ ounce Dubonnet
  Rouge

1 teaspoon dry vermouth
1 dash bitters
1 maraschino cherry

In a mixing glass half-filled with ice cubes, combine the whisky, Chartreuse, Dubonnet, vermouth, and bitters. Stir well. Strain into a cocktail glass. Garnish with the cherry.

611 GREATHEAD

1½ ounces Canadian
  whisky

½ ounce applejack

In a mixing glass half-filled with ice cubes, combine both of the ingredients. Stir well. Strain into a cocktail glass.

612 HEARTY SUSAN

1½ ounces blended
  whiskey

½ ounce cherry brandy
1 maraschino cherry

In a mixing glass half-filled with ice cubes, combine the whiskey and brandy. Stir well. Strain into a cocktail glass. Garnish with the cherry.

613 HORSE FEATHERS

2 ounces blended
  whiskey

2 dashes bitters
4 ounces ginger ale

Pour all of the ingredients into a highball glass almost filled with ice cubes. Stir well.

614 HOT DECK

2 ounces blended
  whiskey
1 ounce green ginger
  wine

½ ounce sweet vermouth

In a mixing glass half-filled with ice cubes, combine all of the ingredients. Stir well. Strain into a cocktail glass.

615 IRISH CANADIAN

1½ ounces Canadian
  whisky

½ ounce Irish Mist

In a mixing glass half-filled with ice cubes, combine both of the ingredients. Stir well. Strain into a cocktail glass.

616 JERSEY GENTLEMAN

1½ ounces blended
  whiskey

½ ounce Pernod
1 ounce pineapple juice

In a shaker half-filled with ice cubes, combine all of the ingredients. Shake well. Strain into a cocktail glass.

617 L.A. COCKTAIL

2 ounces blended
  whiskey
1 teaspoon sweet
  vermouth
½ ounce lemon juice

½ teaspoon superfine
  sugar
1 egg
1 maraschino cherry

In a shaker half-filled with ice cubes, combine the whiskey, vermouth, lemon juice, sugar, and egg. Shake well. Strain into a sour glass. Garnish with the cherry.

618 LA BELLE QUÉBEC

1½ ounces Canadian
  whisky
½ ounce brandy
½ ounce cherry brandy

½ ounce lemon juice
½ teaspoon superfine
  sugar

In a shaker half-filled with ice cubes, combine all of the ingredients. Shake well. Strain into a cocktail glass.

619 LADYLUV

1½ ounces blended
  whiskey
½ ounce dark rum

½ ounce añejo rum
1 teaspoon white crème
  de cacao

In a mixing glass half-filled with ice cubes, combine all of
the ingredients. Stir well. Strain into a cocktail glass.

620 LADY'S COCKTAIL

2 ounces blended
  whiskey

1 teaspoon anisette
1 dash bitters

In a mixing glass half-filled with ice cubes, combine all of
the ingredients. Stir well. Strain into a cocktail glass.

621 MADAME RENÉ

2 ounces blended
  whiskey
½ ounce añejo rum

1 ounce orange juice
1 dash bitters

In a shaker half-filled with ice cubes, combine all of the
ingredients. Shake well. Strain into a cocktail glass.

622 MAJOR BRADBURY

1½ ounces Canadian
  whisky
½ ounce Grand Marnier

1 teaspoon dry vermouth
1 teaspoon sweet
  vermouth

In a mixing glass half-filled with ice cubes, combine all of
the ingredients. Stir well. Strain into a cocktail glass.

623 MANHASSET

1½ ounces blended
  whiskey
1 teaspoon sweet
  vermouth

1 teaspoon dry vermouth
½ ounce lemon juice
½ teaspoon superfine
  sugar

In a shaker half-filled with ice cubes, combine all of the
ingredients. Shake well. Strain into a cocktail glass.

624 MANHATTAN

Besides being a darned good drink, the Manhattan has a rather interesting story to go with it. This cocktail was reportedly developed for Lady Jenny Churchill, a Brooklyn-born woman who married Lord Randolph and gave birth to Winston. The drink was first served at the Manhattan Club in New York, at a banquet given by Lady Jenny in honor of Samuel J. Tilden. Mr. Tilden was a famous lawyer of his time, who prosecuted the Tweed Ring, a group of politicians who stole millions from New York City.

A cherry is the correct garnish for a Manhattan, whereas a twist belongs in a Dry Manhattan; a Perfect Manhattan can take either. The Manhattan is made with sweet vermouth but should not be called a Sweet Manhattan. There is only a Manhattan, a Dry Manhattan (page 189), and a Perfect Manhattan (page 198).

2 ounces blended whiskey	3 dashes bitters
¾ ounce sweet vermouth	1 maraschino cherry

In a mixing glass half-filled with ice cubes, combine the whiskey, vermouth, and bitters. Stir well. Strain into a cocktail glass. Garnish with the cherry.

625 MAPLE LEAF

2 ounces Canadian whisky	1 teaspoon dark crème de cacao
½ ounce Irish Mist	1 ounce heavy cream

In a shaker half-filled with ice cubes, combine all of the ingredients. Shake well. Strain into a cocktail glass.

626 MENDAY'S PERIL

1½ ounces blended whiskey	½ ounce lemon juice
½ ounce cherry brandy	½ ounce orange juice
	2 dashes orange bitters

In a shaker half-filled with ice cubes, combine all of the ingredients. Shake well. Strain into an old-fashioned glass almost filled with ice cubes.

627 MILLIONAIRE

2 ounces blended
  whiskey
½ ounce Cointreau or
  triple sec
½ teaspoon grenadine
1 egg white

In a shaker half-filled with ice cubes, combine all of the
ingredients. Shake well. Strain into a sour glass.

628 MOLEHILL LOUNGER

1½ ounces blended
  whiskey
½ ounce dark crème de
  cacao
1 teaspoon white crème
  de cacao

In a mixing glass half-filled with ice cubes, combine all of
the ingredients. Stir well. Strain into a cocktail glass.

629 MOUNTIE

1½ ounces Canadian
  whisky
½ ounce Campari

In a mixing glass half-filled with ice cubes, combine both
of the ingredients. Stir well. Strain into a cocktail glass.

630 NEW YORK COCKTAIL

2 ounces blended
  whiskey
1 ounce lemon juice
½ teaspoon superfine
  sugar
½ teaspoon grenadine
1 lemon twist

In a shaker half-filled with ice cubes, combine the whiskey,
lemon juice, sugar, and grenadine. Shake well. Strain into
a cocktail glass. Garnish with the lemon twist.

631 OLD-FASHIONED

The classic Old-Fashioned is made with blended whiskey. The original was concocted at the Pendenis Club in Louisville, Kentucky.

There used to be seven distilleries in Louisville, and it is said that a representative from one of them concocted the drink for a retired Civil War general who didn't care much for the taste of whiskey, but who, like a good general should, really did enjoy the effect. Fortunately, though the name of the general and the distillery seem to be lost forever, one longtime employee at the Pendenis does remember that the original Old-Fashioned used branch water, as opposed to tap water. Branch water is merely a southern term for bottled water, so if you are making the drink for a special occasion, open a bottle of whatever designer water you have around. American water is preferred, of course.

Variations include the Bourbon Old-Fashioned (page 25) and the Scotch Old-Fashioned (page 136).

3 dashes bitters	1 orange slice
1 teaspoon water	1 maraschino cherry
1 sugar cube	
3 ounces blended whiskey	

In an old-fashioned glass, muddle the bitters and water into the sugar cube, using the back of a teaspoon. Almost fill the glass with ice cubes and add the whiskey. Garnish with the orange slice and the cherry. Serve with a swizzle stick.

632 OLD GROANER

2 ounces Canadian whisky	½ ounce amaretto

Pour both of the ingredients into an old-fashioned glass almost filled with ice cubes. Stir well.

633 OLD GROANER'S WIFE

2 ounces Canadian
  whisky
½ ounce amaretto
1 ounce heavy cream

In a shaker half-filled with ice cubes, combine all of the ingredients. Shake well. Strain into an old-fashioned glass almost filled with ice cubes.

634 OLD NICK

2 ounces Canadian
  whisky
½ ounce Drambuie
½ ounce orange juice
½ ounce lemon juice
3 dashes orange bitters
1 lemon twist
1 maraschino cherry

In a shaker half-filled with ice cubes, combine the whisky, Drambuie, orange juice, lemon juice, and bitters. Shake well. Strain into an old-fashioned glass almost filled with ice cubes. Garnish with the lemon twist and the cherry.

635 OPENING COCKTAIL

2 ounces blended
  whiskey
½ ounce sweet vermouth
2 teaspoons grenadine

In a mixing glass half-filled with ice cubes, combine all of the ingredients. Stir well. Strain into a cocktail glass.

636 PARK PARADISE

1½ ounces Canadian
  whisky
½ ounce sweet vermouth
1 teaspoon maraschino
  liqueur
1 dash bitters

In a mixing glass half-filled with ice cubes, combine all of the ingredients. Stir well. Strain into a cocktail glass.

637 PERFECT MANHATTAN

2½ ounces blended
  whiskey
½ ounce dry vermouth
½ ounce sweet vermouth
1 dash bitters
1 lemon twist or 1
  marachino cherry

In a mixing glass half-filled with ice cubes, combine the whiskey, dry vermouth, sweet vermouth, and bitters. Stir well. Strain into a cocktail glass. Garnish with the lemon twist or the cherry.

638 POOR TIM

1½ ounces blended
  whiskey
½ ounce dry vermouth
2 teaspoons Chambord

In a mixing glass half-filled with ice cubes, combine all of the ingredients. Stir well. Strain into a cocktail glass.

639 PREAKNESS

1½ ounces blended
  whiskey
½ ounce Bénédictine
1 teaspoon brandy
½ ounce sweet vermouth
2 dashes bitters
1 lemon twist

In a mixing glass half-filled with ice cubes, combine the whiskey, Bénédictine, brandy, vermouth, and bitters. Stir well. Strain into a cocktail glass. Garnish with the lemon twist.

640 PRESBYTERIAN

2 ounces blended
  whiskey
2 ounces ginger ale
3 ounces club soda
1 lemon twist

Pour the whiskey, ginger ale, and club soda into a highball glass almost filled with ice cubes. Stir well. Garnish with the lemon twist.

641 PRINCE RUPERT

1½ ounces blended
  whiskey
½ ounce anisette
1 lemon twist

In a mixing glass half-filled with ice cubes, combine the whiskey with the anisette. Stir well. Strain into a cocktail glass. Garnish with the lemon twist.

642 PURGAVIE

1½ ounces Canadian
  whisky
½ ounce Amer Picon
2 ounces orange juice
2 dashes orange bitters
3 ounces club soda

Pour all of the ingredients into a highball glass almost filled with ice cubes. Stir well.

643 QUEBEC

2 ounces Canadian
  whisky
½ ounce dry vermouth
1 teaspoon Amer Picon
1 teaspoon maraschino
  liqueur

In a mixing glass half-filled with ice cubes, combine all of the ingredients. Stir well. Strain into a cocktail glass.

644 RATTLESNAKE

2 ounces blended
  whiskey
1 teaspoon Pernod
½ ounce lemon juice
½ teaspoon superfine
  sugar
1 egg white

In a shaker half-filled with ice cubes, combine all of the ingredients. Shake well. Strain into a cocktail glass.

645 ROCHDALE COWBOY

1½ ounces blended
  whiskey
½ ounce Southern
  Comfort
½ ounce orange juice
1 teaspoon lemon juice
½ teaspoon superfine
  sugar
1 dash bitters

In a shaker half-filled with ice cubes, combine all of the ingredients. Shake well. Strain into a highball glass almost filled with ice cubes.

646 SAND DANCE

1½ ounces blended   ½ ounce cherry brandy
  whiskey   2 ounces cranberry juice

Pour all of the ingredients into a highball glass almost filled with ice cubes. Stir well.

647 SAN FRANCISCO

1½ ounces blended   ½ ounce Bénédictine
  whiskey   1 ounce lemon juice

In a shaker half-filled with ice cubes, combine all of the ingredients. Shake well. Strain into a cocktail glass.

648 SCREAMIN' HUDSON

1½ ounces Canadian   ½ ounce Drambuie
  whisky   ½ ounce lemon juice

In a shaker half-filled with ice cubes, combine all of the ingredients. Shake well. Strain into a cocktail glass.

649 SCRUMPY STRONG

1 ounce blended whiskey   6 ounces hard cider

Pour both of the ingredients into a highball glass almost filled with ice cubes. Stir well.

650 SEVEN AND SEVEN

2 ounces Seagram's 7   1 lemon twist
  whiskey
5 ounces 7-Up

Pour the whiskey and the soda into a highball glass almost filled with ice cubes. Stir well. Garnish with the lemon twist.

651 SHAKIN' BLUE MONDAY

1½ ounces Canadian
  whisky
½ ounce blueberry
  brandy
1 teaspoon brandy

½ ounce lemon juice
1 teaspoon superfine
  sugar
1 orange slice
1 maraschino cherry

In a shaker half-filled with ice cubes, combine the whisky, blueberry brandy, brandy, lemon juice, and sugar. Shake well. Strain into an old-fashioned glass almost filled with ice cubes. Garnish with the orange slice and the cherry.

652 SHERMAN TANK

2 ounces blended
  whiskey
½ ounce B & B
1 teaspoon lemon juice

1 teaspoon lime juice
½ teaspoon superfine
  sugar
2 dashes bitters

In a shaker half-filled with ice cubes, combine all of the ingredients. Shake well. Strain into a cocktail glass.

653 SOCRATES

1½ ounces Canadian
  whisky
½ ounce apricot brandy

1 teaspoon Cointreau or
  triple sec
1 dash bitters

In a mixing glass half-filled with ice cubes, combine all of the ingredients. Stir well. Strain into a cocktail glass.

654 SPEAKER OF THE HOUSE

1½ ounces Canadian
  whisky
½ ounce ginger wine

1 teaspoon cherry brandy
½ ounce lemon juice
1 maraschino cherry

In a shaker half-filled with ice cubes, combine the whisky, ginger wine, cherry brandy, and lemon juice. Shake well. Strain into a cocktail glass. Garnish with the cherry.

655 SPY CATCHER

1 ounce Canadian whisky   ½ ounce Sambuca

Pour both of the ingredients into a shot glass. Drink it straight back.

656 STILETTO

2 ounces blended
  whiskey
½ ounce amaretto

½ ounce lemon juice
1 teaspoon lime juice

In a shaker half-filled with ice cubes, combine all of the ingredients. Shake well. Strain into an old-fashioned glass almost filled with ice cubes.

657 STRONGARM

2 ounces blended
  whiskey
½ ounce Cointreau or
  triple sec

½ ounce lemon juice

In a shaker half-filled with ice cubes, combine all of the ingredients. Shake well. Strain into a cocktail glass.

658 TEACHER'S PET

1½ ounces blended
  whiskey
½ ounce dry vermouth
1 teaspoon sweet
  vermouth

2 dashes bitters
1 maraschino cherry
1 orange slice

Pour the whiskey, dry vermouth, sweet vermouth, and bitters into an old-fashioned glass almost filled with ice cubes. Stir well. Garnish with the cherry and the orange slice.

659 THUNDERCLAP

1½ ounces blended
  whiskey

1 ounce gin
1 ounce brandy

In a mixing glass half-filled with ice cubes, combine all of the ingredients. Stir well. Strain into a cocktail glass.

660 TIGER JUICE

1½ ounces Canadian
  whisky

½ ounce lemon juice
1 ounce orange juice

In a shaker half-filled with ice cubes, combine all of the ingredients. Shake well. Strain into a cocktail glass.

661 T.L.C.

1½ ounces blended
  whiskey
½ ounce Cointreau or
  triple sec
1 teaspoon Ricard

1 teaspoon Dubonnet
  Rouge
1 dash bitters
1 lemon twist
1 maraschino cherry

In a mixing glass half-filled with ice cubes, combine the whiskey, Cointreau, Ricard, Dubonnet, and bitters. Stir well. Strain into a cocktail glass. Garnish with the lemon twist and the cherry.

662 T.N.T.

1½ ounces blended
  whiskey

1 ounce anisette

In a mixing glass half-filled with ice cubes, combine both of the ingredients. Stir well. Strain into a cocktail glass.

663 TOWER TOPPER

1½ ounces Canadian
  whisky

½ ounce Grand Marnier
½ ounce light cream

In a shaker half-filled with ice cubes, combine all of the ingredients. Shake well. Strain into a cocktail glass.

664 TURTLE

2 ounces Canadian
  whisky

½ ounce Bénédictine

In a mixing glass half-filled with ice cubes, combine both of the ingredients. Stir well. Strain into a cocktail glass.

665 TWIN PEAKS

1½ ounces blended
  whiskey
½ ounce Dubonnet
  Rouge

1 teaspoon Cointreau or
  triple sec
1 lemon twist

In a mixing glass half-filled with ice cubes, combine the whiskey, Dubonnet, and Cointreau. Stir well. Strain into a cocktail glass. Garnish with the lemon twist.

666 TWO TURTLES

2 ounces Canadian
  whisky
½ ounce B & B

½ ounce Cointreau or
  triple sec
1 maraschino cherry

In a mixing glass half-filled with ice cubes, combine the
whisky, B & B, and Cointreau. Stir well. Strain into a
cocktail glass. Garnish with the cherry.

667 WHISKEY COLLINS

2 ounces blended
  whiskey
1 ounce lemon juice
1 teaspoon superfine
  sugar

3 ounces club soda
1 maraschino cherry
1 orange slice

In a shaker half-filled with ice cubes combine the whiskey,
lemon juice, and sugar. Shake well. Strain into a collins
glass almost filled with ice cubes. Add the club soda. Stir
well and garnish with the cherry and the orange slice.

668 WHISKEY COBBLER

1 teaspoon superfine
  sugar
3 ounces club soda
Crushed ice
2 ounces blended
  whiskey

1 maraschino cherry
1 orange slice
1 lemon slice

In an old-fashioned glass, dissolve the sugar in the club
soda. Add crushed ice until the glass is almost full. Add
the whiskey. Stir well. Garnish with the cherry and the
orange and lemon slices.

669 WHISKEY COOLER

2 ounces blended
  whiskey
4 ounces lemon-lime
  soda

1 lemon wedge

Pour the whiskey and soda into a highball glass almost
filled with ice cubes. Stir well. Garnish with the lemon
wedge.

670 WHISKEY CRUSTA

1 tablespoon superfine
  sugar
1 lemon wedge
Peel of 1 orange, cut into
  a spiral
Crushed ice
1½ ounces blended
  whiskey

½ ounce Cointreau or
  triple sec
2 teaspoons maraschino
  liqueur
½ ounce lemon juice

Place the sugar in a saucer. Rub the rim of a wine goblet with the lemon wedge and dip the glass into the sugar to coat the rim thoroughly; discard the lemon. Place the orange peel spiral in the goblet and drape one end of it over the rim. Fill the glass with crushed ice. In a shaker half-filled with ice cubes, combine the whiskey, Cointreau, maraschino liqueur, and lemon juice. Shake well. Strain into the goblet.

671 WHISKEY DAISY

2 ounces blended
  whiskey
1 ounce lemon juice
½ teaspoon superfine
  sugar

½ teaspoon grenadine
1 maraschino cherry
1 orange slice

In a shaker half-filled with ice cubes, combine the whiskey, lemon juice, sugar, and grenadine. Shake well. Pour into an old-fashioned glass. Garnish with the cherry and the orange slice.

672 WHISKEY FIX

1 teaspoon superfine
  sugar
1 ounce lemon juice
2 teaspoons water
Crushed ice

2 ounces blended
  whiskey
1 maraschino cherry
1 lemon slice

In a shaker half-filled with ice cubes, combine the sugar, lemon juice, and water. Shake well. Strain into a highball glass almost filled with crushed ice. Add the whiskey. Stir well and garnish with the cherry and the lemon slice.

673 WHISKEY FLIP

2 ounces blended
  whiskey
1 egg
1 teaspoon superfine
  sugar
1 teaspoon light cream
1/8 teaspoon grated
  nutmeg

In a shaker half-filled with ice cubes, combine the whiskey, egg, sugar, and cream. Shake well. Strain into a sour glass and garnish with the nutmeg.

674 WHISKEY MILK PUNCH

2 ounces blended
  whiskey
1 ounce dark crème de
  cacao
2 ounces milk
1/4 teaspoon grated
  nutmeg

In a shaker half-filled with ice cubes, combine the whiskey, crème de cacao, and milk. Shake well. Strain into a cocktail glass and garnish with the nutmeg.

675 WHISKEY SANGAREE

1 teaspoon superfine
  sugar
2 teaspoons water
1 1/2 ounces blended
  whiskey
Crushed ice
2 1/2 ounces club soda
1/2 ounce tawny port
1 lemon twist
1/8 teaspoon grated
  nutmeg
1/8 teaspoon ground
  cinnamon

In a highball glass, dissolve the sugar in the water and whiskey. Almost fill the glass with crushed ice and add the club soda. Float the port on top. Garnish with the lemon twist and dust with the nutmeg and cinnamon.

676 WHISKEY SLING

1 teaspoon superfine
  sugar
2 teaspoons water
1 ounce lemon juice
2 ounces blended
  whiskey
1 lemon twist

In a shaker half-filled with ice cubes, combine the sugar,

water, lemon juice, and whiskey. Shake well. Strain into a
highball glass. Garnish with the lemon twist.

677 WHISKEY SMASH

4 fresh mint sprigs
1 teaspoon superfine
  sugar
1 ounce club soda

2½ ounces blended
  whiskey
1 lemon twist

In an old-fashioned glass, muddle the mint sprigs lightly
with the sugar and club soda. Fill the glass with ice cubes.
Add the whiskey. Stir well and garnish with the lemon
twist.

678 WHISKEY SOUR

2 ounces blended
  whiskey
1 ounce lemon juice
½ teaspoon superfine
  sugar

1 orange slice
1 maraschino cherry

In a shaker half-filled with ice cubes, combine the whiskey,
lemon juice, and sugar. Shake well. Strain into a sour glass.
Garnish with the orange slice and the cherry.

679 WHISKEY SWIZZLE

1½ ounces lime juice
1 teaspoon superfine
  sugar
2 ounces blended
  whiskey

1 dash bitters
Crushed ice
3 ounces club soda

In a shaker half-filled with ice cubes, combine the lime
juice, sugar, whiskey, and bitters. Shake well. Almost fill
a collins glass with crushed ice and stir until the glass is
frosted. Strain the mixture in the shaker into the glass and
add the club soda. Serve with a swizzle stick.

680 WHISKEY TO GO

1½ ounces blended
  whiskey
½ ounce gin

½ ounce lemon juice
½ teaspoon superfine
  sugar

In a shaker half-filled with ice cubes, combine all of the ingredients. Shake well. Strain into an old-fashioned glass almost filled with ice cubes.

681 WILD JACKALOPE

1½ ounces Canadian
  whisky
½ ounce peppermint
  schnapps

1 teaspoon Pernod
1 lemon twist

In a mixing glass half-filled with ice cubes, combine the whisky, schnapps, and Pernod. Stir well. Strain into an old-fashioned glass almost filled with ice cubes. Garnish with the lemon twist.

10 · TROPICAL DRINKS

What makes a drink tropical? Pineapples, coconuts, orchids, parasols, and plastic monkeys for starters. These exotic potions are guaranteed to transport you to someplace in the Tropics, where vines grow haphazardly around the pillar next to your table and flaming kebabs dance around the dining room in the hands of exotic-looking waiters.

Mai Tais and Zombies are bewitching names for drinks with exceptional ingredients and curious garnishes. They are perfect for a poolside party in the dog days of summer, as an accompaniment to a tropical theme dinner, or to serve at a cocktail party for some favorite friends.

Tropical drinks usually have two things in common: They are great thirst quenchers, containing many exotic fruit juices and ice in great quantities, and they can be very high in alcohol content. These two qualities are rarely found in other drinks, which are generally *either* light thirst quenchers *or* Bacchanalian potions.

Try some of these drinks, sit back with the sun beating on your face, and sip them through a long straw while you imagine some Indiana Jones type of character battling through the perils of the jungle to bring you the exotic ingredients that you just took from your refrigerator. It's a refreshing way to spend a lazy afternoon.

682 AZULUNA

2 ounces light rum	1½ ounces coconut cream
1 ounce blue Curaçao	1 cup crushed ice
4 ounces pineapple juice	1 plastic monkey

In a blender, combine the rum, Curaçao, pineapple juice, and coconut cream with the crushed ice. Blend well at high speed. Pour into a collins glass. Garnish with the monkey.

683 BANANA COLADA

1 ounce dark rum	1 ounce coconut cream
1 ounce light rum	1 cup crushed ice
1 very ripe banana, sliced	1 maraschino cherry
4 ounces pineapple juice	1 pineapple slice

In a blender, combine the dark rum, light rum, banana, pineapple juice, and coconut cream with the crushed ice. Blend well at high speed. Pour into a collins glass. Garnish with the cherry and the pineapple slice.

684 BANANA DAIQUIRI

2 ounces light rum	1 ounce lime juice
½ ounce Cointreau or triple sec	½ teaspoon superfine sugar
1 very ripe banana, sliced	1 cup crushed ice

In a blender, combine all of the ingredients. Blend well. Pour into a collins glass.

685 CARIBBEAN BREEZE

2 ounces dark rum	2 dashes orange bitters
½ ounce crème de bananes	½ teaspoon grenadine
1 teaspoon Rose's lime juice	Crushed ice
6 ounces pineapple juice	1 maraschino cherry
	1 pineapple slice

In a shaker half-filled with ice cubes, combine the rum, crème de bananes, Rose's lime juice, pineapple juice, orange bitters, and grenadine. Shake well. Strain into a collins glass almost filled with crushed ice. Garnish with the cherry and the pineapple slice.

686 CHI CHI

2 ounces vodka
5 ounces pineapple juice
1½ ounces coconut
  cream

1 cup crushed ice
1 maraschino cherry
1 pineapple slice

In a blender, combine the vodka, pineapple juice, coconut cream, and crushed ice. Blend well at high speed. Pour into a collins glass. Garnish with the cherry and the pineapple slice.

687 DISCOVERY BAY

1½ ounces brandy
½ ounce Cointreau or
  triple sec

2 ounces lemon sherbet
2 ounces ginger ale

In a shaker half-filled with ice cubes, combine the brandy, Cointreau, and lemon sherbet. Shake well. Strain into a highball glass almost filled with ice cubes. Top with the ginger ale.

688 FRUIT RUM FRAPPE

1 ounce light rum
½ ounce crème de
  bananes
½ teaspoon crème de
  cassis

½ ounce orange juice
½ cup crushed ice

In a blender, combine all of the ingredients. Blend well. Pour into a cocktail glass.

689 GAUGUIN

2 ounces light rum
1 ounce passion fruit
  syrup
1 ounce lemon juice

1 teaspoon lime juice
½ teaspoon superfine
  sugar

In a blender, combine all of the ingredients with 6 ice cubes. Blend well. Pour into a collins glass.

690 HAWAIIAN COCKTAIL

2 ounces gin
½ ounce Cointreau or
  triple sec

1 ounce pineapple juice

In a shaker half-filled with ice cubes, combine all of the ingredients. Shake well. Strain into a cocktail glass.

691 HONOLULU COCKTAIL

1½ ounces gin
1 teaspoon orange juice
1 ounce pineapple juice
1 teaspoon lime juice

1 teaspoon lemon juice
½ teaspoon superfine
  sugar

In a shaker half-filled with ice cubes, combine all of the ingredients. Shake well. Strain into a cocktail glass.

692 HULA HOOP

1½ ounces gin
1 ounce orange juice

½ ounce pineapple juice

In a shaker half-filled with ice cubes, combine all of the ingredients. Shake well. Strain into a cocktail glass.

693 JAMAICA HOP

1½ ounces Kahlúa
½ ounce white crème de
  cacao

1½ ounces heavy cream

In a shaker half-filled with ice cubes, combine all of the ingredients. Shake well. Strain into a cocktail glass.

694 JAMAICAN FIZZ

2½ ounces dark rum
1½ ounces pineapple
  juice

1 teaspoon superfine
  sugar
4 ounces club soda

In a shaker half-filled with ice cubes, combine the rum, pineapple juice, and sugar. Shake well. Strain into a collins glass almost filled with ice cubes. Add the club soda. Stir well.

695 KING OF KINGSTON

1 ounce gin
½ ounce crème de
  bananes
1 ounce pineapple juice

1 teaspoon grapefruit
  juice
1 teaspoon grenadine
1 ounce heavy cream

In a shaker half-filled with ice cubes, combine all of the ingredients. Shake well. Strain into a cocktail glass.

696 LAZY AFTERNOON

1 ounce dark rum
1 ounce light rum
½ ounce cherry brandy
4 ounces pineapple juice

Crushed ice
1 maraschino cherry
1 pineapple slice

Pour the dark rum, light rum, cherry brandy, and pineapple juice into a highball glass almost filled with crushed ice. Stir well and garnish with the cherry and the pineapple slice.

697 LISTENING TO THE DRUMS OF FEYNMAN

1 ounce dark rum
½ ounce light rum
1 ounce Tia Maria

2 ounces light cream
Crushed ice
⅛ teaspoon nutmeg

In a shaker half-filled with ice cubes, combine the dark rum, light rum, Tia Maria, and cream. Shake well. Strain into an old-fashioned glass almost filled with crushed ice. Dust with the nutmeg.

698 LIZBUTH

1½ ounces light rum
½ ounce amaretto
½ ounce coconut cream

1 ounce pineapple juice
2 ounces half-and-half
1 maraschino cherry

In a blender, combine the rum, amaretto, coconut cream, pineapple juice, and half-and-half with 6 ice cubes. Blend well. Pour into a collins glass and garnish with the cherry.

699 MAI TAI

1 ounce light rum
1 ounce añejo rum
1 ounce Cointreau or
   triple sec
½ ounce lime juice

2 teaspoons orgeat syrup
2 teaspoons grenadine
Crushed ice
1 orchid or paper parasol

In a shaker half-filled with ice cubes, combine the light rum, añejo rum, Cointreau, lime juice, orgeat syrup, and grenadine. Shake well. Strain into an old-fashioned glass half-filled with crushed ice. Float the orchid or parasol on top. Serve with 4 short straws.

700 MICKEY'S FIN

1 ounce dark rum
1 ounce Malibu rum
½ ounce crème de
   bananes

1 ounce pineapple juice
1 ounce orange juice
1 ounce grapefruit juice
1 teaspoon grenadine

In a shaker half-filled with ice cubes, combine all of the ingredients. Shake well. Strain into a collins glass almost filled with ice cubes.

701 PIÑA COLADA

2 ounces light rum
5 ounces pineapple juice
1½ ounces coconut
   cream

1 cup crushed ice
1 maraschino cherry
1 pineapple slice

In a blender, combine the rum, pineapple juice, and coconut cream with the crushed ice. Blend well at high speed. Pour into a collins glass and garnish with the cherry and the pineapple slice.

702 POLYNESIAN COCKTAIL

1 teaspoon powdered
   sugar
1 lime wedge
1½ ounces vodka

½ ounce cherry brandy
½ ounce lime juice
½ ounce lemon juice
1 maraschino cherry

Place the sugar in a saucer. Rub the rim of a cocktail glass with the lime wedge and dip it into the sugar to coat the rim thoroughly; discard the lime. In a shaker half-filled ice cubes, combine the vodka, cherry brandy, lime juice, and lemon juice. Shake well. Strain into the cocktail glass and garnish with the cherry.

703 RASTA'S REVENGE

1 ounce gin
½ ounce dark rum
½ ounce ruby port
½ ounce orange juice

½ ounce lime juice
½ teaspoon superfine
    sugar

In a shaker half-filled with ice cubes, combine all of the ingredients. Shake well. Strain into a cocktail glass.

704 REGGAE

2 ounces vodka
½ ounce crème de
    bananes
1 ounce orange juice
½ ounce grapefruit juice
½ ounce pineapple juice

1 dash orange bitters
½ teaspoon grenadine
1 orange slice
1 pineapple wedge
1 maraschino cherry

In a shaker half-filled with ice cubes, combine the vodka, crème de bananes, orange juice, grapefruit juice, pineapple juice, orange bitters, and grenadine. Shake well. Strain into a highball glass almost filled with ice cubes. Garnish with the orange slice, pineapple wedge, and cherry.

705 SACRIFICE

1 ounce dark rum
1 ounce light rum
½ ounce white crème de
    cacao
1 teaspoon coconut cream
2 ounces pineapple juice

1 ounce cranberry juice
1 ounce orange juice
2 dashes orange bitters
1 cup crushed ice
1 orange slice
1 maraschino cherry

In a blender, combine the dark rum, light rum, crème de cacao, coconut cream, pineapple juice, cranberry juice, orange juice, and orange bitters with the crushed ice. Blend well at high speed. Pour into a collins glass. Garnish with the orange slice and the cherry.

706 SCORPION

1½ ounces añejo rum
½ ounce brandy
1½ ounces orange juice
1 ounce lemon juice

½ ounce orgeat syrup
1 cup crushed ice
1 orange slice
1 maraschino cherry

In a blender, combine the rum, brandy, orange juice, lemon juice, and orgeat syrup with the crushed ice. Blend well at high speed. Pour into an old-fashioned glass. Garnish with the orange slice and the cherry.

707 SHARPLES

1½ ounces dark rum
½ ounce peppermint
schnapps

Crushed ice

Pour both of the ingredients into an old-fashioned glass almost filled with crushed ice. Stir well.

708 STRAWBERRY COLADA

1 ounce dark rum
1 ounce light rum
5 overripe strawberries
4 ounces pineapple juice

1 ounce coconut cream
1 cup crushed ice
1 maraschino cherry
1 pineapple wedge

In a blender, combine the dark rum, light rum, strawberries, pineapple juice, and coconut cream with the crushed ice. Blend well at high speed. Pour into a collins glass and garnish with the cherry and the pineapple wedge.

709 STRAWBERRY DAIQUIRI

2 ounces light rum
½ ounce Cointreau or
triple sec
6 overripe strawberries

1 ounce lime juice
½ teaspoon superfine
sugar
1 cup crushed ice

In a blender, combine all of the ingredients with the crushed ice. Blend well. Pour into a collins glass.

710 SWIMMING ASHORE FOR THE SONGS OF SUNRISE

1½ ounces light rum
½ ounce Cointreau or
   triple sec
3 ounces grapefruit juice
½ ounce orange juice
2 teaspoons grenadine
Crushed ice

In a shaker half-filled with ice cubes, combine all of the ingredients. Shake well. Strain into a highball glass half-filled with crushed ice.

711 TAHITI CLUB

1 ounce light rum
1 ounce dark rum
1 ounce pineapple juice
½ ounce lime juice
½ ounce lemon juice
1 teaspoon maraschino
   liqueur

In a shaker half-filled with ice cubes, combine all of the ingredients. Shake well. Strain into an old-fashioned glass almost filled with ice cubes.

712 THE GREEN-TAILED DRAGON OF THE MAROON MORNING

1½ ounces light rum
½ ounce melon liqueur
1 ounce pineapple juice
½ ounce lime juice
1 teaspoon orgeat syrup
1 cup crushed ice
1 teaspoon cherry brandy

In a blender, combine the rum, melon liqueur, pineapple juice, lime juice, and orgeat syrup with the crushed ice. Blend well at high speed. Pour into an old-fashioned glass. Drop the cherry brandy into the center.

713 TIDAL WAVE

1 ounce light rum
½ ounce dark rum
½ ounce gin
½ ounce vodka
½ ounce tequila
2 ounces pineapple juice
1 ounce orange juice
1 teaspoon grenadine
1 cup crushed ice

Put all of the ingredients into a blender. Blend well. Pour into a collins glass. Stand well away from drinker!

714 TROPICAL RAINSTORM

1½ ounces dark rum
½ ounce cherry brandy
½ ounce lemon juice

1 teaspoon Cointreau or
triple sec

In a shaker half-filled with ice cubes, combine all of the ingredients. Shake well. Strain into a cocktail glass.

715 YELLOW BIRD

1½ ounces light rum
½ ounce Galliano
½ ounce Cointreau or
triple sec

½ ounce lime juice

In a shaker half-filled with ice cubes, combine all of the ingredients. Shake well. Strain into a cocktail glass.

716 ZOCOLO

1 ounce dark rum
½ ounce tequila
2 ounces pineapple juice
2 ounces grapefruit juice

2 ounces club soda
1 orange slice
1 pineapple wedge
1 maraschino cherry

In a shaker half-filled with ice cubes, combine the rum, tequila, pineapple juice, and grapefruit juice. Shake well. Strain into a collins glass almost filled with ice cubes. Add the club soda and stir well. Garnish with the orange slice, pineapple wedge, and cherry.

717 ZOMBIE

1 ounce light rum
1 ounce añejo rum
1 ounce dark rum
½ ounce apricot brandy
2 ounces orange juice
1 ounce pineapple juice
1 ounce lime juice
1 teaspoon superfine
sugar

1 cup crushed ice
2 teaspoons 151° proof
rum
1 orange slice
1 maraschino cherry
1 mint sprig

In a blender, combine the light rum, añejo rum, dark rum, apricot brandy, orange juice, pineapple juice, lime juice, and sugar with the crushed ice. Blend well at high speed. Pour into a collins glass. Float the 151° proof rum on top. Garnish with the orange slice, cherry, and mint sprig.

11 · APERITIFS

The word *aperitif* is actually derived from the Latin word *aperire*, which means "to open." Appropriately, an aperitif is a drink that is used as an opening to a meal, and many drinks can fall into this category. If you choose to drink a quart of stout as a prelude to dinner, then a quart of stout becomes an aperitif (indeed, 12 ounces of good stout makes for a quite superb opening to a meal). Generally speaking, however, aromatized wines and dry sherries are considered to be proper aperitifs. Since dry sherries are discussed in the Wine Drinks chapter, this chapter will deal just with aromatized wines. Wines can be divided into four categories: still, sparkling, fortified, and aromatized.

If you are one of the many people who just can't abide the taste of coffee without some sugar or artificial sweetener in it, then you will understand perfectly how aromatized wines came into being. Sour wine was sweetened with honey or herbs by the ancient Greeks and Romans in order to make it more palatable. The practice of adding herbs to wine in order to preserve their medicinal qualities also played a great part in the creation of aromatized wines.

AROMATIZED WINES

Most aromatized wines are a variation on dry vermouths with a few distinctions:

1. They are generally sweeter, containing more *mistelle* (in simple terms, brandy combined with grape juice).
2. Red aromatized wines are usually made from a red base wine.
3. Quinine is generally added in making aromatized wines.

Examples of popular aromatized wines include: Campari, Dubonnet, Lillet, Cynar, St Raphaël, Punt e Mes, Amer Picon, and Byrrh.

VERMOUTH

Vermouths are aromatized wines, but aromatized wines are not necessarily vermouths. The word *vermouth* comes from the German *wermut,* which literally means "wormwood." Italy produced the first vermouth in the late eighteenth century; it was made from white wines infused with herbs to make a sweetish aromatized wine. In the early nineteenth century, a drier version of vermouth was produced in France and ever since, sweet vermouth is known as Italian vermouth and dry vermouth is known as French, even though both Italy *and* France produce both types of vermouths. Almost every wine-producing nation makes vermouth of both types, sweet and dry, or Italian and French.

The best dry vermouth is made by adding aged *mistelle* (see above) to aged white wine. This mixture is then steeped with herbs, roots, flowers, spices, fruit peels, and probably a host of other ingredients. Each company guards their recipes jealously. This infused wine is then cut with basic wine and brandy is added to it. The mixture is put into vats and chilled until the tartaric acid crystallizes. The vermouth is then drained off and bottled.

Sweet vermouth also is made from white wine, usually sweeter white wines, and sweetening agents are added along with quinine and some caramel for coloring.

718 AGINCOURT

1 ounce sweet vermouth	½ ounce amaretto
1 ounce dry vermouth	1 teaspoon lemon juice

In a shaker half-filled with ice cubes, combine all of the ingredients. Shake well. Strain into a cocktail glass.

719 ALLIED REQUIREMENTS

1½ ounces dry vermouth	½ teaspoon Pernod
1 ounce gin	1 dash bitters

In a mixing glass half-filled with ice cubes, combine all of the ingredients. Stir well. Strain into a cocktail glass.

720 ALLIES COCKTAIL

1 ounce dry vermouth	1 teaspoon kümmel
¾ ounce gin	

In a mixing glass half-filled with ice cubes, combine all of the ingredients. Stir well. Strain into a cocktail glass.

721 AMER PICON COCKTAIL

2 ounces Amer Picon	1 teaspoon grenadine
1½ ounces lime juice	

In a shaker half-filled with ice cubes, combine all of the ingredients. Shake well. Strain into a cocktail glass.

722 AMERICANO

1½ ounces Campari	4 ounces club soda
1½ ounces sweet vermouth	1 lemon twist

Pour the Campari, vermouth, and soda into a highball glass almost filled with ice cubes. Stir well and garnish with the lemon twist.

723 ANTE

1 ounce Dubonnet Rouge   ½ ounce Cointreau or
¾ ounce applejack   triple sec

In a mixing glass half-filled with ice cubes, combine all of
the ingredients. Stir well. Strain into a cocktail glass.

724 APPLE ROUGE

1½ ounces Dubonnet   1 ounce applejack
  Rouge

In a mixing glass half-filled with ice cubes, combine both
of the ingredients. Stir well. Strain into a cocktail glass.

725 BALANCHINE'S BELLE

1½ ounces Dubonnet   ½ ounce dry vermouth
  Rouge   1 lemon twist

In a mixing glass half-filled with ice cubes, combine the
Dubonnet and vermouth. Stir well. Strain into a cocktail
glass. Garnish with the lemon twist.

726 BEANSY'S BATTLEGROUND

1½ ounces sweet   ½ teaspoon Pernod
  vermouth   1 dash bitters
1 ounce brandy
½ ounce peppermint
  schnapps

In a mixing glass half-filled with ice cubes, combine all of
the ingredients. Stir well. Strain into an old-fashioned glass
almost filled with ice cubes.

727 BELLE OF ELLIS ISLAND

2 ounces dry vermouth   ½ teaspoon superfine
½ ounce brandy   sugar
1 teaspoon Cointreau or   2 dashes orange bitters
  triple sec   1 lemon twist

In a shaker half-filled with ice cubes, combine the vermouth, brandy, Cointreau, sugar, and orange bitters. Shake
well. Strain into a cocktail glass. Garnish with the lemon
twist.

728 BIG RED

1 ounce sweet vermouth
¾ ounce dry vermouth
½ ounce sloe gin

2 dashes orange bitters
Crushed ice
1 orange slice

Pour the sweet vermouth, dry vermouth, sloe gin, and orange bitters into an old-fashioned glass two-thirds filled with crushed ice. Stir well and garnish with the orange slice.

729 BITTERSWEET COCKTAIL

1 ounce sweet vermouth
1 ounce dry vermouth

2 dashes orange bitters
1 lemon twist

In a mixing glass half-filled with ice cubes, combine the sweet vermouth, dry vermouth, and orange bitters. Stir well. Strain into a cocktail glass. Garnish with the lemon twist.

730 BLONDE JENNY

1½ ounces dry vermouth
½ ounce gin
½ ounce orange juice

1 dash orange bitters
1 orange slice

In a shaker half-filled with ice cubes, combine the vermouth, gin, orange juice, and orange bitters. Shake well. Strain into a cocktail glass. Garnish with the orange slice.

731 BOSWELLIAN BOOSTER

2 ounces dry vermouth
1 ounce brandy
2 dashes orange bitters
½ ounce lemon juice

½ teaspoon superfine sugar
1 maraschino cherry

In a shaker half-filled with ice cubes, combine the vermouth, brandy, bitters, lemon juice, and sugar. Shake well. Strain into an old-fashioned glass almost filled with ice cubes. Garnish with the cherry.

732 BOYD OF THE LOCH

1½ ounces dry vermouth   1 lemon twist
1 ounce Scotch

In a mixing glass half-filled with ice cubes, combine the vermouth and Scotch. Stir well. Strain into a cocktail glass. Garnish with the lemon twist.

733 BRESNAN

1½ ounces sweet
  vermouth
1 ounce dry vermouth

1 teaspoon crème de
  cassis
½ ounce lemon juice

In a shaker half-filled with ice cubes, combine all of the ingredients. Shake well. Strain into a cocktail glass.

734 BURFENTAILOR

1 ounce sweet vermouth
½ ounce gin
½ ounce brandy
2 teaspoons Pernod

2 teaspoons lemon juice
1 teaspoon grenadine
1 maraschino cherry

In a shaker half-filled with ice cubes, combine the vermouth, gin, brandy, Pernod, lemon juice, and grenadine. Shake well. Strain into an old-fashioned glass almost filled with ice cubes. Garnish with the cherry.

735 BURN'S NIGHT SPECIAL

1½ ounces sweet
  vermouth

1 ounce Scotch whisky
2 teaspoons Bénédictine

In a mixing glass half-filled with ice cubes, combine all of the ingredients. Stir well. Strain into a cocktail glass.

736 CHELSEA

1 ounce dry vermouth
¾ ounce bourbon
1 teaspoon blackberry
  brandy

½ teaspoon Cointreau or
  triple sec
2 teaspoons lemon juice
1 lemon twist

In a shaker half-filled with ice cubes, combine the vermouth, bourbon, blackberry brandy, Cointreau, and lemon juice. Shake well. Strain into a cocktail glass and garnish with the lemon twist.

737 CLARIDGE'S

1 ounce dry vermouth
¾ ounce gin
2 teaspoons apricot
  brandy

2 teaspoons Cointreau or
  triple sec

In a mixing glass half-filled with ice cubes, combine all of the ingredients. Stir well. Strain into a cocktail glass.

738 CUYAHOGA COCKTAIL

½ ounce sweet vermouth
½ ounce dry vermouth

¾ ounce gin
1 lemon twist

In a mixing glass half-filled with ice cubes, combine both vermouths and the gin. Stir well. Strain into a cocktail glass and garnish with the lemon twist.

739 DANCIN' BONES

1½ ounces dry vermouth
2 teaspoons gin

2 teaspoons cherry
  brandy

In a mixing glass half-filled with ice cubes, combine all of the ingredients. Stir well. Strain into a cocktail glass.

740 DIPLOMAT

2 ounces dry vermouth
½ ounce sweet vermouth
½ teaspoon maraschino
  liqueur

1 dash orange bitters
1 maraschino cherry

In a mixing glass half-filled with ice cubes, combine the dry vermouth, sweet vermouth, maraschino liqueur, and orange bitters. Stir well. Strain into a cocktail glass and garnish with the cherry.

741 DRY NEGRONI

1 ounce Campari
1 ounce gin

1 ounce dry vermouth
1 lemon twist

Pour the Campari, gin, and vermouth into an old-fashioned glass almost filled with ice cubes. Stir well and garnish with the lemon twist.

742 DUBONNET FIZZ

2 ounces Dubonnet
  Rouge
1 ounce orange juice
½ ounce lemon juice

2 teaspoons cherry
  brandy
3 ounces club soda

In a mixing glass half-filled with ice cubes, combine the
Dubonnet, orange juice, lemon juice, and cherry brandy.
Shake well. Pour into a highball glass and top with the
club soda. Stir well.

743 DUBONNET COCKTAIL

1½ ounces Dubonnet
  Rouge
½ ounce gin

1 dash bitters
1 lemon twist

In a mixing glass half-filled with ice cubes, combine the
Dubonnet, gin, and bitters. Stir well. Strain into a cocktail
glass and garnish with the lemon twist.

744 EARL OF SARDINIA

1½ ounces Campari
½ ounce crème de cassis
3 ounces grapefruit juice

1 ounce pineapple juice
1 teaspoon grenadine
Crushed ice

In a shaker half-filled with ice cubes, combine all of the
ingredients. Shake well. Strain into an old-fashioned glass
almost filled with crushed ice.

745 EVANS RESCUES THE DAMSEL OF GARSTANG TOWER

1 ounce sweet vermouth
1 ounce dry vermouth
1 ounce gin

½ ounce strawberry
  liqueur
2 dashes orange bitters

In a mixing glass half-filled with ice cubes, combine all of
the ingredients. Stir well. Strain into a cocktail glass.

746 FARTHINGALE

1 ounce sweet vermouth
1 ounce dry vermouth
¾ ounce gin

1 dash bitters
1 lemon twist

In a mixing glass half-filled with ice cubes, combine the sweet vermouth, dry vermouth, gin, and bitters. Stir well. Strain into a cocktail glass and garnish with the lemon twist.

747 FERRARI

2 ounces dry vermouth
¾ ounce amaretto

1 dash bitters
1 lemon twist

Pour the vermouth, amaretto, and bitters into an old-fashioned glass almost filled with ice cubes. Stir well and garnish with the lemon twist.

748 FRENCH KISS

1½ ounces sweet
   vermouth

1½ ounces dry vermouth
1 lemon twist

Pour the sweet vermouth and dry vermouth into an old-fashioned glass almost filled with ice cubes. Garnish with the lemon twist.

749 GADZOOKS

1 ounce dry vermouth
1 ounce apricot brandy
1 ounce gin

2 teaspoons cherry
   brandy
1 teaspoon lemon juice

In a shaker half-filled with ice cubes, combine all of the ingredients. Shake well. Strain into an old-fashioned glass almost filled with ice cubes.

750 GLADYS DELIGHT

2 ounces dry vermouth
1 teaspoon sweet
   vermouth

1 teaspoon grenadine
4 ounces ginger ale
1 lemon twist

Pour the dry vermouth, sweet vermouth, grenadine, and ginger ale into a collins glass almost filled with ice cubes. Stir well and garnish with the lemon twist.

751 GO-FOR-BROKE COCKTAIL

1 ounce dry vermouth
¾ ounce gin
½ teaspoon Cointreau or
  triple sec

1 dash bitters

In a mixing glass half-filled with ice cubes, combine all of the ingredients. Stir well. Strain into a cocktail glass.

752 GRACELAND

1 ounce dry vermouth
1 ounce sweet vermouth
½ ounce Scotch

1 dash bitters
1 lemon twist

In a mixing glass half-filled with ice cubes, combine the dry vermouth, sweet vermouth, Scotch, and bitters. Stir well. Strain into a cocktail glass and garnish with the lemon twist.

753 GREEN GABLES COCKTAIL

Crushed ice
1½ ounces sweet
  vermouth

1 ounce gin
2 teaspoons green
  Chartreuse

In a mixing glass half-filled with crushed ice, combine all of the ingredients. Stir well. Strain into a cocktail glass.

754 HEAD-FOR-THE-HILLS

2 ounces dry vermouth
½ ounce white Curaçao

2 ounces club soda
1 lemon twist

Pour the vermouth, Curaçao, and club soda into an old-fashioned glass almost filled with ice cubes. Stir well and garnish with the lemon twist.

755 HILGERT COCKTAIL

1 ounce dry vermouth
¾ ounce gin
½ teaspoon maraschino
  liqueur

1 teaspoon grapefruit
  juice
1 dash bitters

In a shaker half-filled with ice cubes, combine all of the ingredients. Shake well. Strain into a cocktail glass.

756 JEFF TRACY

1 ounce dry vermouth
1 teaspoon sweet
  vermouth

1 ounce gin
1 ounce cherry brandy
1 maraschino cherry

In a mixing glass half-filled with ice cubes, combine the dry vermouth, sweet vermouth, gin, and cherry brandy. Stir well. Strain into a cocktail glass and garnish with the cherry.

757 JOYCE OF HILLHOUSE

1½ ounces sweet
  vermouth
1 ounce Scotch

1 dash bitters
1 lemon twist

In a mixing glass half-filled with ice cubes, combine the vermouth, Scotch, and bitters. Stir well. Strain into a cocktail glass and garnish with the lemon twist.

758 KAYTEE

1½ ounces dry vermouth
1 ounce dry sherry

½ teaspoon Pernod

In a mixing glass half-filled with ice cubes, combine all of the ingredients. Stir well. Strain into a cocktail glass.

759 KING KENNETH

1½ ounces Campari
½ ounce peach schnapps
1 ounce orange juice

2 teaspoons lemon juice
4 ounces tonic water
1 lemon twist

In a shaker half-filled with ice cubes, combine the Campari, peach schnapps, orange juice, and lemon juice. Shake well. Strain into a collins glass almost filled with ice cubes. Top with the tonic water. Stir well and garnish with the lemon twist.

760 KNOCKOUT COCKTAIL

1 ounce dry vermouth
1 ounce gin
½ ounce anisette

1 teaspoon white crème
de menthe
1 maraschino cherry

In a mixing glass half-filled with ice cubes, combine the vermouth, gin, anisette, and crème de menthe. Stir well. Strain into a cocktail glass and garnish with the cherry.

761 LADY EVELYN

1½ ounces dry vermouth
1 ounce gin

2 teaspoons Cointreau or
triple sec

In a mixing glass half-filled with ice cubes, combine all of the ingredients. Stir well. Strain into a cocktail glass.

762 LADY MADONNA

1½ ounces Dubonnet
Rouge

1 ounce dry vermouth
1 lemon twist

In a mixing glass half-filled with ice cubes, combine the Dubonnet and vermouth. Stir well. Strain into a cocktail glass and garnish with the lemon twist.

763 LEO THE LION

2 ounces dry vermouth
½ ounce brandy

1 teaspoon white crème
de menthe

In a mixing glass half-filled with ice cubes, combine all of the ingredients. Stir well. Strain into a cocktail glass.

764 LILLET COCKTAIL

2 ounces Lillet
½ ounce gin

1 lemon twist

In a mixing glass half-filled with ice cubes, combine the Lillet and gin. Stir well. Strain into a cocktail glass. Garnish with the lemon twist.

765 LYING WITH THE TIGRESS

1½ ounces dry vermouth
1 ounce light rum
¼ teaspoon Rose's lime
   juice

1 dash orange bitters

In a mixing glass half-filled with ice cubes, combine all of the ingredients. Stir well. Strain into a cocktail glass.

766 MAGIQUE

1½ ounces dry vermouth
1 ounce gin

2 teaspoons crème de cassis

In a mixing glass half-filled with ice cubes, combine all of the ingredients. Stir well. Strain into a cocktail glass.

767 MARY'S DELIGHT

1½ ounces sweet
   vermouth

1 ounce brandy
1 dash orange bitters

In a mixing glass half-filled with ice cubes, combine all of the ingredients. Stir well. Strain into a cocktail glass.

768 MATINÉE

1 ounce sweet vermouth
¾ ounce gin
½ ounce green
   Chartreuse

2 tablespoons orange
   juice
1 dash orange bitters

In a shaker half-filled with ice cubes, combine all of the ingredients. Shake well. Strain into a cocktail glass.

769 MAUREEN'S DREAM

1 ounce sweet vermouth
1 ounce dry vermouth

2 teaspoons anisette

In an old-fashioned glass almost filled with ice cubes, combine all of the ingredients. Stir well.

770 MAYFLOWER COCKTAIL

1½ ounces sweet
  vermouth
½ ounce dry vermouth
½ ounce brandy

1 teaspoon Pernod
1 teaspoon Cointreau or
  triple sec
2 dashes orange bitters

In a mixing glass half-filled with ice cubes, combine all of
the ingredients. Stir well. Strain into a cocktail glass.

771 MAYOR BILLY

¾ ounce sweet vermouth
¾ ounce dry vermouth
½ ounce gin

2 teaspoons orange juice
2 dashes orange bitters

In a shaker half-filled with ice cubes, combine all of the
ingredients. Shake well. Strain into a cocktail glass.

772 MERCENARY

2 ounces dry vermouth
½ ounce Armagnac

1 teaspoon green crème
  de menthe

In a mixing glass half-filled with ice cubes, combine all of
the ingredients. Stir well. Strain into a cocktail glass.

773 MOI?

2 ounces dry vermouth
½ ounce gin
2 teaspoons crème de
  cassis

1 ounce lemon juice
4 ounces tonic water
1 lemon wedge

In a shaker half-filled with ice cubes, combine the vermouth, gin, cassis, and lemon juice. Shake well. Strain into
a collins glass almost filled with ice cubes. Top with the
tonic water. Stir well and garnish with the lemon wedge.

774 MUCH FUSS FOR THE CONQUERING HERO

1 ounce sweet vermouth
¾ ounce applejack
2 teaspoons apricot
  brandy

1 teaspoon pineapple
  juice
1 teaspoon lemon juice
2 dashes orange bitters

In a shaker half-filled with ice cubes, combine all of the
ingredients. Shake well. Strain into a cocktail glass.

775 NEGRONI

1 ounce Campari
1 ounce gin

1 ounce sweet vermouth
1 lemon twist

Pour the Campari, gin, and vermouth into an old-fashioned glass almost filled with ice cubes. Stir well and garnish with the lemon twist.

776 PAMMY KAY

1 ounce dry vermouth
½ ounce gin
½ ounce apricot brandy

½ teaspoon lemon juice
½ teaspoon lime juice

In a shaker half-filled with ice cubes, combine all of the ingredients. Shake well. Strain into a cocktail glass.

777 PHOEBE SNOW

2 ounces Dubonnet
  Rouge

1½ ounces brandy
1 teaspoon Pernod

In a mixing glass half-filled with ice cubes, combine all of the ingredients. Stir well. Strain into a cocktail glass.

778 PIGGOT'S PREFERENCE

1½ ounces dry vermouth
½ ounce Southern
  Comfort
2 teaspoons light rum

2 teaspoons Cointreau or
  triple sec
1 dash orange bitters
1 maraschino cherry

In a mixing glass half-filled with ice cubes, combine the vermouth, Southern Comfort, rum, Cointreau, and orange bitters. Stir well. Strain into a cocktail glass. Garnish with the cherry.

779 SACRED MOUNTAIN OF THE PEKINGESE CLOUD GODS

1 ounce dry vermouth
½ ounce Southern Comfort
2 ounces orange juice
2 teaspoons blue Curaçao

Pour the vermouth and Southern Comfort into an old-fashioned glass almost filled with ice cubes. Stir well. Add the orange juice; do not stir. Drop the blue Curaçao into the center of the drink. Add straws and drink from the bottom up.

780 SAME OLD SONG

1 ounce sweet vermouth
½ ounce dry vermouth
1 ounce gin
1 ounce orange juice
1 teaspoon lemon juice
1 dash orange bitters
1 orange slice

In a shaker half-filled with ice cubes, combine the sweet vermouth, dry vermouth, gin, orange juice, lemon juice, and orange bitters. Shake well. Strain into a cocktail glass and garnish with the orange slice.

781 SEETHING JEALOUSY

1 ounce sweet vermouth
½ ounce Scotch
½ ounce cherry brandy
½ ounce orange juice

In a shaker half-filled with ice cubes, combine all of the ingredients. Shake well. Strain into a cocktail glass.

782 SHOOING AWAY THE TRIBES OF THE NIGHT

1 ounce dry vermouth
¾ ounce brandy
½ teaspoon Cointreau or triple sec
¼ teaspoon Ricard
¼ teaspoon cherry brandy
1 dash bitters
1 maraschino cherry
1 orange slice

Pour the vermouth, brandy, Cointreau, Ricard, cherry brandy, and bitters into an old-fashioned glass almost filled with ice cubes. Stir well and garnish with the cherry and the orange slice.

783 STRONG-ARMED CHRIS RETURNS TO THE DEN

1 ounce dry vermouth
1 teaspoon sweet vermouth
¾ ounce white crème de cacao

¾ ounce maraschino liqueur
1 maraschino cherry

In a mixing glass half-filled with ice cubes, combine the dry vermouth, sweet vermouth, crème de cacao, and maraschino liqueur. Stir well. Strain into a cocktail glass. Garnish with the cherry.

784 SWEET NAN

1 ounce sweet vermouth
1 ounce brandy

2 teaspoons Bénédictine

Pour all of the ingredients into an old-fashioned glass almost filled with ice cubes. Stir well.

785 TANNERSWORTH

1 ounce Dubonnet Rouge
½ ounce gin

½ ounce dry vermouth

In a mixing glass half-filled with ice cubes, combine all of the ingredients. Stir well. Strain into a cocktail glass.

786 THANKSGIVING COCKTAIL

1 ounce dry vermouth
¾ ounce gin
¾ ounce apricot brandy

½ teaspoon crème de cassis
½ teaspoon lemon juice

In a shaker half-filled with ice cubes, combine all of the ingredients. Shake well. Strain into a cocktail glass.

787 TRINITY COCKTAIL

1 ounce sweet vermouth
1 ounce dry vermouth

1 ounce gin

In a mixing glass half-filled with ice cubes, combine all of the ingredients. Stir well. Strain into a cocktail glass.

788 TRIPLET COCKTAIL

1 ounce dry vermouth
1 ounce gin
1 ounce peach brandy

2 teaspoons lemon juice
1 maraschino cherry

In a shaker half-filled with ice cubes, combine the vermouth, gin, peach brandy, and lemon juice. Shake well. Strain into a cocktail glass and garnish with the cherry.

789 TRUE TRIXIE

2 ounces Campari
¾ ounce dry vermouth

¾ ounce Cointreau or
triple sec

In a mixing glass half-filled with ice cubes, combine all of the ingredients. Stir well. Strain into an old-fashioned glass almost filled with ice cubes.

790 VERMOUTH CASSIS

2 ounces dry vermouth
2 teaspoons crème de
cassis

1 lemon twist

Pour the vermouth and cassis into a wine goblet with about 4 ice cubes. Stir well and garnish with the lemon twist.

791 VERMOUTH CASSIS TALL

2 ounces dry vermouth
½ ounce crème de cassis

1 lemon twist
4 ounces club soda

Pour the vermouth and cassis into a highball glass almost filled with ice cubes. Top with the club soda. Stir well and garnish with the lemon twist.

792 VERMOUTH COCKTAIL

1½ ounces sweet
vermouth
1½ ounces dry vermouth

2 dashes orange bitters
1 maraschino cherry

In a mixing glass half-filled with ice cubes, combine the sweet vermouth, dry vermouth, and orange bitters. Stir well. Strain into a cocktail glass and garnish with the cherry.

793 WARRIOR

1 ounce sweet vermouth
1 ounce dry vermouth
½ ounce brandy

½ teaspoon Pernod
½ teaspoon Cointreau or
   triple sec

In a mixing glass half-filled with ice cubes, combine all of the ingredients. Stir well. Strain into a cocktail glass.

794 WEDDING BELL COCKTAIL

1 ounce Dubonnet Rouge
¾ ounce gin
2 teaspoons cherry
   brandy

1 tablespoon orange juice
1 dash orange bitters

In a shaker half-filled with ice cubes, combine all of the ingredients. Shake well. Strain into a cocktail glass.

795 WESTERMAN SINGS THE BLUES

1 ounce dry vermouth
½ ounce gin

1 teaspoon Pernod
1 orange slice

In a mixing glass half-filled with ice cubes, combine the vermouth, gin, and Pernod. Stir well. Strain into a cocktail glass and garnish with the orange slice.

796 WILFRED'S WEATHER

1 ounce dry vermouth
¾ ounce gin

½ teaspoon Ricard
1 dash bitters

In a mixing glass half-filled with ice cubes, combine all of the ingredients. Stir well. Strain into a cocktail glass.

797 WYSOOSLER

1 ounce sweet vermouth
¾ ounce gin
¾ ounce green
   Chartreuse

2 dashes orange bitters

In a mixing glass half-filled with ice cubes, combine all of the ingredients. Stir well. Strain into a cocktail glass.

12 · CORDIALS

In America, a cordial, usually served as an after-dinner drink, is what the rest of the world calls a liqueur—a sweetened liquor. In most other English-speaking countries, cordials are concentrated fruit juices with no alcoholic content.

Cordials form the base of some well-known cocktails: the Pink Squirrel, the Apricot Sour, and the Grasshopper. These sweetened liquors were first known to the French as *liqueurs de dessert*, and they are probably as old as any hill you may care to mention. They were originally concocted by the ancient alchemists as potions for medicinal purposes. Infusing alcohol with remedial herbs, spices, fruits, and barks was a good way of preserving their medicinal qualities.

Right up until the end of the eighteenth century, people concocted their own liqueurs at home, adding sugar and fruits from their gardens to brandy or whatever other liquor was available.

PRODUCTION

Cordials can be divided into two basic categories: *fruit cordials*, which can take on the color of the fruit (cherry and blackberry brandy), but may be colorless if made only with the peel or seed of the fruit (triple sec); *plant cordials*, which are generally colorless (anisette), but can take on the color of one of the herbs and roots used in a blend (Bénédictine and Chartreuse).

The rule governing cordial states that a cordial *must* contain at least 2½ percent sugar of any type. In fact, most of them contain 30 to 40 percent sugar. Cordials are made from any base spirit—rum, gin, vodka, or the like—that is then flavored with fruit, roots, herbs, bark, seeds, flowers, peels, or juices. The following methods of introducing these flavors differ from one to another and are usually governed by how much time and money the manufacturer wants to spend.

Maceration: Maceration is similar to infusion and simply means that the flavoring agent is immersed in a base spirit until the flavor is absorbed by that spirit. This process can take as long as a year and is used to flavor liquors with ingredients that would lose flavor if heated.

Infusion: In an infusion, the flavoring agent is steeped in a heated base liquor, and the temperature is maintained for several days. The resultant liqueur is very flavorful and much more inexpensive to produce than macerated liqueurs.

Percolation: This method of flavoring liqueurs may employ hot or cold techniques. The flavoring agent is placed in a sievelike container, and the liquor is then either bubbled through it for weeks at a time or boiled underneath it, so that the vapors rise, collect the flavors, and then condense back into the liquor.

Distillation: This method requires an infused liquor to be redistilled, usually under a vacuum in a pot still.

TYPES OF CORDIALS

A list of all known cordials, or liqueurs, with explanations of their contents could take up a book in itself. Here are a few of the better-known ones, whose names may require explanation.

AMARETTO Usually made in Italy from apricot stones, which produce an almond flavor.

ANIS OR ANISETTE Flavored with aniseed, which imparts a licorice flavor. Replaces the long-banned absinthe.

BENEDICTINE Flavored with 27 herbs, plants, and peels.

CHARTREUSE Flavored with 130 herbs and spices.

COINTREAU A dry orange liqueur that is a form of Curaçao.

CREME DE BANANES Uses artificial banana flavoring.

CREME DE CACAO Flavored with vanilla and cacao (cocoa) beans.

CREME DE CASSIS Flavored with blackcurrants.

CREME DE MENTHE Usually made from peppermint. The green and white varieties differ only in color.

CREME DE NOYAUX Made from fruit stones, producing an almond flavor.

CURAÇAO Flavored with orange peel.

DANZIG GOLDWASSER Flavored with caraway and aniseed with real gold flakes added.

FRANGELICO Flavored with hazelnut berries and herbs.

GALLIANO Flavored with herbs, roots, and spices.

GRAND MARNIER Orange peel steeped in Cognac; an elegant, richer form of Curaçao.

IRISH MIST Flavored with honey and herbs.

KAHLUA Flavored with coffee.

KUMMEL Flavored with caraway seeds.

MARASCHINO Flavored with Dalmatian Marasca cherries.

MALIBU Jamaican rum flavored with coconut.

MIDORI Flavored with Japanese melons.

OUZO Greek aniseed-flavored liqueur; rather drier than anisette.

ROCK AND RYE Rye whiskey flavored with rock candy syrup and fruits.

SAMBUCA Flavored with elderbush, giving a licorice flavor.

SLOE GIN Flavored with sloe berries from the blackthorn bush.

STREGA Flavored with over 70 herbs and barks.

TIA MARIA Flavored with coffee and spices.

TRIPLE SEC A highly refined form of Curaçao.

AMARETTO

798 ALABAMA SLAMMER

1½ ounces amaretto
1 ounce Southern
Comfort

½ ounce sloe gin
½ ounce lemon juice

In a shaker half-filled with ice cubes, combine all of the
ingredients. Shake well. Strain into an old-fashioned glass
almost filled with ice cubes.

799 AMARETTO SOUR

2 ounces amaretto
1 ounce lemon juice
½ teaspoon superfine
sugar

1 orange slice
1 maraschino cherry

In a shaker half-filled with ice cubes combine the amaretto,
lemon juice, and sugar. Shake well. Strain into a sour glass.
Garnish with the orange slice and the cherry.

800 BOCCIE BALL

2 ounces amaretto   5 ounces orange juice

Pour the amaretto and orange juice into a highball glass
almost filled with ice cubes. Stir well.

801 PINK PANTHER

1 ounce amaretto
½ ounce vodka

1 teaspoon grenadine
2 ounces light cream

In a shaker half-filled with ice cubes, combine all of the
ingredients. Shake well. Strain into a cocktail glass.

802 TOASTED ALMOND

1½ ounces amaretto
1 ounce Kahlúa

2 ounces light cream

In a shaker half-filled with ice cubes, combine all of the
ingredients. Shake well. Strain into an old-fashioned glass
almost filled with ice cubes.

APPLEJACK

803 JACK ROSE

2 ounces applejack
1 ounce lemon juice

1 teaspoon grenadine

In a shaker half-filled with ice cubes, combine all of the ingredients. Shake well. Strain into a cocktail glass.

APRICOT BRANDY

804 A.B.C.

1½ ounces apricot
  brandy

1 ounce Scotch
½ ounce sweet vermouth

In a mixing glass half-filled with ice cubes, combine all of the ingredients. Stir well. Strain into a cocktail glass.

805 APRICOT FIZZ

2½ ounces apricot
  brandy
1 ounce lemon juice

½ teaspoon superfine
  sugar
4 ounces club soda

In a shaker half-filled with ice cubes, combine the apricot brandy, lemon juice, and sugar. Shake well. Strain into a collins glass almost filled with ice cubes. Add the club soda. Stir well.

806 APRICOT SOUR

2 ounces apricot brandy
1 ounce lemon juice
½ teaspoon superfine
  sugar

1 orange slice
1 maraschino cherry

In a shaker half-filled with ice cubes, combine the apricot brandy, lemon juice, and sugar. Shake well. Strain into a sour glass. Garnish with the orange slice and the cherry.

807 ON THE SQUARE

1 ounce apricot brandy   ½ ounce Calvados
½ ounce gin

In a mixing glass half-filled with ice cubes, combine all of
the ingredients. Stir well. Strain into a cocktail glass.

808 PARADISE

1½ ounces apricot   1 ounce orange juice
  brandy   ½ teaspoon sweet
½ ounce gin   vermouth

In a mixing glass half-filled with ice cubes, combine all of
the ingredients. Shake well. Strain into a cocktail glass.

BAILEY'S IRISH CREAM

809 BLACKPOOL TOWER

2 ounces Bailey's Irish   ¾ ounce apricot brandy
  Cream   1 teaspoon gin

In a shaker half-filled with ice cubes, combine all of the
ingredients. Shake well. Strain into a cocktail glass.

810 CHERRY KISS

1 ounce Bailey's Irish   1 ounce Chambord
  Cream

Pour the Bailey's into a pousse café glass. Pouring slowly
and carefully over the back of a teaspoon, float the Chambord on top of the Bailey's.

811 DIRTY GIRL SCOUT

1 ounce Bailey's Irish   1 ounce vodka
  Cream   1 teaspoon green crème
1 ounce Kahlúa   de menthe

In a shaker half-filled with ice cubes, combine all of the
ingredients. Shake well. Strain into an old-fashioned glass
almost filled with ice cubes.

812 IRISH FLAG

1 ounce green crème de menthe
1 ounce Bailey's Irish Cream

1 ounce brandy

Pour the crème de menthe into a pousse café glass. Pouring slowly and carefully over the back of a teaspoon, float the Irish cream on the crème de menthe and then the brandy on top of the Irish cream.

813 MORNING WITH THE LEPRECHAUNS

1½ ounces Bailey's Irish Cream
1 ounce Irish whiskey
2 teaspoons cherry brandy

3 ounces cold strong coffee
Crushed ice

Pour all of the ingredients into a highball glass almost filled with crushed ice. Stir well.

B & B

814 B & B STINGER

2½ ounces B & B
½ ounce white crème de menthe

In a mixing glass half-filled with ice cubes, combine the B & B and crème de menthe. Stir well. Strain into a cocktail glass.

BENEDICTINE

815 SILENT MONK

1 ounce Bénédictine
½ ounce Cointreau or triple sec

1 ounce light cream

In a shaker half-filled with ice cubes, combine all of the ingredients. Shake well. Strain into a cocktail glass.

BLUE CURAÇAO

816 BARROW BLUES

1 ounce blue Curaçao
½ ounce light rum
½ ounce añejo rum

1½ ounces pineapple
   juice
1 teaspoon coconut cream

In a shaker half-filled with ice cubes, combine all of the ingredients. Shake well. Strain into an old-fashioned glass almost filled with ice cubes.

CHARTREUSE

817 GOLDEN FLEECE

1½ ounces yellow
   Chartreuse

1 ounce Danzig
   Goldwasser

In a mixing glass half-filled with ice cubes, combine both ingredients. Stir well. Strain into a cocktail glass.

CHERRY BRANDY

818 CHERRIES FROM HEAVEN

1½ ounces cherry brandy
1 ounce lemon juice
1 dash bitters

4 ounces tonic water
1 lime wedge

In a shaker half-filled with ice cubes, combine the cherry brandy, lemon juice, and bitters. Shake well. Strain into a highball glass almost filled with ice cubes. Top with the tonic water. Stir well and garnish with the lime wedge.

819 CHERRY FLASH COLA

1 ounce cherry brandy
½ ounce maraschino
liqueur

4 ounces cola
1 maraschino cherry

Pour the cherry brandy, maraschino liqueur, and cola into a highball glass almost filled with ice cubes. Stir well and garnish with the cherry.

COINTREAU

820 DUVAL

2 ounces Cointreau   1 ounce Sambuca

In a mixing glass half-filled with ice cubes, combine both of the ingredients. Stir well. Strain into a cocktail glass.

CREME DE BANANES

821 BANANARAMA

1 ounce crème de
bananes
½ ounce Cointreau or
triple sec

1 dash bitters
1 ounce light cream

In a shaker half-filled with ice cubes, combine all of the ingredients. Shake well. Strain into a cocktail glass.

822 BANSHEE

1½ ounces crème de
bananes
1 ounce white crème de
cacao

1 ounce light cream

In a shaker half-filled with ice cubes, combine all of the ingredients. Shake well. Strain into a cocktail glass.

CREME DE CACAO

823 GOLDEN CADILLAC

1½ ounces white crème
  de cacao

¾ ounce Galliano
1 ounce light cream

In a shaker half-filled with ice cubes, combine all of the ingredients. Shake well. Strain into a cocktail glass.

824 SLAMDANCER

1 ounce white crème de
  cacao
½ ounce dark crème de
  cacao

½ ounce Kahlúa
2 teaspoons peppermint
  schnapps
1 ounce light cream

In a shaker half-filled with ice cubes, combine all of the ingredients. Shake well. Strain into a cocktail glass.

CREME DE MENTHE

825 CRÈME DE MENTHE FRAPPE

Crushed ice
2 ounces green crème de
  menthe

Fill a pousse café glass with crushed ice and simply pour the crème de menthe into the glass. Using the same method, a frappe may be made from any cordial.

826 DIANA

Crushed ice
2 ounces white crème de
  menthe

½ ounce brandy

Fill a snifter with crushed ice and pour the crème de menthe into the glass. Pouring slowly and carefully over the back of a teaspoon, float the brandy on the crème de menthe.

827 GRASSHOPPER

1 ounce green crème de menthe
1 ounce white crème de cacao
1 ounce light cream

In a shaker half-filled with ice cubes, combine all of the ingredients. Shake well. Strain into a cocktail glass.

CREME DE NOYAUX

828 PINK SQUIRREL

1½ ounces crème de noyaux
½ ounce white crème de cacao
1 ounce light cream

In a shaker half-filled with ice cubes, combine all of the ingredients. Shake well. Strain into a cocktail glass.

DRAMBUIE

829 ROGER SWIMS A MILE

1½ ounces Drambuie
½ ounce blended whiskey
½ ounce dry vermouth
1 lemon twist

In a mixing glass half-filled with ice cubes, combine the Drambuie, whiskey, and vermouth. Stir well. Strain into a cocktail glass. Garnish with the lemon twist.

FRANGELICO

830 END OF MY ROPE

1½ ounces Frangelico
2 teaspoons crème de bananes
1 ounce pineapple juice
1 dash bitters

In a shaker half-filled with ice cubes, combine all of the ingredients. Shake well. Strain into a cocktail glass.

831 FRIAR TUCK

1½ ounces Frangelico
2 teaspoons brandy
1 ounce lemon juice

1 teaspoon grenadine
1 maraschino cherry

In a shaker half-filled with ice cubes, combine the Frangelico, brandy, lemon juice, and grenadine. Shake well. Strain into a cocktail glass. Garnish with the cherry.

GALLIANO

832 GOLDEN DREAM

1½ ounces Galliano
½ ounce Cointreau or
triple sec

½ ounce orange juice
½ ounce light cream

In a shaker half-filled with ice cubes, combine all of the ingredients. Shake well. Strain into a cocktail glass.

GRAND MARNIER

833 B-52

1 ounce Grand Marnier
¾ ounce Kahlúa

½ ounce Bailey's Irish
Cream

In a shaker half-filled with ice cubes, combine all of the ingredients. Shake well. Strain into a cocktail glass.

834 CHUNNEL COCKTAIL

1½ ounces Grand Marnier
1 ounce gin

½ ounce sweet vermouth
1 dash bitters

In a mixing glass half-filled with ice cubes, combine all of the ingredients. Stir well. Strain into a cocktail glass.

KAHLUA

835 COFFEE STICK

1½ ounces Kahlúa   1 ounce heavy cream
½ ounce Sambuca

In a shaker half-filled with ice cubes, combine all of the ingredients. Shake well. Strain into a cocktail glass.

836 DOUGLAS TOWN

2 ounces Kahlúa   ½ ounce lime juice
1 ounce tequila

In a shaker half-filled with ice cubes, combine all of the ingredients. Shake well. Strain into a cocktail glass.

837 KING ALPHONSE

2½ ounces Kahlúa   ½ ounce heavy cream

Pour the Kahlúa into a pousse café glass. Pour the cream slowly and carefully over the back of a teaspoon so that it floats on top of the Kahlúa.

838 MUDDY RIVER

2½ ounces Kahlúa   1½ ounces light cream

In a shaker half-filled with ice cubes, combine the Kahlúa and cream. Shake well. Strain into a cocktail glass.

839 ROOT BEER

1 ounce Kahlúa   ½ teaspoon superfine
1 ounce Galliano   sugar
1 ounce lemon juice   3 ounces cola

In a shaker half-filled with ice cubes, combine the Kahlúa, Galliano, lemon juice, and sugar. Shake well. Strain into a highball glass almost filled with ice cubes. Top with the cola. Stir well. Yes, it tastes like root beer.

840 SOMBRERO

2 ounces Kahlúa   2 ounces light cream

In a shaker half-filled with ice cubes, combine the Kahlúa and cream. Shake well. Strain into a cocktail glass.

841 WITCH'S TIT

2½ ounces Kahlúa   ½ maraschino cherry
½ ounce heavy cream

Pour the Kahlú into a pousse café glass. Pour the cream slowly and carefully over the back of a teaspoon so that it floats on top of the Kahlúa. Place the cherry in the center of the cream.

MELON LIQUEUR (MIDORI)

842 BELLE MELON

1½ ounces melon liqueur   1 ounce light cream
½ ounce vodka

In a shaker half-filled with ice cubes, combine all of the ingredients. Shake well. Strain into a cocktail glass.

843 FOCAL POINT

1½ ounces melon liqueur   ½ ounce lemon juice
1 ounce light rum   1 teaspoon grenadine

In a shaker half-filled with ice cubes, combine the melon liqueur, rum, and lemon juice. Shake well. Strain into a cocktail glass. Drop the grenadine into the center of the drink.

844 GREEN GODDESS

1½ ounces melon liqueur   4 ounces lemon-lime
1 ounce Scotch   soda
1 teaspoon dry vermouth

Pour all of the ingredients into a highball glass almost filled with ice cubes. Stir well.

845 MAN IN THE MELON

1½ ounces melon liqueur
½ ounce vodka
½ ounce Cointreau or
  triple sec

2 ounces lemon-lime
  soda
2 ounces club soda
1 lime wedge

Pour the melon liqueur, vodka, Cointreau, lemon-lime soda, and club soda into a highball glass almost filled with ice cubes. Stir well and garnish with the lime wedge.

846 MELON BALL

1 ounce melon liqueur
1 ounce vodka

3 ounces pineapple juice

Pour all of the ingredients into a highball glass almost filled with ice cubes. Stir well.

PEPPERMINT SCHNAPPS

847 APOCALYPSE

1 ounce peppermint
  schnapps
¾ ounce Kahlúa

½ ounce bourbon
½ ounce vodka

In a mixing glass half-filled with ice cubes, combine all of the ingredients. Stir well. Strain into a cocktail glass.

848 BLUE GLORY

2 ounces peppermint
  schnapps
½ ounce blue Curaçao

5 ounces lemon-lime
  soda

Pour all of the ingredients into a highball glass almost filled with ice cubes. Stir well.

849 PEPPERMINT TWIST

1 ounce peppermint
  schnapps
1 ounce Kahlúa

½ ounce dark crème de
  cacao

In a shaker half-filled with ice cubes, combine all of the ingredients. Shake well. Strain into a cocktail glass.

POUSSE CAFES

850 POUSSE CAFÉ

½ ounce grenadine
½ ounce yellow
  Chartreuse
½ ounce crème de cassis
½ ounce white crème de
  menthe

½ ounce green
  Chartreuse
½ ounce brandy

Starting with the grenadine and adding each ingredient in the order given, pour the liquors slowly and carefully over the back of a teaspoon into a pousse café glass so that each one floats on top of the last one in layers.

851 POUSSE CAFÉ À LA FRANCAISE

½ ounce green
  Chartreuse
½ ounce maraschino
  liqueur

½ ounce cherry brandy
½ ounce kümmel

Starting with the Chartreuse and adding each ingredient in the order given, pour the liquors slowly and carefully over the back of a teaspoon into a pousse café glass so that each one floats on top of the last one in layers.

852 POUSSE CAFÉ STANDISH

½ ounce grenadine
½ ounce white crème de
  menthe

½ ounce Galliano
½ ounce kümmel
½ ounce brandy

Starting with the grenadine and adding each ingredient in the order given, pour the liquors slowly and carefully over the back of a teaspoon into a pousse café glass so that each one floats on top of the last one in layers.

SAMBUCA

853 FERRIS WHEEL

1½ ounces Sambuca   1 lemon twist
1 ounce brandy

In a mixing glass half-filled with ice cubes, combine the Sambuca and brandy. Stir well. Strain into a cocktail glass. Garnish with the lemon twist.

854 SAMBUCA STRAIGHT

2 ounces Sambuca   3 coffee beans

Pour the Sambuca into a brandy snifter and float the coffee beans on top. It is important always to use an odd number of coffee beans, as this is an Italian tradition that shows the guest is welcome. An even number of beans denotes an unwelcome guest.

855 SAMSON

½ ounce black Sambuca   ½ ounce amaretto
  (Opal Nera)   1½ ounces light cream
½ ounce blackberry
  brandy

In a shaker half-filled with ice cubes, combine all of the ingredients. Shake well. Strain into a cocktail glass.

SLOE GIN

856 SLOE GIN FIZZ

2½ ounces sloe gin   4 ounces club soda
1 ounce lemon juice
½ teaspoon superfine
  sugar

In a shaker half-filled with ice cubes, combine the sloe gin, lemon juice, and sugar. Shake well. Strain into a collins glass almost filled with ice cubes. Add the club soda. Stir well.

857 SLOE GIN FLIP

2 ounces sloe gin
1 egg
½ teaspoon superfine
  sugar

½ ounce light cream
⅛ teaspoon grated
  nutmeg

In a shaker half-filled with ice cubes combine the sloe gin, egg, sugar, and cream. Shake well. Strain into a sour glass and garnish with the nutmeg.

858 SLOEHAND JACKSON

1½ ounces sloe gin
½ ounce gin
½ ounce vodka

1 ounce orange juice
½ ounce lemon juice
1 teaspoon grenadine

In a shaker half-filled with ice cubes, combine all of the ingredients. Shake well. Strain into a highball glass almost filled with ice cubes.

SOUTHERN COMFORT

859 BRITISH COMFORT

1½ ounces Southern
  Comfort
½ ounce gin

½ ounce lemon juice
1 ounce orange juice

In a shaker half-filled with ice cubes, combine all of the ingredients. Shake well. Strain into a cocktail glass.

860 SOUTHERN COMFORT MANHATTAN

2 ounces Southern
  Comfort
½ ounce sweet vermouth

3 dashes bitters
1 maraschino cherry

In a mixing glass half-filled with ice cubes, combine the Southern Comfort, vermouth, and bitters. Stir well. Strain into a cocktail glass. Garnish with the cherry.

13 · WINE DRINKS

It is not known when wine was first made, although the date is sure to have been very early in the career of *Homo sapiens*. In addition to the numerous references to wine made in the Old Testament and by the ancient Greeks over 3,000 years ago, there is also evidence, in the form of grape skins and pips, that suggests wine was made by prehistoric man. Pleasure, it seems, came early in the life of our species.

Wine can be divided into four categories: still, sparkling, fortified, and aromatized. Since aromatized wines are dealt with in the Aperitifs chapter, this section will cover the other three. Still wines can themselves be divided into distinct types: To begin with, there is the obvious red, white, and rosé, or blush. Then consider whether the wine is dry, off-dry (or semidry), or sweet. For purposes of mixing, we are concerned here with dry wine, which may actually give the illusion of sweetness if it has a lot of fruitiness to it.

If you're looking for a great bottle of Bordeaux or Cabernet Sauvignon to serve at your dinner party on Saturday night, I refer you to one of the excellent references specializing on fine wines listed in my bibliography at the end of this book. For the bar, I suggest searching your local liquor stores for good quality at a budget price. When it's going to be a large party, don't turn up your nose at jug wines. California, Spain, France, and Italy make some quite respectable wines in quantity. When the wine is to be mixed with other flavorings and liquors, the subtleties of a fine vintage will be lost.

The same goes for sparkling wines. A simple Champagne Cocktail does taste best with an excellent bubbly. But when you begin mixing in a number of other flavors, go for good value. Many countries—and in the case of the United States, states—make fine sparkling wines. Experiment with labels from California, Spain, Italy, and France until you find an inexpensive sparkling wine that has the qualities you enjoy.

Fortified wines include Madeira, port, and sherry. Again, quality and price vary widely, and a fabulously expensive vintage port will be lost in a brew of beverages. Try to find a reliable brand that gives you respectable—but not necessarily exceptional—quality at a decent price.

Since I've told you how other liquors are made, you can read on to learn something about the production of these three types of wine, or skip to page 263 to get right to the recipes.

PRODUCTION

STILL WINE

1. Still wine is simply ordinary noncarbonated wine, as opposed to Champagne and other sparkling wines. The grapes are picked and taken to a pressing house, where they are mechanically or manually pressed and de-stemmed, producing a "must" that is placed in a fermenting vat.
2. If white wine is being made, the skins are removed from the must. Red wines take their color from the grape skins, which also release tannin into the wine. Rosé wines are made by leaving the skins in the must for a short period, to impart some color.

3. The fermentation vats are sealed to prevent oxidization, and fermentation begins utilizing either natural yeast that is present on the grapes or yeast added by the winemaker.

4. Fermentation stops when the yeast dies, that is, when all of the sugar has been utilized by the yeast. In the case of sweet wines, however, some sugar remains in the wine after the yeast dies.

5. The wine is then stored in huge wooden or stainless steel vats, to age and settle. After about six months the wine is racked, that is, drawn off into fresh wooden casks, leaving behind a residue known as the lees.

6. The wine is racked three times during the next year. After the final racking the wine is left to age in wooden casks for periods that differ from wine to wine, winemaker to winemaker.

7. The wine is bottled and shipped or stored for further aging.

CHAMPAGNE

1. The red or white grapes are harvested when fully ripe and taken to pressing houses, where they are pressed twice. The resultant juice, called the *cuvée*, is used only for the best Champagnes.

2. The *cuvée* is stored at a constant temperature while it undergoes its first fermentation. The fermented wine is drawn off into fresh casks, leaving the lees behind, and is chilled to remove bitartrates.

3. After a few months the wine is pumped into blending vats, where it is combined with sugar and yeast to conform with its maker's style. The wine is then bottled, corked, and capped with metal caps similar to those on a beer bottle.

4. The bottles are stored on their sides, in special racks located in chalk caves. Here, the wine undergoes a secondary fermentation due to the added yeast and sugar.

5. During this secondary fermentation sediment appears in the bottle. To collect it and prevent its marring the wine, the bottles are gradually tilted and turned so that the sediment falls onto the bottom of the cork.

6. The neck of the bottle is frozen and the metal cup removed. The cork explodes from the bottle, taking the frozen sediment with it. Sweetened mature wine is added to the bottle, and it is recorked for shipping or storage.

FORTIFIED WINE

Quite simply, this term applies to wine that has been fortified with brandy. Since each type of fortified wine differs from the next, I will briefly describe each of the main varieties.

MADEIRA

Made in Madeira, a tiny island off the coast of Portugal, Madeira is made from fermented grape juice that is fortified with locally produced brandy and then stored at temperatures of up to 140°F for three to six months.

PORT

From the Douro region of Portugal, port is made by adding brandy to wine that is still in the process of fermentation. This halts the process, retaining the sugar not yet used by the yeast and resulting in a sweet fortified wine.

Vintage Port is port that the winemaker decides is good enough to call *vintage*. It must be bottled within two years and should then be aged in the bottle for between 8 and 20 years. These ports have specially treated corks that will not deteriorate quickly, since the bottles are laid down on their sides.

Tawny Port is aged in casks and is repeatedly "fined," that is, clarified by using substances such as egg whites to collect sediment that is suspended in the liquid. This process also takes some of the color out of the port; hence, the longer it is aged, the paler (or tawnier) and drier it becomes.

Ruby Port is not aged for as long as the tawny. It retains much of its original color, fruitiness, and full body.

White Port is made only from white grapes, but it is aged in wooden casks like the ruby and tawny ports and is a drier wine than its sisters.

SHERRY

The word *sherry* is simply an Anglicized version of Jerez, the town around which sherry is produced in the Cadiz region of Spain. Wine is produced from local grapes that are fermented and aged. The wine is then drawn off into casks that are not filled to capacity. At this stage a yeast scum, known as *flor*, should appear on the sherry. The scum is produced by a local, airborne yeast that sometimes develops and sometimes doesn't—it's totally up to Mother Nature. The amount of *flor* that develops will indicate to the winemaker which type of sherry he should produce. At this point he can add the brandy that fortifies the sherry.

Fino (pale, light, and dry) sherry is produced when the scum develops fully.

Manzanilla (dry and crisp) sherry is a fino type that has been aged in the coastal town of Sanlucar de Barrameda.

Amontillado (dry and nutty) sherry results when the *flor* develops only partially.

Oloroso (dark, heavy-bodied, and usually sweetened for export) sherry is produced when the *flor* does not develop at all. Extra brandy is added if the *flor* doesn't look like it will develop, ensuring a batch of oloroso.

Amoroso sherry, also known as cream or brown sherry (sweet), is an oloroso type with sweet wine added.

STORAGE OF WINES

Any white wine—still or sparkling—can be stored unopened in a refrigerator for up to a few months. When storing red wine or white wine for longer periods, however, certain standards should be followed:

Wine should ideally be stored in a dark place at a temperature of no lower than 50° to 55°F. As a general rule the temperature in a wine-storage area should never exceed more than 70°F for wines that will be stored up to 5 years, 65°F if the wine is to be stored for up to 15 years, and 60°F for any period exceeding 15 years.

Humidity in a wine storage area should be kept at around 50 percent in order to prevent cork deterioration and mustiness.

Still and sparkling wines should be stored on their sides in order to keep the corks moist. This prevents air from entering the bottle and, in the case of sparkling wines, gas from escaping.

Except for vintage port, which is specially corked, fortified wines should be kept upright since their high alcohol content can damage the cork.

Once the bottle is opened . . .

HOW TO SERVE WINE

TEMPERATURES

The first rule regarding wine temperature is that wine should be drunk at whatever temperature pleases you most. Having said that, I will now tell you the generally accepted norms of wine temperatures.

White wines should be chilled to between 40° and 50°F. Red wines and fortified wines should be served at room temperature, between 63° and 66°F.

OPENING THE BOTTLE

When selecting a corkscrew, use the type that makes you feel most comfortable. Once a bottle of fine wine is opened it should be drunk immediately. When using cheaper bottles or jug wine for mixed drinks, it is not unheard of to keep an opened bottle for up to a week in the refrigerator, although you should check it, like a good host, before serving. Here's the proper way to open a corked bottle of wine:

1. Remove the foil covering from the neck of the bottle by cutting it with a knife right below the bulge on the neck of the bottle.
2. Wipe off the neck of the bottle to remove any mold that may have developed between the foil and the bottle.
3. Remove the cork gently and smoothly. If you jerk the bottle you may disturb sediment in the wine.
4. After removing the cork wipe the neck again, both inside and out.

For bar wines, especially jugs, you will often find that all you have to do is to unscrew the top.

For sparkling wines:

1. Untwist the wire located on the neck of the bottle and remove it along with the cage that it forms over the cork and the foil that covers the cage.
2. Immediately cover the cork with your thumb to prevent it from flying out.
3. Hold the bottle at a 45-degree angle away from your face and not pointing toward any guest. Serious accidents have occurred with flying corks.
4. Twist the bottle with one hand while holding the cork with the other. The cork should pop out in your hand, not explode to the far reaches of the room.
5. Keep the bottle at the 45-degree angle for a few seconds to help prevent the wine from gushing out of the bottle.
6. Wipe the neck of the bottle, inside and out.

POURING WINE

It could be argued that wine is best enjoyed glugged straight from the bottle while sitting on the ground outside Notre Dame with a loaf of bread and a hunk of good

Gruyère. However, if you wish to follow some basic rules of wine etiquette, they are:

1. Wine should be sampled first by the host. If, after a few seconds, he is not writhing on the floor, the guests may be served. Actually the custom of wine being tasted by the host first was originally to prove to his guests that he was not trying to poison them, a popular practice in the Middle Ages. These days, of course, the host takes a sip from his glass, which he should fill only about one-quarter full, to ensure that the wine is in good condition before serving his guests.

2. The wine can then be poured, from the right side of the guest, to fill about one-third to one-half of the glass. When pouring, the glass should remain on the table. Do not pick it up to bring it to the bottle.

3. The bottle should be twisted slightly after pouring each glass so that the drop of wine lingering on the rim of the bottle coats the rim instead of dropping into the lap of the guest as the bottle is removed.

4. Chilled wines may be kept cold in a wine bucket filled with ice and water. Drape a napkin around the neck of the bottle so that it can be wiped free of dripping water when it is removed for pouring.

5. When pouring sparkling wines, first pour enough wine into the glass so that the froth reaches the top, allow the froth to subside, and then fill the glass.

861 ADONIS COCKTAIL

2 ounces dry sherry   1 dash orange bitters
½ ounce sweet vermouth

In a mixing glass half-filled with ice cubes, combine all of the ingredients. Stir well. Strain into a cocktail glass.

862 ANDALUSIA

2 ounces dry sherry   ½ ounce brandy
½ ounce light rum

In a mixing glass half-filled with ice cubes, combine all of the ingredients. Stir well. Strain into a cocktail glass.

863 BAMBOO

2 ounces cream sherry
½ ounce sweet vermouth

1 ounce lemon juice

In a shaker half-filled with ice cubes, combine all of the ingredients. Shake well. Strain into a cocktail glass.

864 BELLINI

2 ounces peach nectar
½ ounce lemon juice
1 teaspoon grenadine

4 ounces chilled sparkling wine or Champagne

Pour the peach nectar, lemon juice, and grenadine into a Champagne flute. Add the Champagne. Stir well.

865 BETSY ROSS 2

1½ ounces port
1 ounce brandy

2 teaspoons Cointreau or triple sec

In a mixing glass half-filled with ice cubes, combine all of the ingredients. Stir well. Strain into a cocktail glass.

866 BISHOP

3 ounces red wine
1 ounce lemon juice
1½ ounces orange juice

1 teaspoon superfine sugar
1 orange slice

In a shaker half-filled with ice cubes, combine the red wine, lemon juice, orange juice, and sugar. Shake well. Strain into a highball glass almost filled with ice cubes. Garnish with the orange slice.

BOSOM CARESSER
See Brandy, page 39.

867 BUCK'S FIZZ

5 ounces Champagne or sparkling wine
½ ounce Cointreau or triple sec

1 ounce orange juice
½ teaspoon grenadine
1 orange slice

Pour the Champagne, Cointreau, and orange juice into a

Champagne flute. Drop the grenadine into the center of the drink. Stir well. Garnish with the orange slice.

868 CHAMPAGNE COCKTAIL

1 teaspoon granulated
  sugar

3 dashes bitters
6 ounces Champagne

Put the sugar in the bottom of a Champagne flute and soak it with the bitters. Top with the Champagne.

869 CHAMPAGNE FIZZ

1½ ounces gin
1 ounce lemon juice
1 teaspoon superfine
  sugar

3 ounces chilled
  Champagne

In a shaker half-filled with ice cubes combine the gin, lemon juice, and sugar. Shake well. Strain into a Champagne flute. Add the Champagne.

870 CHAMPAGNE JULEP

6 mint leaves
1 teaspoon superfine
  sugar

2 ounces bourbon
4 ounces Champagne

In a mixing glass, combine 4 of the mint leaves with the sugar and a few drops of water. Muddle well. Add the bourbon. Stir well. Strain into a collins glass. Add ice cubes and the Champagne. Garnish with the remaining mint leaves.

871 CLARET COBBLER

1 teaspoon superfine
  sugar
3 ounces club soda
Crushed ice
2½ ounces claret (dry red
  wine)

1 maraschino cherry
1 orange slice
1 lemon slice

In an old-fashioned glass, dissolve the sugar in the club soda. Add crushed ice until the glass is almost full. Add the claret. Stir well. Garnish with the cherry, orange slice, and lemon slice.

872 CREAM SHERRY COBBLER

1 teaspoon superfine sugar	2½ ounces cream sherry
3 ounces club soda	1 maraschino cherry
Crushed ice	1 orange slice
	1 lemon slice

In an old-fashioned glass, dissolve the sugar in the club soda. Add crushed ice until the glass is almost full. Add the sherry. Stir well. Garnish with the cherry, orange slice, and lemon slice.

873 CREAM SHERRY FLIP

2½ ounces cream sherry	1 teaspoon light cream
1 whole egg	⅛ teaspoon grated nutmeg
1 teaspoon superfine sugar	

In a shaker half-filled with ice cubes, combine the sherry, egg, sugar, and cream. Shake well. Strain into a sour glass and garnish with the nutmeg.

874 CREAM SHERRY SANGAREE

1 teaspoon superfine sugar	½ ounce Bénédictine
2 teaspoons water	1 lemon twist
2 ounces cream sherry	⅛ teaspoon grated nutmeg
Crushed ice	⅛ teaspoon ground cinnamon
2½ ounces club soda	

In a highball glass, dissolve the sugar in the water and sherry. Almost fill the glass with crushed ice and add the club soda. Float the Bénédictine on top. Garnish with the lemon twist and a dusting of nutmeg and cinnamon.

875 FEROCIOUS FLIP

1½ ounces brandy	½ ounce light cream
1 ounce ruby port	⅛ teaspoon grated nutmeg
1 whole egg	
1 teaspoon superfine sugar	

In a shaker half-filled with ice cubes, combine the brandy,

port, egg, sugar, and cream. Shake well. Strain into a sour glass and garnish with the nutmeg.

876 FRENCH REVOLUTION

2 ounces brandy
½ ounce framboise

3 ounces chilled
    Champagne

In a mixing glass half-filled with ice cubes, combine the brandy and framboise. Stir well. Strain into a Champagne flute. Add the Champagne.

877 HILLARY WALLBANGER

4 ounces dry white wine
2 ounces orange juice
½ ounce Galliano

In a collins class almost filled with ice cubes, combine the wine and orange juice. Stir well. Float the Galliano on top.

878 KING'S PEG

1 ounce brandy

5 ounces Champagne

Pour the brandy and the Champagne into a Champagne flute.

879 KIR

6 ounces dry white wine
½ ounce crème de cassis

1 lemon twist

Pour the wine and cassis into a wine glass. Stir well. Garnish with the lemon twist.

880 KIR ROYALE

6 ounces Champagne or
    sparkling wine

½ ounce crème de cassis
1 lemon twist

Pour the Champagne and cassis into a Champagne flute. Stir well. Garnish with the lemon twist.

881 LICENCED VICTUALER'S CHAMPAGNE COCKTAIL

1 teaspoon granulated
  sugar
3 dashes bitters

½ ounce brandy
6 ounces Champagne

Put the sugar in the bottom of a Champagne flute and soak it with the bitters. Pour the brandy over the sugar. Top with the Champagne.

882 MADEIRA M'DEAR

1½ ounces Madeira
1 ounce brandy
½ ounce dry vermouth

1 teaspoon sweet
  vermouth
1 lemon twist

Pour the Madeira, brandy, dry vermouth, and sweet vermouth into an old-fashioned glass almost filled with ice cubes. Stir well. Garnish with the lemon twist.

883 MIMOSA

5 ounces Champagne or
  sparkling wine
½ ounce Cointreau or
  triple sec

1 ounce orange juice
1 orange slice

Pour the Champagne, Cointreau, and orange juice into a Champagne flute. Stir well. Garnish with the orange slice.

884 NELSON'S BLOOD

5 ounces Champagne or
  sparkling wine

1 ounce tawny port

Pour the Champagne and port into a Champagne flute. Stir well.

885 PORT AND BRANDY

1½ ounces port

1 ounce brandy

Pour the port and the brandy into a snifter. Stir well.

886 PORTUGUESE DAISY

2 ounces ruby port
1 ounce brandy
1 ounce lemon juice
½ teaspoon superfine
  sugar
½ teaspoon grenadine
1 lemon wedge

In a shaker half-filled with ice cubes, combine the port, brandy, lemon juice, sugar, and grenadine. Shake well. Pour into an old-fashioned glass. Garnish with the lemon wedge.

887 PORT WINE FLIP

2½ ounces ruby port
1 whole egg
1 teaspoon superfine
  sugar
½ ounce light cream
⅛ teaspoon grated
  nutmeg

In a shaker half-filled with ice cubes, combine the port, egg, sugar, and cream. Shake well. Strain into a sour glass and garnish with the nutmeg.

888 PORT WINE SANGAREE

1 teaspoon superfine
  sugar
2 teaspoons water
2 ounces tawny port
Crushed ice
2½ ounces club soda
½ ounce brandy
1 lemon twist
⅛ teaspoon grated
  nutmeg
⅛ teaspoon ground
  cinnamon

In a highball glass, dissolve the sugar in the water and port. Almost fill the glass with crushed ice and add the club soda. Float the brandy on top. Garnish with the lemon twist and a dusting of nutmeg and cinnamon.

889 QUEEN'S COUSIN

1 ounce vodka
½ ounce Grand Marnier
½ ounce lime juice
2 dashes bitters

1 teaspoon Cointreau or
 triple sec
3 ounces sparkling white
 wine or Champagne

In a shaker half-filled with ice cubes, combine all of the ingredients except for the wine. Shake well. Strain into a large wine glass. Add the wine and stir well.

890 RED WINE COOLER

4 ounces red wine
2 ounces lemon-lime
 soda

2 ounces ginger ale
1 lemon twist
1 orange slice

Pour the wine, lemon-lime soda, and ginger ale into a highball glass almost filled with ice cubes. Stir well. Garnish with the lemon twist and the orange slice.

891 RUBY PORT COBBLER

1 teaspoon superfine
 sugar
3 ounces club soda
Crushed ice

2 ½ ounces ruby port
1 maraschino cherry
1 orange slice
1 lemon slice

In an old-fashioned glass, dissolve the sugar in the club soda. Add crushed ice until the glass is almost full. Stir well. Garnish with the cherry, orange slice, and lemon slice.

892 SPRITZER

5 ounces white wine
2 ounces club soda

1 lemon twist

Pour the wine and soda into a collins glass almost filled with ice cubes. Stir well. Garnish with the lemon twist.

893 WHITE WINE COOLER

4 ounces dry white wine
2 ounces lemon-lime soda

1 lemon twist
1 orange slice

Pour the wine and the soda into a highball glass almost filled with ice cubes. Stir well. Garnish with the lemon twist and the orange slice.

14 · BEER AND BEER CONCOCTIONS

Although drinks made with beer are not referred to as cocktails, there are some recipes in this chapter, such as the Black and Tan and the Snake Bite, that make for some very interesting drinking. The history of beer is anything but brief. The ancient Egyptians brewed beer 6,000 years ago; it has been brewed by every society on every continent since then, and—who knows?—probably before then. Beer is an alcoholic beverage that is available to people who have an abundance of grain but are without plentiful amounts of fruit for making wine. Beer is the ancestor of whiskey, which, in very simple terms, is just distilled beer.

It is very doubtful that brewing beer predates winemaking, but it can safely be said that beer has been with us for as long as civilized man has been around. The practice of putting hops into beer for flavor was probably introduced by the Dutch in the fifteenth century. The addition of these leaves from the mulberry family served not only to flavor the beer, but also acted as a preservative.

Beer was brought to the United States by the Pilgrims and was brewed by individual households. The first large commercial brewery was owned by William Penn, the founder of Pennsylvania.

PRODUCTION

1. Barley is malted, that is, germinated to produce an enzyme that can convert the rest of the starch into fermentable sugar.
2. The malt is roasted to stop the germination process. Roasting takes place for different lengths of time depending on what type of beer is being brewed. The longer the malt is roasted, the darker the malt and, hence, the darker the beer.
3. The roasted malt is then ground into grist and mixed with water and other cooked cereals in a mash tun, where the starches are converted into fermentable sugars.
4. The mash is stirred within the mash tun, dissolving soluble material from the malt and cereals. The amount of time given to this stirring determines the amount of solubles absorbed into the water and therefore governs the end product.
5. The mash is transferred to a lauter tun, which has moving rakes that move it around, further breaking down the grist and cereal. When the rakes stop, the grist falls to the bottom, and the liquid, now called "wort," sieves through it and through the slotted base of the tun.
6. Hops are added to the wort in a brewing kettle. It is boiled and then strained to remove the hops.
7. The hot wort is cooled and put into a fermenting vat where brewer's yeast is added and the beer is allowed to ferment. Some brewer's yeast ferments on the top of the wort and produces ale, while others ferment on the bottom and result in lager.
8. Finally the beer is cooled in storage vats in order to separate it from the yeast and other solids still present, and carbonated.

LAGERS

Lagers are differentiated by the types of yeasts used in making them and are aged for longer periods than ales. They are light in body and can be divided into several types:

PILSNER

The only true Pilsner is brewed in Pilsen, Czechoslovakia. It is flowery and dry. The word *Pilsner* on any beer not from Pilsen merely implies that the style of Pilsen beer has been copied.

BOCK

Dark, strong, and sweet, Bock beer can be, although rarely is, top fermented, when it becomes an ale.

MALT LIQUOR

A term applied to any malt beverage that is too high in alcohol content to be defined as a beer within the legal limits of any given state.

ALES

Generally described as having a full body and a heavy hop flavor, ale is top fermented and can be divided into several types:

STOUT

Dark, very malty, and rather bitter, stout has roasted barley added to it for color and flavor.

PORTER

Basically stout with a lower alcohol content, porter is known for having a rich coffeelike flavor.

BITTER

Also known as amber ale, it is flavored heavily with hops. Bitter ale derives its name from its bitter taste.

BROWN ALE

Sweet and dark in color.

CREAM ALE

A light-bodied ale, sometimes blended with a lager.

SCOTCH ALE

Dark and heavily flavored with malt, brewed in Scotland.

PALE ALE

Light-colored ale, often a bottled variety of bitter.

MILD

Lightly hopped, sweeter ale, dark in color.

BARLEY WINE

Usually sold in six-ounce bottles, this dark, strong, sweet ale is usually too high in alcohol to be designated an ale, although it is top-fermented beer.

SAKE

Although saké is usually known as a rice wine, it is in the literal sense a beer. Made from rice that is fermented twice, with a different yeast used each time, saké is a clear uncarbonated beer with a high alcohol content. It is traditionally served warm in small Japanese cups known as *sakazuki*.

894 ALE FLIP

1 ounce lemon juice
12 ounces ale
¼ teaspoon ground
  ginger
1 tablespoon granulated
  sugar
1 egg yolk
1 ounce brandy

In a saucepan over moderate heat, heat the lemon juice with 2 ounces of the ale, the ginger, and the sugar until the sugar is dissolved. In a bowl, beat the egg yolk into the brandy. Beat the lemon juice mixture into the egg yolk mixture and pour it into a beer mug. Add the rest of the ale and stir well.

895 BLACK AND TAN

6 ounces ale   6 ounces stout

Carefully pour the ale into a Pilsner or beer mug, trying not to raise too much head. Pour the stout into the ale.

896 BLACK VELVET

12 ounces stout
4 ounces chilled
  Champagne or sparkling
  wine

Pour the stout, then the Champagne into a large beer mug.

897 BLACK VELVETEEN

12 ounces stout   4 ounces hard cider

Pour the stout, then the cider into a large beer mug.

898 DEPTH CHARGE

1½ ounces peppermint   12 ounces ale or lager
schnapps

Pour the schnapps, then the ale into a Pilsner or beer mug.

899 DOG'S NOSE

1 ounce gin   12 ounces ale

Pour the gin, then the ale into a Pilsner or beer mug.

900 GINGER BEER SHANDY

4 ounces ginger beer   12 ounces chilled ale or
lager

Pour the ginger beer into a Pilsner or beer mug. Carefully add the ale.

901 LAGER AND BLACK

1½ ounces Ribena   12 ounces chilled lager
blackcurrant syrup

Pour the Ribena, then the lager into a Pilsner or beer mug.

902 LAGER AND LIME

1½ ounces Rose's lime   12 ounces chilled lager
juice

Pour the Rose's lime juice, then the lager into a Pilsner or beer mug.

903 LEMON TOP

12 ounces chilled ale or   2 ounces lemon-lime
lager   soda

Pour the ale into a Pilsner or beer mug. Top with the soda.

904 RED EYE

3 ounces tomato juice   12 ounces ale or lager

Pour the tomato juice, then the ale into a Pilsner or beer mug.

905 SHANDY

4 ounces lemon-lime
  soda

12 ounces chilled ale or
  lager

Pour the soda into a Pilsner or beer mug. Carefully add the ale.

906 SNAKE BITE

6 ounces ale or lager

6 ounces hard cider

Pour the ale, then the cider into a Pilsner or beer mug.

907 STOUT AND BLACK

1½ ounces Ribena
  blackcurrant syrup

12 ounces stout

Pour the Ribena, then the stout into a Pilsner or beer mug.

908 STOUT SANGAREE

2 teaspoons superfine
  sugar
2 teaspoons water
12 ounces stout
1 ounce ruby port

⅛ teaspoon grated
  nutmeg
⅛ teaspoon ground
  cinnamon

In a beer mug, dissolve the sugar in the water. Carefully pour the stout to give a ½-inch head. Float the port. Garnish with the nutmeg and the cinnamon.

15 · HOT DRINKS

Irish Coffee, Hot Buttered Rum, Tom and Jerry: I think that these drinks stir a memory in most of us—a memory of a certain Christmas with the whole family present, sitting around a roaring log fire with a group of friends on a skiing trip, or maybe sneaking into a bar on an icy, windy afternoon to savor a hot drink before carrying on with the chores of the day.

One of my favorite memories of the coastal town where I was raised is that of the cold and blustery days when the rain actually *did* come down in torrents, and the Irish Sea would cascade over the sea walls onto the promenade. On these days, I would don my warmest and most weatherproof clothes, slip a small flask of dark rum into my pocket, and go for a solitary stroll with the sea. After walking for about 20 minutes along the shore, I would make my way, drenched to the bone, to a small, seedy café on Nutter Road (that always seemed quite appropriate) and order a hot malted milk. I would slip the rum into my drink and wrap my hands around the mug, trying to get some feeling back into them, and let the vapors of hot rum and malted milk rise to my nose. In my fantasy I had braved the elements and survived, and this was my reward.

The secret to making good hot drinks is a simple one:

Don't skimp. Don't use canned whipped cream on an Irish Coffee if you can lay your hands on some cold heavy cream to pour gently over the back of a teaspoon. When the drink is made, spend some time enjoying the aroma; savor the whole experience of the drink. It will warm the cockles of your heart.

909 BEDROOM FARCE

1 ounce dark rum
½ ounce bourbon
2 teaspoons Galliano
4 ounces hot chocolate

2 ounces heavy cream,
  whipped
¼ teaspoon grated
  bittersweet chocolate

Pour the rum, bourbon, Galliano, and hot chocolate into an Irish coffee glass. Spoon the cream carefully so that it floats on top of the drink. Garnish with the grated chocolate.

910 BLACK STRIPE

2 ounces dark rum
1 tablespoon molasses
1 teaspoon honey

2 ounces boiling water
1 lemon twist

Pour the run, molasses, honey, and hot water into an Irish coffee glass. Stir well. Garnish with the lemon twist.

911 BLUE BLAZER

2 ½ ounces Scotch
2 ounces boiling water
1 teaspoon granulated
  sugar

1 lemon twist

Heat the Scotch and pour it into a silver tankard. Pour the boiling water into another silver tankard. Carefully ignite the Scotch and, *very carefully,* pour it into the second tankard while it is still blazing. Pour the flaming drink very carefully back and forth between the tankards 4 or 5 times. Add the sugar and stir. Garnish with the lemon twist.

BROWN BETTY
See Party Punches, page 290.

912 CALYPSO COFFEE

4 ounces hot coffee
1½ ounces Tia Maria

½ ounce dark rum
2 ounces heavy cream

Pour the coffee into an Irish coffee glass. Add the Tia Maria and rum and stir. Pour the cream carefully over the back of a teaspoon so that it floats on top of the drink.

913 CANDLE IN THE WINDOW

2 ounces light rum
2 teaspoons bourbon
1 teaspoon dark crème de cacao

1 teaspoon cherry brandy
4 ounces hot coffee
2 ounces heavy cream

Pour the rum, bourbon, crème de cacao, cherry brandy, and coffee into an Irish coffee glass. Pour the cream carefully over the back of a teaspoon so that it floats on top of the drink.

914 CARIBBEAN COFFEE

4 ounces hot coffee
1 teaspoon granulated sugar

2 ounces dark rum
2 ounces heavy cream

Pour the coffee into an Irish coffee glass. Add the sugar and stir to dissolve it. Add the rum and stir. Pour the cream carefully over the back of a teaspoon so that it floats on top of the drink.

915 CHOCOLATE CORVETTE

1½ ounces dark rum
½ ounce dark crème de cacao

4 ounces hot chocolate
2 ounces heavy cream

Pour the rum, crème de cacao, and hot chocolate into an Irish coffee glass. Pour the cream carefully over the back of a teaspoon so that it floats on top of the drink.

916 CHOCOLATE VICE

1½ ounces dark rum
½ ounce bourbon
½ ounce dark crème de
    cacao

4 ounces hot chocolate
2 ounces heavy cream,
    whipped

Pour the rum, bourbon, crème de cacao, and hot chocolate into an Irish coffee glass. Spoon the cream carefully on top of the drink.

917 COFFEE ROYALE

4 ounces hot coffee
1 teaspoon granulated
    sugar

2 ounces brandy
2 ounces heavy cream

Pour the coffee into an Irish coffee glass. Add the sugar and stir to dissolve. Add the brandy and stir. Pour the cream carefully over the back of a teaspoon so that it floats on top of the drink.

918 COMFORTING COFFEE

4 ounces hot coffee
1 ounce Southern
    Comfort
1 ounce bourbon

1 teaspoon dark crème de
    cacao
2 ounces heavy cream

Pour the coffee into an Irish coffee glass. Add the Southern Comfort, bourbon, and crème de cacao and stir. Pour the cream carefully over the back of a teaspoon so that it floats on top of the drink.

919 DeROSIER's 19th HOLE

1 ounce añejo rum
½ ounce bourbon
2 teaspoons dark crème
    de cacao

2 teaspoons Drambuie
4 ounces hot coffee
2 ounces heavy cream

Pour the rum, bourbon, crème de cacao, Drambuie, and coffee into an Irish coffee glass. Pour the cream carefully over the back of a teaspoon so that it floats on top of the drink.

920 FIVE BEFORE FLYING

½ ounce bourbon
½ ounce Southern
  Comfort
½ ounce crème de
  bananes

2 teaspoons brandy
2 teaspoons white crème
  de cacao
4 ounces coffee
2 ounces heavy cream

Pour the bourbon, Southern Comfort, crème de bananas, brandy, crème de cacao, and coffee into an Irish coffee glass. Pour the cream carefully over the black of a teaspoon, so that it floats on top of the drink.

GLÖGG
See Party Punches, page 293.

921 GOOD GOLLY

1½ ounces dark rum
½ ounce Galliano
2 teaspoons dark crème
  de cacao

4 ounces hot coffee
2 ounces heavy cream

Pour the rum, Galliano, crème de cacao, and coffee into an Irish coffee glass. Stir well. Pour the cream carefully over the back of a teaspoon so that it floats on top of the drink.

922 GRACIOUS ENJEE

1½ ounces bourbon
½ ounce Southern
  Comfort

2 teaspoons dark crème
  de cacao
4 ounces hot malted milk

Pour all of the ingredients into a coffee mug. Stir well.

923 HOT BUTTERED RUM

1 teaspoon brown sugar
4 ounces boiling water
1 whole clove
2 ounces dark rum

1 teaspoon unsalted
  butter
⅛ teaspoon grated
  nutmeg

In an Irish coffee glass, combine the brown sugar with the boiling water. Stir until the sugar is dissolved. Add the clove and the rum. Float the butter on the top and dust with the nutmeg.

924 HOT DARING DYLAN

1½ ounces tequila
1 ounce Kahlúa
4 ounces Mexican hot
  chocolate

2 ounces heavy cream

Pour the tequila, Kahlúa, and hot chocolate into an Irish coffee glass. Stir well. Pour the cream carefully over the back of a teaspoon so that it floats on top of the drink.

925 HOT MOLLIFIER

1½ ounces dark rum
½ ounce Tia Maria

4 ounces hot coffee
2 ounces heavy cream

Pour the rum, Tia Maria, and coffee into an Irish coffee glass. Stir well. Pour the cram carefully over the back of a teaspoon so that it floats on top of the drink.

926 HOT PENNY RUM

1½ ounces añejo rum
½ ounce bourbon
2 teaspoons dark crème
  de cacao

4 ounces hot coffee
2 ounces heavy cream

Pour the rum, bourbon, crème de cacao, and coffee into an Irish coffee glass. Pour the cream carefully over the back of a teaspoon so that it floats on top of the drink.

927 HOT PIPER

2 ounces tequila
2 teaspoons lemon juice

½ ounce dark crème de
  cacao
4 ounces hot coffee

Pour all of the ingredients into an Irish coffee glass. Stir well.

HOT WHISKEY PUNCH
See Party Punches, page 294.

928 HOT ZULTRY ZOË

1½ ounces tequila
½ ounce Galliano
4 ounces Mexican hot
  chocolate

2 ounces heavy cream

Pour the tequila, Galliano, and hot chocolate into an Irish coffee glass. Stir well. Pour the cream carefully over the back of a teaspoon so that it floats on top of the drink.

929 IRISH COFFEE

4 ounces hot coffee
1 teaspoon granulated
  sugar

2 ounces Irish whiskey
2 ounces heavy cream

Pour the coffee into an Irish coffee glass. Add the sugar and stir to dissolve it. Add the whiskey and stir. Pour the cream carefully over the back of a teaspoon so that it floats on top of the drink.

930 ITALIAN COFFEE

4 ounces hot coffee
1½ ounces amaretto

½ ounce brandy
2 ounces heavy cream

Pour the coffee into an Irish coffee glass. Add the amaretto and brandy and stir. Pour the cream carefully over the back of a teaspoon so that it floats on top of the drink.

931 JACK ROBERTS' TREAT

4 ounces hot chocolate
2 ounces brandy
½ ounce dark crème de
  cacao

2 ounces heavy cream

Pour the hot chocolate into an Irish coffee glass. Add the brandy and crème de cacao and stir. Pour the cream carefully over the back of a teaspoon so that it floats on top of the drink.

932 MEXICAN COFFEE

4 ounces hot coffee   2 ounces heavy cream
2 ounces Kahlúa

Pour the coffee into an Irish coffee glass. Add the Kahlúa
and stir. Pour the cream carefully over the back of a teaspoon so that it floats on top of the drink.

933 MONASTERY COFFEE

4 ounces hot coffee   2 ounces Bénédictine
½ teaspoon granulated   2 ounces heavy cream
  sugar

Pour the coffee into an Irish coffee glass. Add the sugar
and stir to dissolve. Add the Bénédictine and stir. Pour the
cream carefully over the back of a teaspoon so that it floats
on top of the drink.

934 MONK'S ROPE COFFEE

4 ounces hot coffee   2 ounces heavy cream
1½ ounces Frangelico
½ ounce dark crème de
  cacao

Pour the coffee into an Irish coffee glass. Add the Frangelico and crème de cacao and stir. Pour the cream carefully
over the back of a teaspoon so that it floats on top of the
drink.

935 MORLEY'S DRIVER

1½ ounces dark rum   4 ounces hot coffee
½ ounce cherry brandy   2 ounces heavy cream
2 teaspoons dark crème
  de cacao

Pour the rum, cherry brandy, crème de cacao, and coffee
into an Irish coffee glass. Stir well. Pour the cream carefully
over the back of a teaspoon so that it floats on top of the
drink.

MULLED PORT
See Party Punches, page 294.

936 PRINCE CHARLES COFFEE

4 ounces hot coffee   2 ounces heavy cream
2 ounces Drambuie

Pour the coffee into an Irish coffee glass. Add the Drambuie and stir. Pour the cream carefully over the back of a teaspoon so that it floats on top of the drink.

937 SQUIRE RACINE

1½ ounces dark rum   4 ounces hot malted milk
½ ounce Southern
  Comfort

Pour all of the ingredients into a coffee mug. Stir well.

938 RITCHIE RITCHIE

1½ ounces añejo rum   4 ounces hot coffee
2 teaspoons dark crème   2 ounces heavy cream
  de cacao   ¼ teaspoons ground
2 teaspoons white crème   cinnamon
  de cacao

Pour the rum, dark crème de cacao, white crème de cacao, and coffee into an Irish coffee glass. Pour the cream carefully over the back of a teaspoon so that it floats on top of the drink. Dust with the cinnamon.

939 SOUTHFORK COFFEE

4 ounces hot coffee   2 ounces heavy cream
1½ ounces bourbon
½ ounce dark crème de
  cacao

Pour the coffee into an Irish coffee glass. Add the bourbon and crème de cacao and stir. Pour the cream carefully over the back of a teaspoon so that it floats on top of the drink.

940 TOM AND JERRY

1 whole egg, separated
1/8 teaspoon baking soda
2 tablespoons superfine
sugar
2 ounces plus 1 teaspoon
light rum

6 ounces hot milk
1/2 ounce brandy
1/8 teaspoon grated
nutmeg

In a mixing bowl, whisk the egg white until it forms soft peaks. In another bowl, whisk the yolk until it becomes frothy. Fold the white into the yolk. Add the baking soda, sugar, and 1 teaspoon of the rum. Whisk it all together to form a stiff batter. Pour the batter into a warm beer mug and dissolve it in 1/4 cup of the hot milk. Add the rest of the rum and the brandy. Fill the mug with the rest of the milk, stir, and sprinkle the nutmeg on top.

941 WHISKEY-ALL-IN

2 ounces blended
whiskey
1 teaspoon superfine
sugar

2 teaspoons lemon juice
2 ounces boiling water
1 lemon twist
1 whole clove

Combine the whiskey, sugar, lemon juice, and hot water in an Irish coffee glass. Stir well. Garnish with the lemon twist and the clove.

16 · PARTY PUNCHES

The recipes in this chapter are for classic punches—Glögg, Wassail, and Fish House Punch—that are made in quantity to serve large groups of people. Drinks like the popular Planter's Punch, which is usually made individually, can be found in the appropriate liquor chapters (Rum for Planter's Punch).

There are two explanations for the origin of the word *punch*. One says that it is just an abbreviation of the word *puncheon*, which is a huge cask that holds about 70 gallons of liquid (although the amount varies depending on what part of the world you are in). The more likely explanation, however, is that it comes from the Hindu or Persian word *panch*, which means "five," and denotes that at least five ingredients are present.

The oldest-known punch is a rum punch made in Jamaica in the mid-seventeenth century that was simply rum, sugar, water, and orange juice. I know that there are only four ingredients there, but that's the way history is. It offers sound and logical explanations one minute and tears them down the next. Maybe punch got its name from the way it hits you.

Serving punch at a party puts less strain on the host or hostess. It can be made in advance and there is no need for a bartender to make lots of different drinks for every-body. If you are serving punch, however, make sure that you have some nonalcoholic drinks available for the folks who like to stay sober.

Punch should be served in a bowl with a large block of ice in it to keep it chilled; ice cubes water down the punch, since they dissolve quickly. The block of ice can be made simply by taking the metal dividers out of your ice tray, or just by freezing water in a well-cleaned milk or juice carton.

942 AMBASSADOR'S PUNCH

MAKES 8 (6-OUNCE) PUNCH CUPS

1 quart chilled eggnog	3 ounces dark crème de
5 ounces brandy	cacao
4 ounces dark rum	1 whole nutmeg

Whisk the eggnog, brandy, rum, and crème de cacao together in a large punch bowl. Add 1 large block of ice. Grate a little nutmeg onto the top of each drink when serving.

943 BOMBAY PUNCH

MAKES 50 (6-OUNCE) PUNCH CUPS

1 cup lemon juice	¼ cup cherry brandy
½ cup lime juice	4 (750-ml) bottles chilled
1 cup superfine sugar	Champagne or
1 liter brandy	sparkling wine
1 liter sherry	2 liters chilled club soda
½ cup Cointreau or triple	3 oranges, cut into slices
sec	24 maraschino cherries
½ cup maraschino	
liqueur	

Stir the lemon juice, lime juice, and sugar together in a large punch bowl until the sugar is dissolved. Add the brandy, sherry, Cointreau, maraschino liqueur, cherry brandy, Champagne, and club soda. Stir well. Add 1 large block of ice and garnish with the orange slices and the cherries.

944 BROWN BETTY

MAKES 8 (10-OUNCE) BEER MUGS

½ cup brown sugar
1 lemon, sliced
4 whole cloves
1 cinnamon stick
½ teaspoon grated
nutmeg
¼ teaspoon ground
ginger

2¼ cups water
12 ounces (1½ cups)
brandy
4 (12-ounce) bottles
amber ale, such as Bass
ale

In a large nonreactive saucepan set over medium-high heat, place the brown sugar, lemon slices, cloves, cinnamon stick, nutmeg, ginger, and water. Stir frequently to dissolve the sugar. Let the mixture come to a boil, turn the heat down to medium, and simmer for 10 minutes. Add the brandy and ale and heat but do not boil. Serve in beer mugs, with a lemon slice in each drink.

945 CHAMPAGNE RUM PUNCH

MAKES 30 (6-OUNCE) PUNCH CUPS

1 liter light rum
1 liter añejo rum
1 (750-ml) bottle sweet
vermouth
1 (750-ml) bottle
Champagne or
sparkling wine

1 quart orange juice
1 cup cranberry juice
2 oranges, cut into slices

In a large punch bowl, combine the light rum, añejo rum, vermouth, Champagne, orange juice, and cranberry juice. Stir well. Add 1 large block of ice and garnish with the orange slices.

946 CIDER PUNCH

MAKES 18 (6-OUNCE) PUNCH CUPS

1½ quarts hard cider
4 ounces Drambuie
4 ounces dry sherry
2 ounces lemon juice
8 ounces (1 cup) club soda

3 apples, cored and thinly sliced
1 teaspoon grated nutmeg

In a large punch bowl, place the cider, Drambuie, sherry, lemon juice, and club soda. Stir well. Add 1 large block of ice. Garnish with the apple slices and sprinkle the nutmeg on top.

947 CLARET PUNCH

MAKES 30 (6-OUNCE) PUNCH CUPS

2 cups lemon juice
1 cup superfine sugar
3 (750-ml) bottles claret (dry red wine)
12 ounces (1½ cups) brandy
4 ounces apricot brandy

4 ounces bourbon
8 ounces (1 cup) Cointreau or triple sec
1 quart club soda
2 cups cold tea
3 oranges, cut into slices

Stir the lemon juice and sugar together in a large punch bowl until the sugar is dissolved. Add the claret, brandy, apricot brandy, bourbon, Cointreau, club soda, and cold tea. Stir well. Add 1 large block of ice and garnish with the orange slices.

948 CREOLE CHAMPAGNE PUNCH

MAKES 36 (6-OUNCE) PUNCH CUPS

1 pineapple, peeled and
 cored
2 cups lemon juice
1 cup superfine sugar
2 (750-ml) bottles
 Champagne
1 (750-ml) bottle dry
 white wine

4 ounces Cointreau or
 triple sec
2 ounces brandy
1 quart club soda
2 pints strawberries,
 hulled and quartered

Take half of the peeled and cored pineapple and chop it
finely. Thinly slice the other half. Stir the lemon juice and
sugar together in a large punch bowl until the sugar is
dissolved. Add the chopped pineapple, Champagne, white
wine, Cointreau, brandy, and club soda. Stir well. Add 1
large block of ice and garnish with the sliced pineapple
and the strawberries.

949 EGGNOG

MAKES 6 (6-OUNCE) PUNCH CUPS

4 eggs
2 teaspoons vanilla
 extract

$1/4$ cup superfine sugar
1 quart milk
1 whole nutmeg

In a large bowl, whisk together the eggs with the vanilla
extract, sugar, and 1 cup of the milk until the sugar is
dissolved and the mixture is well blended. Add the rest of
the milk, whisking constantly. Grate some nutmeg onto
each cup of eggnog as it is served.

950 FISH HOUSE PUNCH

MAKES 30 (6-OUNCE) PUNCH CUPS

2 cups lemon juice
1 cup superfine sugar
2 liters dark rum
1 liter brandy

12 ounces ($1^1/2$ cups)
 peach brandy
1 quart club soda

Stir the lemon juice and sugar together in a large punch
bowl until the sugar is dissolved. Add the rest of the ingredients. Stir well. Add 1 large block of ice.

951 FRANK DAVIS PUNCH

MAKES 36 (6-OUNCE) PUNCH CUPS

1 cup lemon juice
½ cup superfine sugar
1 liter chilled gold tequila
2 (750-ml) bottles chilled
Champagne or
sparkling wine

4 (750-ml) bottles chilled
sauternes
1 large honeydew melon,
cut into melon balls

Stir the lemon juice and sugar together in a large punch bowl until the sugar is dissolved. Add the tequila, Champagne, and sauternes. Stir well. Add 1 large block of ice and garnish with the melon balls.

952 GLÖGG

MAKES 8 (4-OUNCE) IRISH COFFEE CUPS

12 ounces (1½ cups)
brandy
1 (375-ml) bottle dry red
wine
8 whole cloves
3 cardamon pods,
crushed

1 cinnamon stick
½ cup raisins
½ cup blanched almonds
¾ cup granulated sugar
2 teaspoons brown sugar

In a large nonreactive saucepan, place the brandy, wine, cloves, crushed cardamon pods, cinnamon stick, raisins, almonds, and granulated sugar. Set over medium-high heat and stir frequently to dissolve the sugar. Just before the mixture boils, carefully ignite it by touching a burning match to the surface.* Sprinkle the brown sugar onto the flames. After 10 seconds, extinguish the flames by covering the pan with its lid. To serve, spoon some raisins and almonds out of the mixture into the Irish coffee cups before adding the Glögg.

*Be extremely careful when igniting the liquid; it is best to have a household fire extinguisher handy when dealing with this amount of liquid.

953 HOT WHISKEY PUNCH

MAKES 8 (6-OUNCE) IRISH COFFEE GLASSES

4 lemons, peeled and cut
  into slices (reserve
  the peel)
1 cup granulated sugar

2 cinnamon sticks
8 whole cloves
1 liter blended or Irish
  whiskey

In a large nonreactive saucepan, place the lemon peel, sugar, cinnamon sticks, cloves, and 3 cups of water. Set over medium-high heat and stir frequently to dissolve the sugar. Let the water come to a boil, turn the heat down to medium, and simmer for 10 minutes. Strain the mixture and return it to the pan. Add the whiskey and heat but do not boil. Serve in Irish coffee glasses with a slice of peeled lemon in each.

954 MULLED PORT

MAKES 6 (6-OUNCE) IRISH COFFEE GLASSES

2 oranges, peeled and cut
  into slices (reserve
  the peel)
12 whole cloves
$\frac{1}{2}$ teaspoon ground mace
$\frac{1}{2}$ teaspoon grated
  nutmeg

$\frac{1}{2}$ teaspoon ground
  allspice
1 cinnamon stick
$\frac{1}{4}$ cup granulated sugar
1 (750-ml) bottle ruby or
  tawny port

In a large nonreactive saucepan, place the orange peel, cloves, mace, nutmeg, allspice, cinnamon stick, sugar, and 2 cups of water. Set over medium-high heat and stir frequently to dissolve the sugar. Let the water come to a boil, turn the heat down to medium, and simmer for 10 minutes. Strain the mixture and return it to the pan. Add the port and heat but do not boil. Serve in Irish coffee glasses with a slice of peeled orange in each.

955 ORCHARD PUNCH

MAKES 24 (6-OUNCE) PUNCH CUPS

1 liter applejack
2 cups orange juice
5 ounces grapefruit juice
2 ounces grenadine
½ ounce orange bitters

1 quart lemon-lime soda
1 quart ginger ale
1 orange, cut into slices
1 apple, cut into slices

In a large punch bowl, combine the applejack, orange juice, grapefruit juice, grenadine, and orange bitters. Stir well. Add the lemon-lime soda and ginger ale and stir again. Add 1 large block of ice. Garnish with the orange and apple slices.

956 SUNSET PUNCH

MAKES 22 (6-OUNCE) PUNCH CUPS

2 cups lemon juice
1 cup superfine sugar
2 (750-ml) bottles chilled
  Champagne or
  sparkling wine
6 ounces maraschino
  liqueur

8 ounces Cointreau or
  triple sec
3 ounces cherry brandy
3 ounces brandy
2 cups cold tea
2 oranges, cut into slices
24 maraschino cherries

Stir the lemon juice and sugar together in a large punch bowl until the sugar is dissolved. Add the Champagne, maraschino liqueur, Cointreau, cherry brandy, brandy, and cold tea. Stir well. Add 1 large block of ice and garnish with the orange slices and the cherries.

957 TARTAN CHAMPAGNE PUNCH

MAKES 25 (6-OUNCE) PUNCH CUPS

4 ounces Drambuie
½ cup superfine sugar
4 ounces brandy
4 ounces maraschino
  liqueur
3 (750-ml) bottles chilled
  Champagne or
  sparkling wine

16 ounces (2 cups) club
  soda
3 oranges, peeled and
  sliced

Stir the Drambuie and sugar together in a large punch bowl until the sugar is dissolved. Add the brandy, maraschino liqueur, Champagne, and club soda. Stir well. Add 1 large block of ice and garnish with the peeled orange slices.

958 TEXAS BAR PUNCH

MAKES 20 (6-OUNCE) PUNCH CUPS

2 (750-ml) bottles ruby
  port
1 liter ginger ale

1 liter lemon-lime soda
1 lemon, sliced
1 orange, sliced

In a large punch bowl, place the port, ginger ale, and soda. Stir well. Add 1 large block of ice and garnish with the lemon and orange slices.

959 VI'S JAMAICAN PUNCH

MAKES 35 (6-OUNCE) PUNCH CUPS

1 pineapple, peeled and
  cored
2 cups lemon juice
½ cup superfine sugar
1 (750-ml) bottle light
  rum
1 (750-ml) bottle añejo
  rum
16 ounces (2 cups) dark
  rum

1 quart pineapple juice
1½ quarts orange juice
1 teaspoon grated nutmeg
1 teaspoon ground
  cinnamon
½ teaspoon ground mace
½ teaspoon ground
  allspice
12 ounces (1½ cups)
  club soda

Take half of the peeled and cored pineapple and chop it finely. Thinly slice the other half. Stir the lemon juice and sugar together in a large punch bowl until the sugar is dissolved. Add the chopped pineapple, light rum, añejo rum, dark rum, pineapple juice, orange juice, nutmeg, cinnamon, mace, allspice, and club soda. Stir well. Add 1 large block of ice and garnish with the pineapple slices.

960 WEDDING BELL PUNCH

MAKES 32 (6-OUNCE) PUNCH CUPS

2 cups lemon juice
1 cup superfine sugar
16 ounces (2 cups) bourbon
12 ounces (1½ cups) añejo rum
4 ounces crème de cacao
1 split (187 ml) chilled Champagne

2 liters dry red wine
8 ounces sweet vermouth
16 ounces (2 cups) club soda
16 ounces (2 cups) ginger ale
2 oranges, cut into slices
2 pints strawberries, hulled and quartered

Stir the lemon juice and sugar together in a large punch bowl until the sugar is dissolved. Add the bourbon, rum, crème de cacao, Champagne, red wine, vermouth, club soda, and ginger ale. Stir well. Add 1 large block of ice and garnish with the orange slices and the strawberries.

17 · NONALCOHOLIC DRINKS

As mentioned in the introduction to this book, not drinking alcohol is much more common these days. The nondrinkers among us should be catered to. For the past few years more and more celebrities have come forth admitting their addiction to booze. Betty Ford was one of the first, and many other well-known figures have followed. These people have helped to take the stigma away from alcoholism, making it much easier for recovering alcoholics to function in a society that no longer thinks those who have drinking problems are merely weak willed or simply irresponsible. I dedicate this chapter to the brave folk in the public eye who have come forth and bared their souls, showing the general public that even the most upstanding citizen can fall prey to the disease of alcoholism.

I would also like to take time here to mention that if a person tells you that they don't drink alcohol, then you should take some steps to make sure that you don't serve them any by accident. One of the most common mistakes is to add bitters to a glass of tonic water or club soda along with a wedge of lime. While this makes a rather refreshing cocktail, bitters usually contain about 50 percent alcohol and should be avoided by the strict teetotaler. The trick is to read all labels; they will tell you how much alcohol, if any, is contained in a product. Nonalcoholic beers and wines all contain a trace of alcohol, although, by law, it must be less than one-half of one percent. Check with your nondrinking guest before you serve it.

On the lighter side now, this chapter contains dozens of nonalcoholic drinks, some old standards like the Shirley Temple, along with some lesser-known drinks, such as a Flying Fairbrother and a favorite Indian concoction called a Lassi. If you are throwing a party, plan to have something different for your nondrinking friends to quaff. Try to remember that, if they used to drink, they would probably prefer something not too sweet—say, homemade lemonade or store-bought ginger beer.

961 ATOMIC CAT

4 ounces orange juice   4 ounces tonic water

Pour the orange juice and tonic water into a highball glass almost filled with ice cubes. Stir well.

962 BANANA BRACER

1 very ripe banana, cut   1 ounce coconut cream
   into chunks.   ½ cup crushed ice
3 ounces milk   1 maraschino cherry
1 ounce pineapple juice

In a blender, combine the banana, milk, pineapple juice, and coconut cream with the crushed ice. Blend well. Pour into a collins glass and garnish with the cherry.

963 BATMAN COCKTAIL

6 ounces orange juice   1 orange slice
½ teaspoon grenadine

Pour the juice and grenadine into a collins glass almost filled with ice cubes. Stir well. Garnish with the orange slice.

964 BLASTER BATES

1 very ripe banana
1/4 cup blueberries
1/4 cup raspberries

2 ounces chilled milk
4 ounces chilled orange
juice

Place all of the ingredients into a blender. Blend well. Pour into a collins glass.

965 BROOKE SHIELDS

4 ounces lemon-lime
soda
2 ounces ginger ale

1 teaspoon grenadine
1 orange slice

Pour both sodas and the grenadine into a highball glass almost filled with ice cubes. Stir well and garnish with the orange slice.

966 CAESAR MAKES SENSE

6 ounces orange juice
1 teaspoon grenadine

1 scoop vanilla ice cream
1 orange slice

In a blender, combine the orange juice, grenadine, and ice cream with 6 ice cubes. Blend well. Pour into a collins glass and garnish with the orange slice.

967 CARRY'S CARIBE

6 ounces crushed
pineapple
1 tablespoon honey
2 teaspoons coconut
cream

3 ounces pineapple juice
1 cup crushed ice

In a blender, combine all of the ingredients. Blend well at high speed. Pour into a collins glass.

968 COCONAPPLE

4 ounces pineapple juice
1 ounce coconut cream

1/2 cup crushed ice

In a blender, combine all of the ingredients. Blend well. Pour into a collins glass.

969 CRANBERRY COOLER

4 ounces cranberry juice
2 ounces grape juice
2 ounces lemon-lime
  soda

1 lime wedge

Pour the cranberry juice, grape juice, and lemon-lime soda into a highball glass almost filled with ice cubes. Stir well and garnish with the lime wedge.

970 CRANBERRY LASSI

2 ounces plain yogurt
5 ounces cranberry juice
1 ounce lemon juice

2 teaspoons granulated
  sugar

Place all of the ingredients into a blender and blend thoroughly. Pour into a collins glass almost filled with ice cubes.

971 CROW'S NEST

4 ounces orange juice
1 ounce cranberry juice

1 whole egg
1/2 teaspoon grenadine

In a shaker half-filled with ice cubes, combine all of the ingredients. Shake well. Strain into an old-fashioned glass almost filled with ice cubes.

972 ELEPHANT CHARGER

2 ounces orange juice
2 ounces milk
1 ripe peach, peeled and
  sliced
1 very ripe banana,
  chopped

1/4 cup raspberries
2 scoops vanilla ice
  cream

In a blender, combine all of the ingredients. Blend well. Pour into a collins glass.

973 FLAMINGO

4 ounces cranberry juice
2 ounces pineapple juice
½ ounce lemon juice

2 ounces club soda
1 lime wedge

In a shaker half-filled with ice cubes, combine the cranberry juice, pineapple juice, and lemon juice. Shake well. Strain into a highball glass. Top with the club soda. Stir well and garnish with the lime wedge.

974 FLYING FAIRBROTHER

2 ounces grapefruit juice
1 ounce orange juice
1 ounce cranberry juice

1 teaspoon honey
3 ounces ginger ale

In a shaker half-filled with ice cubes, combine the grapefruit juice, orange juice, cranberry juice, and honey. Shake well. Strain into a collins glass almost filled with ice cubes. Top with the ginger ale. Stir well.

975 GOLDEN NEST

4 ounces orange juice
1 ounce cranberry juice

1 egg yolk
½ teaspoon grenadine

In a shaker half-filled with ice cubes, combine all of the ingredients. Shake well. Strain into an old-fashioned glass almost filled with ice cubes.

976 LASSI

2 ounces plain yogurt
6 ounces water
⅛ teaspoon salt

¼ teaspoon roasted
    cumin seeds

Place the yogurt, water, and salt into a blender and blend thoroughly. Pour into a collins glass almost filled with ice cubes. Add the cumin seed and stir thoroughly.

977 LEMONADE

2 teaspoons granulated
  sugar
2 ounces lemon juice

6 ounces water or club
  soda
1 lemon wedge

In a collins glass, dissolve the sugar in the lemon juice. Fill the glass with ice cubes and add the water or club soda. Garnish with the lemon wedge.

978 LIME TONIC

1 ounce Rose's lime juice
6 ounces tonic water

1 lime wedge

Pour Rose's lime juice and tonic water into a highball glass almost filled with ice cubes. Stir well and garnish with the lime wedge.

979 LIMEADE

2 teaspoons granulated
  sugar
3 ounces lime juice

5 ounces water or club
  soda
1 lime wedge

In a collins glass, dissolve the sugar in the lime juice. Fill the glass with ice cubes and add the water or club soda. Garnish with the lime wedge.

980 ORANGEADE

1 teaspoon granulated
  sugar
1 ounce lemon juice
5 ounces fresh orange
  juice

2 ounces club soda
1 orange slice

In a collins glass, dissolve the sugar in the lemon juice. Fill the glass with ice cubes and add the orange juice and the club soda. Stir well and garnish with the orange slice.

981 PEACHY HANES

2 ounces peach nectar
6 ounces chilled ginger
  beer

Place the peach nectar in the bottom of a beer mug. Slowly stir in the ginger beer.

982 PENZANCE COCKTAIL

2 ounces fresh orange   6 ounces ginger beer
  juice   1 lemon wedge

Pour the orange juice and ginger beer into a beer mug with a few ice cubes. Stir well. Garnish with the lemon wedge.

983 POMEGRANATE SODA

1 ounce lemon juice   1 teaspoon grenadine
6 ounces club soda

Pour the lemon juice and club soda into a collins glass almost filled with ice cubes. Stir well. Drop the grenadine into the center of the drink.

984 PUSSYFOOT

2 ounces orange juice   1 teaspoon grenadine
2 ounces lemon juice   1 egg yolk
1 ounce lime juice

In a shaker half-filled with ice cubes, combine all of the ingredients. Shake well. Strain into an old-fashioned glass almost filled with ice cubes.

985 ROSE AND THISTLE

1 very ripe banana, sliced   6 ounces milk
½ cup ripe strawberries

In a blender with 6 ice cubes, combine all of the ingredients. Blend well. Pour into a collins glass.

986 ROY ROGERS

4 ounces ginger ale
2 ounces lemon-lime
  soda

1 teaspoon grenadine
1 maraschino cherry
1 orange slice

Pour the ginger ale, lemon-lime soda, and grenadine into a highball glass almost filled with ice cubes. Stir well. Garnish with the cherry and the orange slice.

987 RUSSIAN DENIM

3 ounces orange juice
1 ounce cranberry juice
½ teaspoon grenadine

1 egg yolk
2 ounces club soda

In a shaker half-filled with ice cubes, combine the orange juice, cranberry juice, grenadine, and egg yolk. Shake well. Strain into a highball glass almost filled with ice cubes. Top with the club soda. Stir well.

988 SAFE SCRUMPY

2 ounces lemon juice
1 whole egg
1 teaspoon superfine
  sugar

6 ounces apple cider

In a shaker half-filled with ice cubes, combine the lemon juice, egg, and sugar. Shake well. Strain into a highball glass half-filled with ice cubes. Top with the cider. Stir well.

989 SHIRLEY TEMPLE

4 ounces lemon-lime
  soda
2 ounces ginger ale

1 teaspoon grenadine
1 maraschino cherry
1 orange slice

Pour the lemon-lime soda, ginger ale, and grenadine into a highball glass almost filled with ice cubes. Stir well. Garnish with the cherry and the orange slice.

990 SILVER NEST

4 ounces orange juice
1 ounce cranberry juice

1 egg white
½ teaspoon grenadine

In a shaker half-filled with ice cubes, combine all of the ingredients. Shake well. Strain into an old-fashioned glass almost filled with ice cubes.

991 SWEET LASSI

2 ounces plain yogurt
6 ounces water
2 teaspoons granulated
  sugar

¼ teaspoon orange flower
  water
2 drops rosewater

Place all of the ingredients into a blender and blend thoroughly. Pour into a collins glass almost filled with ice cubes.

992 TOMATO LASSI

2 ounces plain yogurt
2 ounces tomato juice
4 ounces water

⅛ teaspoon salt
¼ teaspoon celery seed

Place the yogurt, tomato juice, water, and salt into a blender and blend thoroughly. Pour into a collins glass almost filled with ice cubes. Add the celery seed and stir thoroughly.

993 VIRGIN BANANA COLADA

1 very ripe banana, cut
  into chunks
6 ounces pineapple juice
1½ ounces coconut
  cream

1 cup crushed ice
1 maraschino cherry
1 pineapple wedge

In a blender, combine the banana, pineapple juice, and coconut cream with the crushed ice. Blend well at high speed. Pour into a collins glass. Garnish with the cherry and the pineapple wedge.

994 VIRGIN BELLINI

3 ounces peach nectar
1 teaspoon grenadine
1 ounce lemon juice

4 ounces chilled club
soda

Pour the peach nectar, grenadine, and lemon juice into a
Champagne flute. Add the club soda. Stir well.

995 VIRGIN BULLSHOT

7 ounces beef bouillon
1/8 teaspoon black pepper
1 dash Worcestershire
sauce

1 dash Tabasco sauce
1 lemon wedge

In a shaker half-filled with ice cubes, combine the bouil-
lon, pepper, Worcestershire, and Tabasco. Shake well.
Strain into a highball glass almost filled with ice cubes.
Garnish with the lemon wedge.

996 VIRGIN CLAMATO COCKTAIL

5 ounces tomato juice
3 ounces clam juice
1/8 teaspoon black pepper
1 dash Worcestershire
sauce

1 dash Tabasco sauce
1 lemon wedge

In a shaker half-filled with ice cubes, combine the tomato
juice, clam juice, pepper, Worcestershire, and Tabasco.
Shake well. Strain into a highball glass almost filled with
ice cubes. Garnish with the lemon wedge.

997 VIRGIN MARY

7 ounces tomato juice
1/2 ounce lemon juice
1/8 teaspoon black pepper
1/8 teaspoon salt
1/8 teaspoon celery seed

3 dashes Worcestershire
sauce
1 dash Tabasco sauce
1 celery rib
1 lime wedge

In a shaker half-filled with ice cubes, combine the tomato
juice, lemon juice, pepper, salt, celery seed, Worcestershire, and Tabasco. Shake well. Strain into a highball glass
almost filled with ice cubes. Garnish with the celery rib
and the lime wedge.

998 VIRGIN PIÑA COLADA

7 ounces pineapple juice   1 maraschino cherry
2 ounces coconut cream   1 pineapple wedge
1 cup crushed ice

In a blender, combine the pineapple juice and coconut cream with the crushed ice. Blend well at high speed. Pour into a collins glass. Garnish with the cherry and the pineapple wedge.

999 VIRGIN STRAWBERRY COLADA

7 very ripe strawberries   1 cup crushed ice
5 ounces pineapple juice   1 maraschino cherry
1½ ounces coconut   1 pineapple wedge
  cream

In a blender, combine the strawberries, pineapple juice, and coconut cream with the crushed ice. Blend well at high speed. Pour into a collins glass. Garnish with the cherry and the pineapple wedge.

1000 WAVEBENDER

1 ounce orange juice   1 teaspoon grenadine
½ ounce lemon juice   5 ounces ginger ale

In a shaker half-filled with ice cubes, combine the orange juice, lemon juice, and grenadine. Shake well. Strain into a highball glass almost filled with ice cubes. Top with the ginger ale. Stir well.

1001 YELLOWJACKET

2 ounces pineapple juice   1½ ounces lemon juice
2 ounces orange juice

In a shaker half-filled with ice cubes, combine all of the ingredients. Shake well. Strain into an old-fashioned glass almost filled with ice cubes.

18 · VERSATILE COCKTAILS

A bone of contention has arisen over the root of the word *cocktail*, an interesting name for a mixture of beverages, don't you think? Here, then, are some of the possible origins of the word:

1. A derivation of the French word *coquetier*, or a double-sided egg cup that was used by a New Orleans pharmacist for serving mixed drinks.
2. A derivation of the phrase "cock your tail," meaning "keep your spirits up."
3. A pro-Revolutionary tavern keeper during the War of Independence stole chickens from a nearby farm owned by British sympathizers to feed Washington's troops. She used the feathers from the chickens to garnish the drinks in her tavern and was toasted by French-speaking customers, who shouted, "Vive le cocktail!" That's really farfetched.
4. It used to be customary to dock the tail of horses of mixed breed so that they would not be confused with the thoroughbreds. These horses were then known as being "cocktailed." Since a cocktail is a mixture of liquors but is not "pure" in itself, mixed drinks became known as cocktails. This one gets my vote.

Here is a handy little list of versatile cocktails that can be made with a variety of liquors. These drinks are mostly classics from the Twenties and Thirties that have survived the test of time. Differences among them are often slight, but you absolutely must know the difference between a Daisy and a Fancy if you want to impress. All of these generic recipes appear as specific drinks elsewhere in the book.

COBBLER

1 teaspoon superfine sugar	2 ounces desired liquor
	1 maraschino cherry
3 ounces club soda	1 orange slice
Crushed ice	1 lemon slice

In an old-fashioned glass, dissolve the sugar in the club soda. Add crushed ice until the glass is almost full. Add the liquor. Stir well. Garnish with the cherry, orange slice, and lemon slice.

COLLINS

2 ounces desired liquor	3 ounces club soda
1 ounce lemon juice	1 maraschino cherry
1 teaspoon superfine sugar	1 orange slice

In a shaker half-filled with ice cubes, combine the liquor, lemon juice, and sugar. Shake well. Strain into a collins glass almost filled with ice cubes. Add the club soda. Stir and garnish with the cherry and the orange slice.

COOLER

2 ounces desired liquor	1 lemon wedge
4 ounces lemon-lime soda	

Pour the liquor and soda into a highball glass almost filled with ice cubes. Stir well. Garnish with the lemon wedge. N.B.: Wine coolers (red or white) should be made with 4 ounces wine to 2 ounces soda.

CRUSTA

1 tablespoon superfine sugar	1½ ounces desired liquor
1 lemon wedge	½ ounce Cointreau or triple sec
Peel of 1 orange, cut into a spiral	2 teaspoons maraschino liqueur
Crushed ice	½ ounce lemon juice

Place the sugar in a saucer. Rub the rim of a wine goblet with the lemon wedge and dip the glass into the sugar to coat the rim thoroughly; discard the lemon. Place the orange peel spiral into the goblet and drape one end over the rim of the glass. Fill the glass with crushed ice. In a shaker half-filled with ice cubes, combine the desired liquor, Cointreau, maraschino liqueur, and lemon juice. Shake well. Strain into the goblet.

DAISY

2 ounces desired liquor	½ teaspoon grenadine
1 ounce lemon juice	1 maraschino cherry
½ teaspoon superfine sugar	1 orange slice

In a shaker half-filled with ice cubes, combine the liquor, lemon juice, sugar, and grenadine. Shake well. Pour into an old-fashioned glass. Garnish with the cherry and the orange slice.

FANCY

2 ounces desired liquor	2 dashes bitters
½ teaspoon Cointreau or triple sec	1 lemon twist
¼ teaspoon superfine sugar	

In a shaker half-filled with ice cubes, combine the liquor, Cointreau, sugar, and bitters. Shake well. Strain into a cocktail glass and garnish with the lemon twist.

FIX

1 teaspoon superfine sugar	Crushed ice
1 ounce lemon juice	2 ounces desired liquor
2 teaspoons water	1 maraschino cherry
	1 lemon slice

In a shaker half-filled with ice cubes, combine the sugar, lemon juice, and water. Shake well. Strain into a highball glass almost filled with crushed ice. Add the liquor. Stir well and garnish with the cherry and the lemon slice.

FIZZ

2½ ounces desired liquor	4 ounces club soda
1 ounce lemon juice	
1 teaspoon superfine sugar	

In a shaker half-filled with ice cubes, combine the liquor, lemon juice, and sugar. Shake well. Strain into a collins glass almost filled with ice cubes. Add the club soda. Stir well.

FLIP

2 ounces desired liquor	½ ounce light cream
1 whole egg	⅛ teaspoon grated
1 teaspoon superfine sugar	nutmeg

In a shaker half-filled with ice cubes, combine the liquor, egg, sugar, and cream. Shake well. Strain into a sour glass and garnish with the nutmeg.

FRAPPE

Crushed ice	2 ounces desired cordial

Fill a pousse café glass with crushed ice and simply pour the cordial into the glass.

HIGHBALL

What is a highball? Well, first, it's a drink that is served in a highball glass; second, it's quick to make; and third, it's whatever liquor you desire mixed with water or soda. Of these three qualities, speed is the most important.

In the nineteenth century, when a train was running behind schedule, a ball would be placed high up on a tall pole in the railway station to signal the driver and engineer to travel at full speed. Hence, the term *highball* was first connected to speed and was later given to a drink that can be made quickly. The basic rules of a highball are:

Use only one liquor.
Use only one mixer.
Use only one garnish or none at all.
Make the drink quickly.

Examples of a Highball include a Bourbon and Branch (page 22), Brandy and Soda (page 39), Gin and Tonic (page 64), and Scotch and Water (page 134).

MIST

Crushed ice   2½ ounces desired liquor

Fill an old-fashioned glass with crushed ice and simply pour the desired liquor into the glass.

RICKEY

2 ounces desired liquor   1 lime wedge
5 ounces club soda

Pour the liquor and club soda into a highball glass almost filled with ice cubes. Stir well. Garnish with the lime wedge.

SANGAREE

1 teaspoon superfine sugar	½ ounce tawny port
2 teaspoons water	1 lemon twist
1½ ounces desired liquor	⅛ teaspoon grated nutmeg
Crushed ice	⅛ teaspoon ground cinnamon
2½ ounces club soda	

In a highball glass, dissolve the sugar in the water and liquor. Almost fill the glass with crushed ice and add the club soda. Float the port on top. Garnish with the lemon twist and a dusting of the nutmeg and cinnamon.

SLING

1 teaspoon superfine sugar	1 ounce lemon juice
2 teaspoons water	2 ounces desired liquor
	1 lemon twist

In a shaker half-filled with ice cubes, combine the sugar, water, lemon juice, and liquor. Shake well. Pour into a highball glass. Garnish with the lemon twist.

SMASH

4 fresh mint sprigs	2½ ounces desired liquor
1 teaspoon superfine sugar	1 orange slice
1 ounce club soda	1 maraschino cherry

In an old-fashioned glass, muddle the mint sprigs lightly with the sugar and club soda. Fill the glass with ice cubes. Add the desired liquor. Stir well and garnish with the orange slice and the cherry.

SOUR

2 ounces desired liquor	1 orange slice
1 ounce lemon juice	1 maraschino cherry
½ teaspoon superfine sugar	

In a shaker half-filled with ice cubes, combine the liquor, lemon juice, and sugar. Shake well. Strain into a sour glass and garnish with the orange slice and the cherry.

SWIZZLE

1½ ounces lime juice
1 teaspoon superfine
  sugar
2 ounces desired liquor

1 dash bitters
Crushed ice
3 ounces club soda

In a shaker half-filled with ice cubes, combine the lime juice, sugar, liquor, and bitters. Shake well. Almost fill a collins glass with crushed ice. Stir until the glass is frosted. Strain the mixture in the shaker into the glass and add the club soda. Serve with a swizzle stick.

BIBLIOGRAPHY

In order to research this book thoroughly I consulted many publications which I list here and heartily recommend for further reading on the world of drinks and bartendering.

THE GENTLEMAN'S COMPANION by Charles H. Baker Jr. (Crown Publishers).

WHY DRINKING CAN BE GOOD FOR YOU by Morris Chafetz, M.D. (Stein and Day).

GROSSMAN'S GUIDE TO WINES, BEERS, AND SPIRITS by Harold J. Grossman (Charles Scribner's Sons).

SPIRITS AND LIQUEURS by Peter Hallgarten (Faber & Faber).

THE POCKET BARTENDER'S GUIDE by Michael Jackson (Simon & Schuster).

MICHAEL JACKSON'S COMPLETE GUIDE TO SINGLE MALT SCOTCH by Michael Jackson (Running Press).

HUGH JOHNSON'S POCKET ENCYCLOPEDIA OF WINE by Hugh Johnson (Simon & Schuster).

ALEXIS LICHINE'S NEW ENCYCLOPEDIA OF WINES & SPIRITS by Alexis Lichine (Alfred A. Knopf).

THE DICTIONARY OF DRINK AND DRINKING by Oscar A. Mendelsohn, B.Sc., F.R.I.C., F.R.A.C.I. (Hawthorne Books, Inc.).

FRANK SCHOONMAKER'S ENCYCLOPEDIA OF WINE by Frank Schoonmaker (Hastings House).

INDEX